Rethinking Organizational Diversity, Equity, and Inclusion

Rethinking Organizational Diversity, Equity, and Inclusion

A Step-by-Step Guide for Facilitating Effective Change

Edited by
William J. Rothwell, Phillip L. Ealy,
and Jamie Campbell

Routledge
Taylor & Francis Group

A PRODUCTIVITY PRESS BOOK

First published 2022
by Routledge
605 Third Avenue, New York, NY 10158

and by Routledge
2 Park Square, Milton Park, Abingdon, Oxon, OX14 4RN

Routledge is an imprint of the Taylor & Francis Group, an informa business

ISBN: 9781032027333 (hbk)
ISBN: 9781032027289 (pbk)
ISBN: 9781003184935 (ebk)

DOI: 10.4324/9781003184935

Typeset in Garamond
by Deanta Global Publishing Services, Chennai, India

William J. Rothwell dedicates this book to his wife *Marcelina*, his daughter *Candice*, his son *Froilan*, his grandsons *Aden* and *Gabriel*, and his granddaughters *Freya* and *Lina*.

Phillip L. Ealy dedicates this book to his parents *James* and *Linda*, his wife *Michelle*, and kids *Cain*, *Phillip*, and *Terrell*.

Jamie Campbell dedicates this book to his parents *Wilhemena* and *Claude*, his wife *Kimberly*, and his daughters *Grace*, *Vivian*, and *Lillian*.

Contents

Preface

Many people find themselves challenged to set up a program related to diversity, equity, and inclusion (DE&I) in their organizations. Often they are woefully unprepared to do it. They may enjoy the trust and confidence of their immediate organizational superiors, but do not necessarily have any clue how to set up, launch, and sustain an enduring corporate culture change that will inspire appreciation for differences in all its forms. If they fail in their efforts, they could prompt disappointment – and even diversity fatigue or troublesome backlashes.

While much has been published about organizational change, it remains true that most organizational change efforts fail to live up to management or worker expectations. There is a great risk that DE&I efforts could end up as one of those change disappointments.

The Purpose of the Book

This book offers a step-by-step, systematic approach to implementing an organizational change to encourage diversity, equity, and inclusion. While many approaches to organizational change could work to help facilitate DE&I efforts, the editors and contributing authors of this book favor the use of Organization Development (OD). OD is a planned approach to change, relying on behavioral science principles to facilitate – rather than impose or coerce – change.

An effective DE&I change effort meets the needs of the organization and its people. It relies on a positive view of people and a strong effort to encourage participation and inclusion in all aspects of organizational change during start up, implementation, and evaluation. Long-term efforts –called *interventions* to emphasize that they require thought and take time – lead to corporate culture change, an important goal.

This book provides readers with a comprehensive, step-by-step approach to implement DE&I efforts within their organizations.

The Target Audience for the Book

This book is written for anyone who seeks to implement DE&I change efforts. That would include:

- *Chief Diversity Officers* (CDOs) who coordinate and facilitate DE&I programs.
- *DE&I program managers, directors, and human resource professionals* tasked to facilitate the implementation of DE&I programs.
- *Managers* and *workers* who participate in DE&I change efforts and often help to shape them.
- *Teachers* or *professors* who teach about implementing DE&I change efforts.
- *Consultants* who facilitate DE&I change efforts.

The Organization of the Book

This book is organized in four parts. It provides a step-by-step approach to implementation. Part I provides the foundation for DE&I; Part II describes a step-by-step approach to implementing DE&I; Part III looks to the future of DE&I; and Part IV offers resources to support implementation of DE&I. The book is based on a model that a DE&I program facilitator may use to facilitate the implementation of a DE&I effort. See the change model appearing in Figure Frontmatter 1 to guide program facilitators. That model is also an important organizing scheme for this book.

Examined in more detail, the book consists of this Preface to summarize the book, an Acknowledgments to thank contributors, an Advance Organizer to help readers assess on which chapters they may wish to focus attention. An Overview entitled "What's in a Name?" introduces DE&I change efforts and offers reflections on the importance of what organizational leaders should call the change efforts centered on DE&I. Chapter 1 provides a framework and set of tools for facilitating transformative learning, a process of mindfully recognizing and compassionately challenging unhelpful habits of mind, increasing the likelihood that your efforts have a genuine and sustainable impact. Chapter 2 examines the first step in a step-by-step approach to facilitate a change effort in an organization to implement a DE&I program. It covers *"Step 1: Defining Your Organization's Culture, Values, and Goals."* It walks professionals and leaders through identifying or defining their organization's culture, values, and goals. Chapter 3 examines *"Step 2: Clarifying the Role of Diversity, Equity, and Inclusion in Shaping Culture."* Incoming diversity practitioners must enter workspaces ready to assess organizational policies, practices, structures, and reward systems. These three areas constitute an organization's culture and allow leaders to gauge system-readiness for change. Before individual roles can be defined, diversity leaders must lead the work of shaping an inclusive and equitable climate that provides support to experienced and emergent leaders. Chapter 4 examines *"Step 3: Identifying Who Has Authority to Change Culture."* In that chapter, professionals learn that change happens easily when those with the authority to change are involved. Identifying those individuals and getting them to lead or support the change is important. Chapter 5 looks at *"Step 4: Identifying and Defining the Pipeline."* Change practitioners learn that they cannot increase diversity if there is no diversity in the pipeline. Understanding where talent comes from – and where it doesn't come from – will allow change practitioners to plant seeds that can lead to diversity change. Chapter 6 looks at *"Step 5: Developing Talent."* It examines ways to build diverse talent. Chapter 7 focuses on *"Step 6: Navigating Emotions and Other Relational Dynamics,"* reviewing dynamics that emerge for stakeholders during DE&I initiatives. It offers ways of successfully navigating, supporting, and leveraging both positive and challenging sentiments to overcome roadblocks and garner momentum needed to move DE&I initiatives forward. Chapter 8, entitled *"Step 7: Showcasing Your Organization's Talent,"* describes how to give talented, diverse people opportunities for growth that raises their visibility with decision-makers. Change practitioners will learn how to examine their practices to ensure equity in opportunities. Chapter 9, entitled *"Step 8: Promoting Your Organization's Talent,"* discusses ways to reduce bias and other factors that prevent otherwise qualified candidates from getting fair promotion opportunities. Chapter 10, entitled *"Step 9: Developing Employee Resource Groups,"* discusses the importance of affinity groups in increasing inclusion. Chapter 11, entitled *"Step 10: Evaluating Your Processes,"* teaches change practitioners about seeking process improvement in what they do. They learn how to develop and measure metrics that clearly show

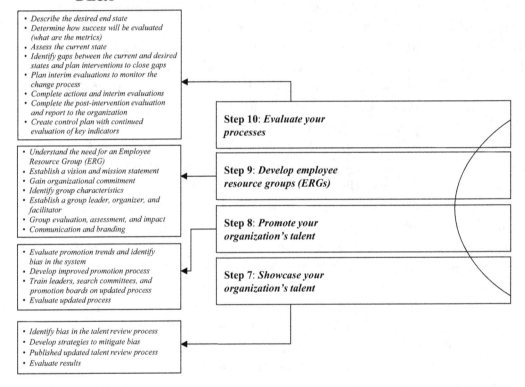

Substeps in Implementing DE&I

- Describe the desired end state
- Determine how success will be evaluated (what are the metrics)
- Assess the current state
- Identify gaps between the current and desired states and plan interventions to close gaps
- Plan interim evaluations to monitor the change process
- Complete actions and interim evaluations
- Complete the post-intervention evaluation and report to the organization
- Create control plan with continued evaluation of key indicators

Step 10: *Evaluate your processes*

- Understand the need for an Employee Resource Group (ERG)
- Establish a vision and mission statement
- Gain organizational commitment
- Identify group characteristics
- Establish a group leader, organizer, and facilitator
- Group evaluation, assessment, and impact
- Communication and branding

Step 9: *Develop employee resource groups (ERGs)*

Step 8: *Promote your organization's talent*

- Evaluate promotion trends and identify bias in the system
- Develop improved promotion process
- Train leaders, search committees, and promotion boards on updated process
- Evaluate updated process

Step 7: *Showcase your organization's talent*

- Identify bias in the talent review process
- Develop strategies to mitigate bias
- Published updated talent review process
- Evaluate results

Figure 1   The diversity, equity, and inclusion (DE&I) roadmap model.

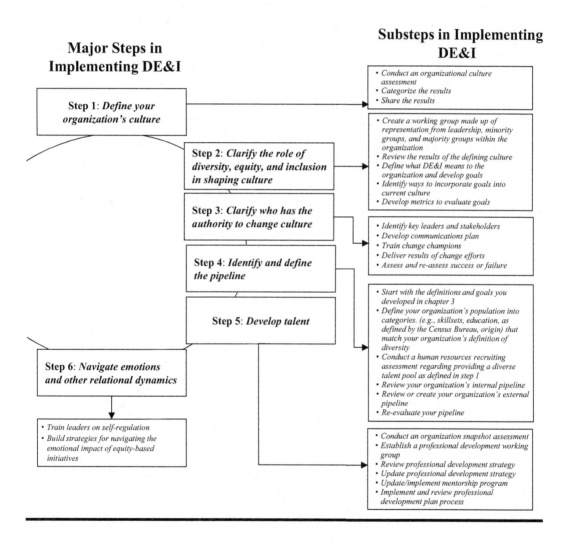

**Major Steps in
Implementing DE&I**

**Substeps in Implementing
DE&I**

Step 1: *Define your
organization's culture*

- *Conduct an organizational culture
  assessment*
- *Categorize the results*
- *Share the results*

Step 2: *Clarify the role of
diversity, equity, and inclusion
in shaping culture*

- *Create a working group made up of
  representation from leadership, minority
  groups, and majority groups within the
  organization*
- *Review the results of the defining culture*
- *Define what DE&I means to the
  organization and develop goals*
- *Identify ways to incorporate goals into
  current culture*
- *Develop metrics to evaluate goals*

Step 3: *Clarify who has the
authority to change culture*

- *Identify key leaders and stakeholders*
- *Develop communications plan*
- *Train change champions*
- *Deliver results of change efforts*
- *Assess and re-assess success or failure*

Step 4: *Identify and define
the pipeline*

Step 5: *Develop talent*

- *Start with the definitions and goals you
  developed in chapter 3*
- *Define your organization's population into
  categories. (e.g., skillsets, education, as
  defined by the Census Bureau, origin) that
  match your organization's definition of
  diversity*
- *Conduct a human resources recruiting
  assessment regarding providing a diverse
  talent pool as defined in step 1*
- *Review your organization's internal pipeline*
- *Review or create your organization's external
  pipeline*
- *Re-evaluate your pipeline*

Step 6: *Navigate emotions
and other relational dynamics*

- *Train leaders on self-regulation*
- *Build strategies for navigating the
  emotional impact of equity-based
  initiatives*

- *Conduct an organization snapshot assessment*
- *Establish a professional development working
  group*
- *Review professional development strategy*
- *Update professional development strategy*
- *Update/implement mentorship program*
- *Implement and review professional
  development plan process*

how the organization is performing. Chapter 12 looks at diversity, equity, and inclusion in emerging markets.

The book ends with five appendices. Appendix A, the Glossary, defines important terms used throughout the book. Appendix B gives readers an instrument to use to audit the culture for its support of DE&I. Appendix C provides useful resources that can carry the reader beyond this book to information of value in setting up and implementing a DE&I program. Appendix D offers Frequently Asked Questions (FAQs) about DE&I programs. Appendix E consists of tools, linked sequentially to the steps in the model governing the book, to help readers guide the application of theory into practice.

The step-by-step model guiding the book is presented here for the first time. It is the major organizing device for the book. Note that the tools in Appendix E are based on this model and provide readers with ways to translate what they read in the book immediately into on-the-job application.

By William J. Rothwell, Phillip L. Ealy, and Jamie Campbell

Acknowledgments

The editors appreciate all those who contributed to this project.

William J. Rothwell wants to express his special thanks to Phillip L. Ealy and Jamie Campbell for their excellent ability to herd cats – and academics always have that feline quality about them. They put the project plan together and were mindful of deadlines and publisher requirements while also shouldering the responsibilities of writing their chapters. Dr. Rothwell would also like to thank Aileen Zaballero for reviewing the book while in draft as well as Farhan Sadique, his graduate assistant, for his help with this book.

William J. Rothwell
State College, Pennsylvania

Phillip L. Ealy
State College, Pennsylvania

Jamie Campbell
State College, Pennsylvania

About the Editors and Contributing Authors

The Editors

William J. Rothwell, PhD, SPHR, SHRM-SCP, RODC, CPTD Fellow, is Distinguished Professor in the Master of Professional Studies in Organization Development and Change program and also in the PhD program of Workforce Education and Development at the Pennsylvania State University. He has authored, coauthored, edited, and coedited 127 books since 1987. His recent books since 2017 include *Organization Development (OD) Interventions: Executing Effective Organizational Change* (Routledge, 2021); *Virtual Coaching to Improve Group Relationships: Process Consultation Reimagined* (Routledge, 2021); *The Essential HR Guide for Small Business and Start Ups* (Society for Human Resource Management, 2020); *Increasing Learning and Development's Impact through Accreditation* (Palgrave, 2020); *Adult Learning Basics, 2nd ed.* (Association for Talent Development, 2020) *Workforce Development: Guidelines for Community College Professionals*, 2nd ed. (Rowman-Littlefield, 2020); *Human Performance Improvement: Building Practitioner Performance*, 3rd ed. (Routledge, 2018); *Innovation Leadership* (Routledge, 2018), *Evaluating Organization Development: How to Ensure and Sustain the Successful Transformation* (CRC Press, 2017), *Marketing Organization Development Consulting: A How-To Guide for OD Consultants* (CRC Press, 2017), and *Assessment and Diagnosis for Organization Development: Powerful Tools and Perspectives for the OD Practitioner* (CRC Press, 2017).

Phillip L. Ealy, MPS, is a retired U.S. Army Officer where he spent time integrating women into previously restricted combat arms roles. He also developed U.S. and foreign militaries, building international coalitions. He works as the coaching coordinator for the Children, Youth, and Families at Risk (CYFAR) grant program. In this role, Ealy trains and develops coaches that work with land-grant universities on implementing government-funded programs for local communities.

Ealy holds a Master of Professional Studies in Organization Development and Change and is finishing a PhD in Workforce Education and Development with an emphasis in human resource development and organization development from the Pennsylvania State University. He holds an undergraduate degree in communications from West Virginia State University.

Jamie Campbell, MEd, serves as the Assistant Dean for Diversity Enhancement Programs at the Smeal College of Business. He has served as a panelist on topics ranging from social justice to students' issues, and has been a keynote speaker for various leadership programs. He also serves as an advisor to several student organizations within the Smeal College of Business and continues to mentor graduates working in Fortune 500 companies. Campbell is a 1995 graduate of Morehouse College where he obtained his BA in sociology. He obtained his MEd with concentrations in adult education and instruction education from Central Michigan University in 2003. He is a PhD student in the Workforce Education and Development program with concentrations in organization design and human resource development at the Pennsylvania State University. His research focuses on succession planning as a form of crisis management.

The Contributing Authors

S. Ron Banerjee, MPS, CCP, CFS, CLTC, is a financial advisor specializing in the tax-exempt markets for Voya Financial Advisors, Inc. Banerjee is also a Training and Development Officer for the Center for Independent Living of Central Pennsylvania. He is a PhD student in the Workforce Education and Development program with a human resource development focus at the Penn State University and received his Master of Professional Studies in Organization Development and Change from the same university. Banerjee is a Prosci® certified change professional with ADKAR® and large-scale change expertise. Banerjee is a decorated veteran of the U.S. Navy and has been nationally recognized by the U.S. Veterans Administration as an advocate for disabled veterans. Banerjee is also an active community leader holding board and leadership positions in a variety of organizations including the Organization Development Network, Meals on Wheels of State College, the International Fraternity of Phi Gamma Delta, and the Penn State University World Campus Alumni Society.

William Brendel, EdD, is Assistant Professor of Organization Development and Change at Penn State University. His research investigates how the ancient wisdom tradition of mindfulness practice may be integrated with the field of OD as a transformative approach to leadership development, team-based innovation, and inclusive organizational cultures. He is also the CEO of the Transformative Learning Institute, an OD consulting firm, which has helped dozens of organizations cultivate mindful, innovative, and high-performing workforces. Brendel earned his doctorate in adult learning and leadership at Columbia University and is also a member of the board of trustees for the Organization Development Network.

Marie Carasco, PhD, MBA, GPHR, SHRM-SCP, is the founder and chief social scientist of Talent en Floré LLC, an executive coaching practice supporting individuals interested in personal or professional change (see www. talentenflore.com). She has served as a trusted advisor to C-level leadership teams managing task forces for large-scale global change initiatives and human resources strategy, including diversity initiatives in multiple sectors.

Carasco is an International Coach Federation Professional Certified Coach (PCC) and has deep functional expertise in high-potential leader development and appreciative change management using multiple interventions for individual, group, and organization-wide planned change. She teaches masters-level courses in organizational behavior, global diversity, group processes, and leadership studies. Her research and professional interests are in leader development, identity and belonging, organization development (OD) competencies, HR strategy, and qualitative research methods. She also advises startup and small business leaders on HR strategy.

She holds a PhD in Workforce Education and Development with an emphasis in human resource development and organization development from the Pennsylvania State University and an Executive MBA in organizational behavior and coaching from the University of Texas at Dallas Naveen

Jindal School of Management. She also holds an undergraduate degree in psychology and a graduate degree in industrial-organizational psychology from CUNY-Brooklyn College.

She is the coauthor of *The Essential HR Guide for Small Businesses and Start-ups* (Society for Human Resource Management, 2020) and has authored book chapters in *Evaluating Organization Development: How to Ensure and Sustain the Successful Transformation* (CRC Press, 2017), *Marketing Organization Development Consulting: A How-To Guide for OD Consultants* (CRC Press, 2017), and *Organization Development (OD) Interventions: Executing Effective Organizational Change* (Productivity Press Taylor & Francis Group, in press).

Farhan Sadique, MS, is a recognized student leader and a PhD student in the Workforce Education & Development program at Penn State University. He previously received a master's degree from Pittsburg State University. Sadique is a globally experienced, value-driven professional with years of experience in management with a successful track record. He is passionate about studying innovative organization development (OD) and change management approaches. Even though his research interest primarily focuses on the sustainability of retail organizations, he has successfully contributed to related research outcomes, including an open-source model for OD application, OD career assessment tools, evaluation capacity development, and employee work engagement.

Wayne Gersie, PhD, is the inaugural Vice President for Diversity and Inclusion (VPDI) and a Research Assistant Professor in the Department of Cognitive & Learning Sciences at Michigan Technological University. In his VPDI role he is responsible for providing vision, strategic leadership, and thoughtful change management for campus diversity, equity, inclusion and sense of belonging (DEIS) initiatives. Gersie works collaboratively with Michigan Tech faculty, staff, students, alumni, and external constituents to advance the University's commitment to all aspects of diversity and inclusion. His senior leadership role includes communicating the value proposition of educational and innovation impacts of DEIS initiatives on the University's overall performance related scholarship and research. Additionally, he coaches University leaders to become culturally proficient in order to promote and sustain culturally responsive leadership.

Prior to joining Michigan Tech, Gersie served as Assistant Research Professor and Chief Diversity Officer for the Applied Research Laboratory at The Pennsylvania State University. He is the is the founder and principal of Oasis Strategic Consulting LLC. He has earned his PhD in Workforce Education and Development, with emphasis on Human Resources, and a MEd in Counselor Education, both from Penn State. Additionally, he holds certificates from the Harvard University Institute for Management and Leadership Education, Cambridge, Massachusetts, Cornell University School of Industrial and Labor Relations and Center for Creative Leadership in Colorado Springs, Colorado.

Catherine Haynes, PhD, GCDF, EEO, is a retired U.S. Army Noncommissioned Officer with dual PhD in Workforce Education and Development and in comparative international education from the Pennsylvania State University. She holds a master's degree in human resource development and organization development; her undergraduate degree is in hotel, restaurant, and institution management from the Pennsylvania State University. She is certified in Global Career Development and Facilitation (GCDF). Haynes is a graduate of the Defense Equal Opportunity Management Institute (DEOMI) and is an Equal Employment Opportunity (EEO) Counselor. She is also a Fulbright Scholar.

As a human capital manager, Haynes was responsible for the successful operation and implementation of all human resources functions for soldiers and civilian employees, including training, employee relations, evaluations, and professional development. As the EEO Counselor, she was the senior counsel to commanders on all aspects pertaining to EEO and served as an advocate for employee issues. Haynes is appointed as Co-Chair of the Carlisle Barracks Retiree Council. The council provides insights on retiree concerns to the U.S. Army Installation Management Command Army.

Her recent publications include works in organization development fundamentals: *Managing Strategic Change* (ATD Press, 2014), *Optimizing Talent in the Federal Workforce* (Management Concepts, 2014), and *The Competency Toolkit*, 2 vols, 2nd ed. (HRD Press, 2015).

Barbara R. Hopkins, MS, is the Associate Vice President of Academic Affairs at Northern Virginia Community College (NOVA), one of the largest institutions of higher education in the country. In her long career at NOVA, she has held multiple leadership positions and participated in projects at the institutional, state-wide, and national levels. Before beginning her tenure at NOVA, she had an accounting career, which included owning her own practice. Hopkins has also been highly active in the business community and the public school system. She holds a master's degree in accounting and is working toward a Doctor of Education in higher education leadership to be an even larger contributor to resolving Community College issues nation-wide.

Norm J. Jones, PhD, a nationally recognized leader in higher education, educational equity and access, and organization development. He holds a PhD in Workforce Education and Development and a master's degree in public administration from Pennsylvania State University, and BA degree in English from Morehouse College.

His professional service includes membership on many Boards of Trustees: the Pennsylvania Historical and Museum Commission, the Organization Development Network, the Liberal Arts Diversity Officers (LADO), and the Consortium on High Achievement and Success (CHAS). He also serves on the editorial review boards of the Organization Development Practitioner, the *Journal of African American Males in Education*, and the *Mellon Mays Undergraduate Fellowship Journal*.

Michele McBride, MPS, is Director of Organization Development at Keller Williams Realty International's Pennsylvania Region. She is responsible for the assessment of organizational needs as it relates to the franchise systems of Keller Williams Realty International. She also oversees the design, implementation, and evaluation of programs that facilitate the professional development and continuous learning of sales associates, emerging leaders, and office leaders. This includes directing the implementation of systematic change initiatives through the creation and reinforcement of talent management initiatives and talent development programs.

McBride holds a Master of Professional Studies in Organization Development and Change and is a PhD student in the Workforce Education and Development program at Penn State University. She has two BAs in psychology and political science from Penn State University.

Christina Pettey, MPS, PHR, SHRM-SCP, is the Chief People Officer for Kwik Lok Corporation. She has over 15 years of experience in human resources and continuous improvement specializing in using a blended approach to improve interactions between people and processes to improve organizations.

Pettey holds a bachelor's degree in psychology from the University of Washington and a Master of Professional Studies in Organization Development and Change from Penn State University. She is a certified Six Sigma Black Belt and professional in human resources and SHRM-SCP.

Advance Organizer

By William J. Rothwell

Complete the following Organizer before you read the book. Use it as a diagnostic tool to help you assess what you most want to know about OD interventions – and where you can find it in this book *fast*.

The Organizer

Directions

Read each item in the Organizer below. Spend about 10 minutes on the Organizer. Be honest! Think of DE&I change efforts/interventions as you would like to practice them. Then indicate whether you would like to learn more about DE&I change efforts to develop yourself professionally. For each item in the center column, indicate with a *Y* (for Yes), *N/A* (for Not Applicable), or *N* (for No) in the left column whether you would like to develop yourself. When you finish, score and interpret the results using the instructions appearing at the end of the Organizer. Then be prepared to share your responses with others you know to help you think about what you most want to learn about DE&I interventions that rely on facilitated change. To learn more about one item below, refer to the number in the right column to find the chapter in which the subject is discussed.

The Questions

Circle your response for each item below:	*I would like to develop myself to:*	*Chapter in the book in which the topic is covered:*
Y N/A N 1.	Review why the name of a DE&I effort is strategically important.	*Overview: What's in a name?*
Y N/A N 2.	Use a framework and tools to facilitate transformative learning as it applies to DE&I.	*1*
Y N/A N 3.	Mount a change effort in an organization to implement DE&I efforts.	*2*
Y N/A N 4.	Assess organizational policies, practice, structures, and reward systems as they affect DE&I.	*3*
Y N/A N 5.	Involve decision-makers and other stakeholders in the implementation of a DE&I program.	*4*
Y N/A N 6.	Identify and define the talent pipeline of the organization.	*5*
Y N/A N 7.	Develop diverse talent.	*6*
Y N/A N 8.	Overcome roadblocks that stand in the way of successful implementation of DE&I programs.	*7*
Y N/A N 9.	Know how to showcase and sponsor diverse talent.	*8*
Y N/A N 10.	Reduce bias in organizational promotion decisions.	*9*
Y N/A N 12.	Use affinity groups in a DE&I program/change effort.	*10*
Y N/A N 11.	Know how to apply process improvement principles to DE&I efforts.	*11*
Y N/A N 13.	Address trends in DE&I issues.	*12*

_____ **Total**

Scoring and Interpreting the Organizer

Give yourself *1 point for each Y* and a *0 for each N or N/A* listed above. Total the points from the *Y* column and place the sum in the line opposite to the word **Total** above. Then interpret your score:

Score

13–12 = Congratulations! This book is just what you need.
points Read about the issue(s) you marked *Y.*

11–9 = You have great skills in DE&I change efforts already,
points but you also have areas where you could develop
professionally. Read those chapters marked *Y.*

8–5 = You have skills in DE&I, but you could
points still benefit to build skills in selected areas.

4–0 = You believe you need little development in
points planning, implementing, and evaluating DE&I change
efforts.

ESTABLISHING THE FOUNDATION FOR DE&I

Part I consists of the Overview only. It establishes a foundation for DE&I, encouraging readers of this book to engage the managers and workers in their organizations to clarify the philosophy guiding DE&I in their organization(s).

DOI: 10.4324/9781003184935-1

Overview: What's in a Name?

William Brendel

Contents

Why We Chose Diversity, Equity, and Inclusion (DE&I)

The acronym DE&I does not come without debate. Compelling cases exist for adding terms such as "Justice" (National Health Foundation 2021), "Belonging" (McGregor 2019), "Accessibility" (American Alliance of Museums 2021), and "Engagement" (The National Council 2020). Some also suggest changing the order of terms, placing "Equity" or "Justice" in front of "Inclusion" or "Diversity." Though definitions vary depending on the source, DE&I continues to be the most prevalent terminology in professional associations, including the Organization Development Network (2021), Association for Talent Development (2021), the Society for Human Resource Management (2021), and the Society for Industrial and Organizational Psychology (2021). DE&I is also widely referenced in management literature, including the *Harvard Business Review* and *Forbes*, and consulting outlets like Deloitte (2021) and McKinsey & Company (2021). According to a recent Indeed.com job search, over 4,344 positions in the United States include "DE&I" in their titles (2021). Therefore, to be consistent and relatable, we have adopted the acronym "DE&I" for this book.

DOI: 10.4324/9781003184935-2

How We Collectively Define DE&I

The authors of this book also agree that although our definitions of DE&I differ slightly – as is to be expected – what is universal to them all is the intentional, organization-wide effort to restore, cultivate, and sustain *humanity* at work. Humanity is an anchoring term that implies diversity, equity, and inclusion, and a host of related synonyms: compassion, kindness, fairness, charity, and generosity. Humanity is also something we all innately share, belong to, and it bears a sacred responsibility to improve, protect, and celebrate at work. As we utilize the term DE&I, our meaning differs little from the definitions provided by the outlets noted above.

Customizing Your Naming Convention

Given the sheer number of histories, cultures, and languages throughout the world, arriving at a single acronym that conveys DE&I would, paradoxically, require a certain level discrimination, inequity, and exclusion. Even the relatively small number of contributors to this book, who hold much in common, must sacrifice some of their preferences for consistent terminology. You will undoubtedly face the same challenge. Because OD practitioners value learning and collaboration as part of successful change efforts (Yoon et al. 2020), your organization can benefit by using this naming opportunity as:

1. An object lesson that invites employees to enter dialogue around the definitions, associations, relevance, and intersectionality of these terms.
2. A continuous improvement endeavor that leaves space for additional reframing and renaming as new research and organizational discoveries are provided.
3. A chance to translate these terms from statements in employee handbooks to generative questions that encourage experiential learning, professional growth, and genuine acceptance.

To assist you with adopting, creating, or revising your terminology, we offer the following "DE&I Kickoff Naming Tool" (see Overview Addendum Tool 1), which includes helpful framing, questions to discuss, and a decision-making framework. The following tool presents the ideal facilitation; however, we realize that due to pressures and unique differences in your organization this may not be possible.

OVERVIEW TOOL 1: KICKOFF TOOL FOR CHOOSING AND DEFINING TERMINOLOGY

OVERVIEW

This meeting is your *kickoff* to an ongoing process of dialogue, consensus building, appreciation, and ownership of DE&I efforts across all levels of your organization. Your objective is to convene a diverse group of internal stakeholders to suggest, reflect, refine, and decide upon the title/acronym associated with your DE&I efforts.

1. **Select Your Participants**: Invite a diverse group of representatives from your executive leadership team, including the CEO, Human Resources, Employee Resource Groups (ERG), high-potential emerging leaders, Training & Development, and other individuals who have formal or informal influence. Ensure that your group has as much diverse representation as possible.

2. **Prepare Your Slides**: Ask participants to email you their personal understanding of the terms "Diversity, Equity, and Inclusion." Ask them to describe the core concepts, observable behaviors, and feelings associated with each word. Also ask that they send additional words you should consider for your official title/acronym and have them define these as well. Review participant submissions and create a handout that lists all keywords in the order of their frequency. Place a star next to descriptive words used by professional associations. Create a second slide with blank columns under the headings "Primary Terms," "Secondary Terms," and "Change Initiatives."

3. **Facilitate Dialogue**: Discuss and sort terms in the following way:

    a. *Primary Terms* are those you will utilize in your title; begin with the terms diversity, equity, and inclusion.

    b. *Secondary Terms* are more specific behavioral- and change-oriented, and may be more suitable for your vision or mission. Discuss whether any terms on your list are synonyms, antonyms, or are part of the definition of diversity, equity, and inclusion. If any of your words are not directly related to diversity, equity, and inclusion, consider adding them to your list of Primary Terms.

    c. *Change Initiatives* are words that are associated with primary and secondary terms but imply larger strategic objectives. Align these with primary/secondary terms.

4. **Finalizing Your Acronym**: Before deciding on your acronym, discuss the following:

   a. ***Vision and Mission***: Discuss whether any terms are critical to your organization's mission; it may be worth including these in your Primary Terms list. For instance, "Accessibility" is particularly important in healthcare and education. If you are a social justice organization, consider including the word "Justice" in your acronym.

   b. ***Global Meaning***: Discuss how well each of your terms translates in different parts of the world. Even if you are not a global organization, the chances are that you have a multicultural workforce.

   c. ***Order of Terms***: Decide on the order of primary terms used in your official title/acronym. Order conveys importance. Reflect on your dialogue for guidance on your final decision.

Works Consulted

American Alliance of Museums. n.d. "Definitions of Diversity, Equity, Accessibility, and Inclusion." Accessed June 26, 2021. https://www.aam-us.org/programs/diversity-equity-accessibility-and-inclusion/facing-change-definitions/

Association for Talent Development. n.d. "DE&I Discussion Series." Accessed June 26, 2021. https://www.td.org/de-i-discussion-series

Deloitte. n.d. "Diversity Equity & Inclusion Transparency Report." Accessed June 26, 2021. https://www2.deloitte.com/us/en/pages/about-deloitte/articles/diversity-equity-inclusion-transparency-report.html

Forbes. n.d. "HR Transformation: Why Diversity Equity and Inclusion Is Here to Stay." Accessed June 26, 2021. https://www.forbes.com/sites/sap/2021/05/24/hr-transformation-why-diversity-equity-and-inclusion-is-here-to-stay/?sh=2936b0f428cb

Harvard Business Review. n.d. "Update your DE&I Playbook." Accessed June 26, 2021. https://hbr.org/2020/07/update-your-dei-playbook

Indeed.com. n.d. "Job Search for 'Diversity Equity and Inclusion'." Accessed June 26, 2021. https://www.indeed.com/jobs?q=diversity+equity+and+inclusion&l=USA

McGregor, Jenna. 2019. "First There Was 'Diversity.' Then 'Inclusion.' Now HR Wants Everyone to Feel Like They 'Belong.'" *The Washington Post* (December). Accessed June 26, 2021. https://www.washingtonpost.com/business/2019/12/30/first-there-was-diversity-then-inclusion-now-hr-wants-everyone-feel-like-they-belong/

McKinsey & Company. n.d. "Insights to Guide Organizations in 2021, Part 3." Accessed June 26, 2021. https://www.mckinsey.com/business-functions/organization /our-insights/the-organization-blog/insights-to-guide-organizations-in -2021-part-3

National Health Foundation. n.d. "Justice, Equity, Diversity, and Inclusion." Accessed June 26, 2021. https://nationalhealthfoundation.org/people-culture/ justice-equity-diversity-inclusion

Organization Development Network. n.d. "DE&I Resources." Accessed June 26, 2021. https://www.odnetwork.org/page/dei-resources

Society for Human Resource Management. n.d. "Introduction to the Human Resources Discipline of Diversity, Equity & Inclusion." Accessed June 26, 2021. https://www.shrm.org/resourcesandtools/tools-and-samples/toolkits/pages/ introdiversity.aspx

Society for Industrial and Organizational. n.d. "Psychology 'Business Resources for Diversity, Equity & Inclusion'." Accessed June 26, 2021. https://www.siop.org/ Business-Resources/Diversity-Equity-Inclusion

The National Council Website. 2020. "We Need More Than Inclusion: Reframing Engagement to Foster Diversity and Equity." Accessed June 26, 2021. https:// www.thenationalcouncil.org/BH365/2020/10/23/we-need-more-than-inclusion -reframing-engagement-to-foster-diversity-and-equity/

Yoon, Hyung Joon, Sasha B. Farley, and Cesar Padilla. 2020. "Organization Development Values from a Future-Oriented Perspective: An International Delphi Study." *The Journal of Applied Behavioral Science.* (September). 57(3), 323–349. doi:10.1177/0021886320957351.

A STEP-BY-STEP APPROACH TO IMPLEMENTING A DE&I EFFORT

Implementing a DE&I effort is a corporate culture change effort. Many people tasked with facilitating the implementation of DE&I efforts find a step-by-step approach helpful to guide what they do. This part provides a flexible, step-by-step approach to facilitate the change effort required to implement a DE&I effort.

The model for implementing a DE&I effort requires organizations to do the following:

- *Step 1*: Defining your organization's culture
- *Step 2*: Clarifying the role of diversity, equity, and inclusion in shaping culture
- *Step 3*: Clarifying who has the authority to change culture
- *Step 4*: Identifying and defining the pipeline
- *Step 5*: Developing talent
- *Step 6*: Navigating emotions and other relational dynamics
- *Step 7*: Showcasing your organization's talent
- *Step 8*: Promoting your organization's talent
- *Step 9*: Developing Employee Resource Groups
- *Step 10*: Evaluating your processes

DOI: 10.4324/9781003184935-3

OVERVIEW TOOL 1: KICKOFF TOOL FOR CHOOSING AND DEFINING TERMINOLOGY

OVERVIEW

This meeting is your *kickoff* to an ongoing process of dialogue, consensus-building, appreciation, and ownership of DE&I efforts across all levels of your organization. Your objective is to convene a diverse group of internal stakeholders to suggest, reflect, refine, and decide upon the title/acronym associated with your DE&I efforts.

1. **Select Your Participants**: Invite a diverse group of representatives from your executive leadership team, including the CEO, Human Resources, Employee Resource Groups (ERG), high-potential emerging leaders, Training & Development, and other individuals who have formal or informal influence. Ensure that your group has as much diverse representation as possible.

2. **Prepare Your Slides**: Ask participants to email you their personal understanding of the terms "Diversity, Equity, and Inclusion." Ask them to describe the core concepts, observable behaviors, and feelings associated with each word. Also ask that they send additional words you should consider for your official title/acronym and have them define these as well. Review participant submissions and create a handout that lists all keywords in the order of their frequency. Place a star next to descriptive words used by professional associations. Create a second slide with blank columns under the headings "Primary Terms," "Secondary Terms," and "Change Initiatives."

3. **Facilitate Dialogue**: Discuss and sort terms in the following way:
   a. ***Primary Terms*** are those you will utilize in your title; begin with the terms diversity, equity, and inclusion.
   b. ***Secondary Terms*** are more specific behavioral- and change-oriented, and may be more suitable for your vision, mission. Discuss whether any terms on your list are synonyms, antonyms, or are part of the definition of Diversity, Equity, and Inclusion. If any of your words are not directly related to Diversity, Equity, and Inclusion, consider adding them to your list of Primary Terms.
   c. ***Change Initiatives*** are words that are associated with primary and secondary terms but imply larger strategic objectives. Align these with primary/secondary terms.

4. **Finalizing Your Acronym**: Before deciding on your acronym, discuss the following:

   a. ***Vision and Mission***: Discuss whether any terms are critical to your organization's mission; it may be worth including these in your Primary Terms list. For instance, "Accessibility" is particularly important in health care and education. If you are a social justice organization, consider including the word "Justice" in your acronym.
   b. ***Global Meaning***: Discuss how well each of your terms translates in different parts of the world. Even if you are not a global organization, the chances are that you have a multicultural workforce.
   c. ***Order of Terms***: Decide on the order of primary terms used in your official title/acronym. Order conveys importance. Reflect on your dialogue for guidance on your final decision.

Chapter 1

Facilitating Transformative Learning

William Brendel

Contents

DOI: 10.4324/9781003184935-4

The violets in the mountains have broken the rocks.

–Tennessee Williams

Moving Mountains

"It's like moving a mountain!" I'll never forget those words shared by one of my favorite clients, the first Chief Diversity and Inclusion Officer in his organization's history. He fought for every inch of progress in his first two years. Like Atlas, he carried the entire weight of this noble cause for his organization since no one else seemed to care as deeply. His position, which reported directly to the CEO, seemed doomed from the start. No lever seemed large enough to nudge the organization's policies, systems, and culture in the "right" direction. So, he turned to bigger devices, including provocative organizational assessments and training sessions that addressed problems head-on and handed employees "foolproof" practices they could use when they returned to work. This direct approach should have made things crystal clear! By now, employees should know why they have a moral obligation to change and could use simple tools handed to them on a silver platter.

However, the hardening of hearts continued. Rumors spread that his approach was offending employees and backfiring. Reports of racial insensitivity, bias, and sometimes overt discrimination seemed to be on the rise. Everything my client had ever learned about management theory, training delivery, and behavioral conditioning only seemed to escalate the problem. When every tool at one's disposal fails, it may be time to step outside of the paradigm in which they were created. What if my client's metaphor of moving mountains with the right shovel, drill, or bulldozer were replaced with the imagery of a steady gardener, planting seeds – small questions, invitations, and intriguing reflections – which, with the help of some skillful tending, sprout roots on their own? What if these roots could reach their *own* depths, like a field of violets, collectively permeating the bedrock of systemic racism, exclusion, and in DE&I?

This inside-out, self-directed process is the central feature of *Transformative Learning Theory* (Mezirow 2000), which would suggest that leaders focus less on levers and more on how they position the fulcrum; in other words, the way they balance their leadership approach, power, agency, and action. Transformative Learning is a theory that calls all employees, beginning with DE&I leaders themselves, to accept and transform the way their anxieties, assumptions, attachments, and awareness impact change.

Chapter Overview

Following a brief reflection on the current state of DE&I in the United States, and an overview of Transformative Learning Theory, this chapter will walk you through five steps, which I utilize with great success as both the CEO and principal consultant at the *Transformative Learning Institute*. I share these approaches and their tools freely and encourage you to integrate them with your work so that it works best for you. At the conclusion of this chapter, I will bring these steps to life with a real client case. One caveat that accompanies any step-by-step approach is that transformation is seldom linear or permanent. Depending on how far along your organization is in creating conditions for Transformative Learning, you may find that some steps are less critical than others. Some may require revisiting. Some will call for extra care and additional phases of discussion and reflection. However, each step requires continuous devotion. This five-step approach assumes that DE&I initiatives can only be considered "transformative" when employees move beyond mere compliance and *authentically* embody change. The following outline describes the frameworks, tools, and transitions between each step.

1. ***Establish and Encourage Mindfulness Practice***
   Develop an everyday practice that includes nonjudgmentally noticing how your assumptions, anxieties, and attachments drive your interpretations and behavior.
2. ***Balance Your Leadership Approach***
   Take and administer the *Balanced Leadership Inventory* (BLI) to your closest DE&I allies to understand and identify areas of imbalance in learning, leadership, strategy, organizational design, and employee engagement.
3. ***Identify and Reflect on Sources of Imbalance***
   For each area of imbalance indicated on the BLI, facilitate the *4 Lines of Inquiry Tool* to critically reflect upon ways your collective assumptions, anxieties, and attachments may be hampering your DE&I efforts.
4. ***Assess Transformative Learning Agility***
   Administer the *Transformative Learning Agility Assessment* (TLA) to teams outside of DE&I who will help you transform different pockets of

your organization. This will establish a baseline for understanding the team's potential to collectively transform their assumptions, anxieties, and attachments.

5. ***Prime Transformative Dialogue***

Finally, depending on the lowest scoring items on the TLA, utilize the *P.R.I.M.E.* approach to set the stage for transformative dialogue within each team, which includes encouragement and coaching around permeability, reflectiveness, inclusion, a measured approach, and emotional capability to change.

The Current DE&I Landscape

If you currently find yourself stumbling or even causing additional anxiety through your DE&I work, you are not alone. The story I shared above is more common than you might think. To understand the necessity of the steps I will present, consider the following. U.S. companies now invest close to US$ 8 billion per year on DE&I (Kirkland and Bohnet 2017), a fixture in 234 of the S&P 500 companies, which presents current job seekers with over 46,000 open positions (Glassdoor.com 2021). Unlike traditional organizational functions, the center of gravity for DE&I spans beyond the organization, including racial tensions and surreal flashpoints that pervade society. As a discipline, DE&I struggles to stem the voluntary attrition of minorities who feel suffocated by the silence of their colleagues.

The potential impact of DE&I on organizational performance is enormous, but it still breathes an experimental air, which in some pockets is turning stale. Look no further than Google, which invested over US$ 264 million into DE&I in 2014 and 2015. By 2019, black employees still comprised just 3.3% of their workforce, with only 2.6% holding leadership positions (Newkirk 2019). Deloitte's 2019 State of Inclusion Survey reveals a shortcoming of a more insidious nature: even though 73% of employees feel comfortable addressing bias in the workplace when they perceive it, only 29% stand up in the moment on behalf of themselves or their coworkers (Cooper and Horn 2019). To make matters worse, Gallup reports that the gender gap has barely advanced over the last decade (Miller and Adkins 2016). These findings could not be more frustrating for DE&I leaders who often feel stuck with no real alternative levers for moving the needle.

Five Steps toward Transformative Learning

While many powerful definitions have surfaced over the past four decades, I would like to first offer my favorite academic definition, followed by my own definition, which has proven helpful in the practical sphere of DE&I. According to Dean Elias, Transformative Learning involves "the expansion of consciousness … facilitated through consciously directed processes such as appreciatively accessing and receiving the symbolic contents of the unconscious and critically analyzing underlying premises" (Elias 1997, 1). Three practical processes that one might derive from this definition include a person's ability to influence awareness (theirs or others), observe features of emotion and cognition without self-judgment, and reflect upon the validity and helpfulness of these features.

Transformative Learning involves shifting, expanding, receiving insight from, and applying awareness helped by mindfulness practice and other contemplative approaches (Brendel, Samarin, and Sadique, 2021) that focus awareness on assumptions, anxieties, and attachments; particularly those that yield outcomes that stand in contrast to our stated values and intentions. The more we bring these features of mind into the foreground of awareness and without judgment, the less likely we are to over-identify with our beliefs and the more likely we are to reflect critically upon them without the hindrance of guilt, bias, or self-cynicism. If we adopt this transformative paradigm, the job of a DE&I leader is not to prescribe or inculcate solutions but rather to invite and guide employees through a process of self-directed practices to identify and examine unhelpful, self-preserving beliefs; in *their own words*, developing creative and meaningful solutions, and taking charge of leading change themselves.

Step 1: Establish and encourage applied mindfulness practice

Our everyday language and behavior are often propelled forward automatically through the tacit momentum of our assumptions, anxieties, and attachments. Without clarity, these 3 As will instinctively affect the way you frame and guide employee learning, leadership, strategy, design, and engagement (Figure 1.1). Therefore, the first step in transforming DE&I is to dive inward, cultivating an awareness of your specific 3 As by applying mindfulness practice, which is defined as an "awareness that emerges by paying attention on purpose, in the present moment, and without judgment" (Kabat-Zinn 2003,

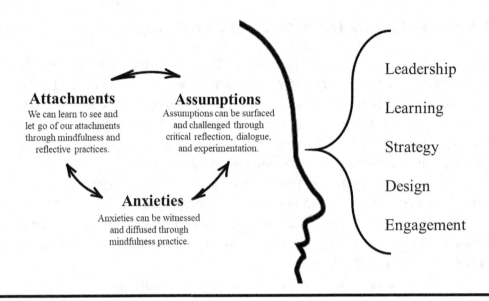

Figure 1.1   The 3 As of DE&I leadership. The author has incorporated this assessment with the permission of the Transformative Learning Institute, LLC.

145). To make this definition practical in the space of DE&I, your first (and continuous step) is to practice paying attention to your anxieties, assumptions, and attachments with intention, in each of your present-moment interactions, and without judgment.

Mindfulness practice creates mental elbow room required to surface, reflect upon, and change our behaviors in "real time" without experiencing a threat to our identity. It creates a distance from which we can see and let go of unhealthy attachments regarding control. Creating this space is necessary if we are to respond thoughtfully, rather than react. It is a movement from clenching one's hands to opening them, which makes it more likely that we are able to genuinely apologize for an unfounded comment we have just made, allow ourselves to be persuaded by others in dialogue, let go of a great idea and bear witness to what another person is saying, act with grace when attacked, and to forgive others. Absent such awareness, DE&I practitioners are also susceptible to developing and leading an approach to change fraught with imbalance. To remind yourself of what to be "mindful of," keep this 3 As framework handy and take purposeful pauses as you read through the remainder of this book. Observe and embrace what "comes up" for you, without judgment, and examine whether the way you orchestrate meaning around DE&I may be unintentionally hampering the goals you and your organizational allies have set for yourselves.

Observe Your Anxieties

Driven by uncertainty and the feeling of losing control, anxieties comprise a mix of fears, nervousness, and physical distress (Spielberger 2013). We are more likely to react than respond to anxieties and stress because they compel us to recoil, fight, or even freeze (Maack, Buchanan, and Young 2014, 117–27). At the individual level, anxieties often result in a self-referential "what's-in-it-for-me" orientation, status quo seeking language, and stubborn avoidance behaviors. Anxieties may also stem from the fear of speaking up, reinforcing a negative stereotype through one's own behavior, or causing general discomfort around race conversations (Kent 2021).

Noteworthy interactions between an anxious individual and their social environment must also be mindfully observed (Bandura 1988, 77–98). Left unaddressed, group anxieties can suddenly escalate as they attract and feed off each other (Parkinson and Simmons 2012, 462–79). This can cause defensive organizational behaviors (Fennessey 1962, 470–1), including turf wars, political subterfuge, scapegoating, and even sabotage. Research has demonstrated that when threat is anticipated, individuals adhere to a *Conservatism Bias*, in which they take a "better safe than sorry" approach, which manifests in self-censorship (de Jong and Vroling 2014, 22–43). It is also responsible for a walk-on-eggshells attitude that prevents transformative dialogue that can lead to fundamental improvements in DE&I.

Notice Your Assumptions

Assumptions include orienting views or perspectives about one's world. Combined with anxiety, assumptions drive our interpretation of reality and provide us with an operational anchor for how we see ourselves, others, and what is within or outside of our control. As we accumulate memories from experience, assumptions cluster into belief systems reinforced from within but also by those we surround ourselves with. In this way, we seek the opinions of like-minded individuals (Oswald and Grosjean 2004). This powerful feature of organizational life is just one manifestation of *Confirmation Bias* (Nickerson 1998, 175–200), a psychological mechanism that selectively observes and interprets information, so it validates preexisting beliefs.

Assumptions and anxieties ride on interpretations of the past. *Negativity Bias* also presents an enormous challenge to Transformative Learning in the DE&I space. Negativity Bias refers to the way individuals pay attention to, and remember, negative experiences over neutral or positive ones, which leads to narrow-minded first impressions and decision-making (Hilbig 2009, 983–6). When repeatedly exposed to judgment, Negativity Bias is even shown to decrease an individual's belief in their abilities (Müller-Pinzler et al. 2019, 1–15). To transform hearts and minds, DE&I leaders must simultaneously address anxieties through a compassionate lens while also subtly inviting individuals to seek porosity in their assumptions: enough as to warrant critical reflection. Maintaining this level of balance within both the DE&I practitioner and their stakeholders is essential to Transformative Learning.

Let Go of Your Attachments

What Conservatism, Negativity, and Confirmation Biases share is their affinity for ego, gained or lost from the perspective of "I, me, and mine." For this chapter, I define attachment as any fixation with specific assumptions, anxieties, memories, and narratives, particularly those that revolve around unsatiated needs of ego and control. Attachments make critical reflection difficult because they are often an obsessive, ruminative quality of mind that makes it difficult to assume different perspectives and entertain alternative beliefs. Similarly, they make genuine dialogue difficult because they excite a grasping and clinging quality of mind, which leads to an unyielding "my way or the highway" mindset, often at a great cost. Attachments also manifest in the escalation of commitment, whereby an individual has poured so much energy and time into a project that even though all signs suggest they should stop what they are doing, they continue to the detriment of the organization (Brockner 1992, 39–61).

Attachments, particularly to selfhood (Van Gordon et al. 2018, 892–6) and the need to have a distinct organizational identity, can lead to a great deal of personal suffering in the face of DE&I, including depression and even self-loathing. Some have said that "All beings are addicted to existence, addicted to being, being something" (Amaro 2021, 1). Even when we learn of ego attachment, the temptation to stand out as superior to one's peers can be irresistible. One of the deepest forms of attachment is *Unconscious Bias* (Ross 2020), which includes automatic mental associations and preferences for or against one group or thing instead of another. In the workplace, unconscious biases produce innumerable organizational inequities for traditionally marginalized populations, including a decreased likelihood of being hired, mentored, presented with growth opportunities, considered for promotion, included in informal networks, and rewarded fairly for performance.

Step 2: Balance your DE&I leadership approach

If you are new or well-versed in change initiatives that aim to improve upon DE&I, the five areas of imbalance introduced below may seem strikingly familiar. As DE&I practitioners are compelled to engage resistance in a balanced fashion (Wasserman 2008, 175–200), I define imbalance as a strong preference about how change *should* be led, which stems from the 3 As and demand a more egoic and controlling approach. The areas in which these imbalances arise include *learning, leadership, strategy, organizational design*, and *employee engagement*. To address each area in the assessment below, I use the metaphor of planting, cultivating, and tending to flowers. At first, this may sound like a soft solution to a hard problem, but later in this chapter, you will be introduced to a case that demonstrates how patience, nonjudgment, and trust can break their way deep into the bedrock of an institution, rendering systemic forms of oppression untenable.

EXHIBIT 1-1: BALANCED LEADERSHIP INVENTORY

OVERVIEW

When it comes to leading DE&I efforts, the need for psychological safety and control can vary widely between individuals. In some instances, our anxieties, attachments, and assumptions inform strong preferences for the way DE&I leaders approach organizational leadership, learning, strategy, design, and engagement. The following assessment is designed to raise awareness and help you reflect upon your own preferences, their origins, and impact on DE&I efforts. The results of this assessment can inform the way you address your own areas of imbalance by comparing them to the case study and testing the *4 Lines of Inquiry* tool.

INSTRUCTIONS

1. For each set of statements listed below, circle the number that most closely resembles your approach. Example: When it comes to leading DE&I efforts, to what degree do you Correct versus Cultivate? If you lean entirely toward "Correct," circle the number 1. If you lean entirely toward "Cultivate," circle the number 5. If you lean mostly but not entirely toward "Correct," circle the number 2. If you lean mostly but not entirely toward "Cultivate," circle the number 4. If you find yourself doing both in equal measure, circle the number 3.

2. Next, assume a bird's-eye view, noting which of the five areas reflect your strongest preference(s), and jot down the anxieties, attachments, or assumptions that you suspect are behind these preferences. What evidence (observations, behaviors, communications) suggest that biases (Negativity, Confirmation, and Unconscious) are reinforcing your anxieties, attachments, and assumptions.

3. Finally, using a different shape (square, star, or check mark), indicate the preference of your stakeholders. Note how similar or different they are from yours. What evidence (observations, behaviors, communications) would suggest anxieties, attachments, and assumptions that would drive imbalance on their part.

Correcting	Leadership	Cultivating
A preventative orientation in which DE&I creates mandatory processes, policies, and recourse that prevent employees from making mistakes	1 2 3 4 5	A promotional orientation in which DE&I promotes and celebrates change as growth opportunities driven by employees
Preaching	**Learning**	**Planting**
A prescriptive approach in which DE&I assumes the role of expert who must prescribe a specific language, set of mental models, and behaviors for DE&I work that must be taken without question and adhered to	1 2 3 4 5	A facilitated approach in which DE&I assists employees in developing their own language and critical thinking capacity by planting simple questions, engaging narratives, and challenging employees to seek deeper meaning in the unique context of their lives
Upending	**Strategy**	**Inviting**
A provocative approach in which DE&I speaks truth to power through agitation, critiquing established norms, and compelling employees to accept blame for systemic racism and in DE&I	1 2 3 4 5	An accepting approach in which DE&I gives unconditional positive regard to all employees, with an invitation to enter difficult conversations to the extent that individuals are emotionally prepared to do so

Centralizing	Design	Spreading
An exclusive approach in which DE&I is concentrated in a department, center or individual, that oversees and drives all DE&I work, which creates a dependency upon their knowledge, skills, expertise, and resources. Anxieties revolve around structure and hierarchy	1 2 3 4 5	An inclusive approach in which DE&I is seen as a vibrant, interdisciplinary hub supporting learning and innovation offshoots that directly infuse DE&I knowledge, skills, and abilities into local strategies, norms, and decisions
Judging	**Engagement**	**Tending**
A deficit orientation in which DE&I focuses on identifying and communicating problem areas	1 2 3 4 5	An appreciative approach in which DE&I tends directly to employee hopes and growth opportunities while honoring positive changes (both big and small)

The author has incorporated this assessment with the permission of the Transformative Learning Institute, LLC (2021).

Step 3: Identify and reflect on sources of imbalance

Unlike other business functions, DE&I may reach its heights by generating more questions and motivation from *within* than answers and requirements from above. Slow and steady growth from within has always been key to deep and lasting change. Sometimes the roots of real change run into stubborn obstacles but instead of wasting time trying to break through, DE&I leaders must themselves practice patience and open-mindedness. With the right guidance, these roots will seek their depth, and faster than you might expect. Inquiry is essential to Transformative Learning, because it can drive a fundamental shift in the way things get done, why we do them in the first place, and how we view our roles, behaviors, mindfulness, agency, and efficacy.

The Four "Ifs"

To guide transformation around the five forms of imbalance described above, a DE&I professional can practice guiding employees, leaders, and teams across four lines of inquiry. Each line of inquiry addresses one or more of the 3 As. By first identifying areas of imbalance and then guiding employees, leaders, and teams through these lines of inquiry, DE&I professionals can help to collectively restore a balanced, inclusive, self-directed, consensus-driven, and sustainable approach to change. For each line of inquiry, I include guiding questions that can be asked in a variety of ways depending on the language common in your organization. Modify these questions as needed, so you and your colleagues comfortably identify your assumptions, anxieties, and attachments around DE&I.

"If … then …"

"If … then …" provides a nonthreatening way of simply describing, clarifying, and reflecting upon taken-for-granted assumptions around your current processes. The goal here is to verbalize assumptions and surface logic between causes and effects. You will know you are asking the right "If … then …" questions if the answers should seem obvious and not worth asking. These questions are asked in the spirit of a beginner's mind and are an attempt to level set – particularly when a process that has always seemed to work is failing. To get started, complete the following sentence: If I am to succeed as a DE&I leader, then I must _____. Based on your answer:

a. When did you first recognize the value of this approach?
b. What would you compare this approach to and why?
c. How might the outcomes of this approach be described differently by various stakeholders?
d. Do you believe the results will be sustainable?

"As if …"

"As if …" builds upon previous descriptions of basic process assumptions by challenging the premise behind them. The big question is whether you have framed the problem or solution properly. It also creates a space for questions about individual differences, marginalization, and creating unfair advantages. This is the space where you can expect to surface assumptions about ego and control. Complete the following sentence: As if these approaches are the most effective or appropriate means for _____. Based on your answer:

a. Could individual differences make this approach easier for some and more difficult for others?
b. Does this approach unintentionally marginalize, disenfranchise, or put anyone in an otherwise uncomfortable position?
c. Which does this approach not address or serve well?
d. How might those with formal power be seen to benefit from this approach?
e. Does this approach address symptoms rather than root causes?

"What if ... ?"

Next, enter the space of anxieties and attachments by asking questions in the spirit of a thought experiment, so you are curiously wondering aloud if the assumptions and anxieties you have so far explored may be producing unintentional negative consequences. These thought experiments follow the "What if ... ?" line of inquiry. Complete the following sentence: What if this approach unintentionally _____? Based on your answer:

a. How does this approach impact personal responsibility?
b. What are ways this approach might backfire?
c. Could this approach reinforce some problems it purports to solve?
d. Is there any possibility this approach might create new anxieties that make fundamental change even harder?
e. Are we framing any assumption in a dualistic (either/ or) versus flexible (both/and) manner?

"If only ..."

As you move through the first three lines of inquiry you will notice that a shared desire to "fix" or "test" your way of doing things gains steam. The goal of "If only …" is to expand awareness (i.e., transcend our assumptions, anxieties, and attachments) to reframing, revising, eliminating, or supplementing specific characteristics of your approach. It is also a space where you ask yourself how you now look at your Self in new ways. How must I not only change what I am doing but also viewing myself. With careful practice, you, and those you have guided through these four lines of inquiry, are ready to plan and test the way you have reframed both objective and subjective reality surrounding DE&I. Complete the following sentence: If only we could (actually) change _____. Based on your answer:

a. What are the ways that we can address the deeper anxieties and attachments not readily changeable through this approach?
b. What are the ways to help this initiative take on a life of its own while also remaining consistent with our DE&I vision?
c. What can we do to balance both technical and organic aspects of the change we seek?
d. What inherent paradoxes exist and how can we enable our employees to appreciate and utilize them as additional sources of insight rather than frustration?
e. What personal attachments and anxieties have surfaced that are present and potentially responsible for other forms of imbalance?

EXHIBIT 1-2: TRANSFORMATIVE LEARNING AGILITY SELF-ASSESSMENT

To complete this assessment, rate how much you agree with each of the following statements when it comes to your experience with discussions you have with colleagues around strategies that center on DE&I. Key: 1 = never; 2 = sometimes; 3 = about half the time; 4 = most of the time; 5 = always					
1. When I share my views, I also genuinely suggest that my perspectives may be incomplete and ask for feedback.	1	2	3	4	5
2. When I share my assessment of a situation, I also genuinely suggest that my perspectives may be altogether incorrect and ask for feedback.	1	2	3	4	5

	1	2	3	4	5
3. When I hear a perspective that makes me uncomfortable, I first turn inward and examine my own anxieties, attachments, and assumptions.	1	2	3	4	5
4. When I find myself forming a somewhat negative judgment about a colleague, I consider whether I may be subconsciously attributing something to her or him that I really don't like about myself.	1	2	3	4	5
5. I help others explore their own assumptions more often than I actively examine my own.	1	2	3	4	5
6. I tend to speak in a definitive fashion (This is how I see things, I believe this, People should ...), more than an exploratory fashion (I wonder if, Is it possible that, Perhaps I am wrong about ...)	1	2	3	4	5
7. I am confident that my understanding of who I am is more complete than incomplete.	1	2	3	4	5
8. When it comes to working in a group setting, I believe that there is neither "good" nor "bad" ideas, only thinking makes it so.	1	2	3	4	5

The author has incorporated this assessment with the permission of the Transformative Learning Institute, LLC.

Step 4: Assess transformative learning agility

Not everyone will be ready or capable of entering these lines of inquiry with the same acceptance, flexibility, or fervor. For some employees, assumptions, anxieties, and attachments have been formed through distressing experiences, leaving behind post-traumatic residue that makes it very difficult to address certain topics. For others, engaging in discussion around the 3 As is a well-honed skill. Therefore, respect how much they are ready and willing to engage in dialogue, and drawing from this understanding, create the right blend of questions. I have developed and utilize the following self-assessment as a baseline and follow-up measure when coaching others through Transformative Learning in the sphere of DE&I. It gauges the level and degree to which individuals maintain an open-mindedness around change.

Step 5: Prime transformative dialogue

Transformative Learning is one of the most widely studied areas of adult education, and throughout the literature (Cranton and Taylor 2011, 214–23) one must prime five dynamics for dialogue to be transformative. I remember these five areas by the mnemonic P.R.I.M.E. and rely on them when customizing and leading the transformative dialogue on DE&I issues.

1. *Permeability* refers to how much we are open to information that does not confirm our biases, including accurate and complete information and the subjective realities of others.
2. *Reflectiveness* refers to how capable we are of addressing our mental schemas, the influence of power and authority on the way we make meaning, and the relevance of power, authority, and coercion.
3. *Inclusion* refers to how much we are open to alternative points of view, which involves empathy, curiosity, and care regarding how others think and feel.
4. *Measured approach* refers to how capable we are of weighing evidence and assessing arguments objectively.
5. *Emotional capability* refers to how willing and safe we feel about seeking understanding and agreement toward a tentative best judgment that may be tested and validated further.

When forming and empowering teams to help carry out DE&I work in their areas of the organization, ask them to review and reflect on the elements of P.R.I.M.E. together. Have members brainstorm what it would look like, feel like, and sound like if the team excelled at each area. What specific behaviors, interactions, and feelings are involved? Next, bake each element into the team's norms and ask individual members to commit to developing at least one area they would like to improve. Finally, have members discuss what the technical, political, and cultural barriers and enablers are – both in the team and in the organization at large – for each component of P.R.I.M.E. After mapping these forces that help or hinder genuine dialogue, discuss and commit to ways of utilizing or enhancing each of the enablers and eliminating the barriers. Finally, encourage each team to share the processes and behaviors they develop in service to P.R.I.M.E. and share them with other teams facilitating DE&I dialogue throughout your organization.

Case Study

In less than 4 years, Briana Joyner would rise from an HR Generalist position to become the first woman of color to serve as the Director of Human Resources and earn the concurrent role of Chief Inclusion Officer at the Minnesota Historical Society (MNHS). What makes Briana's accomplishments special is her balanced approach to transforming assumptions, anxieties, and attachments surrounding DE&I work at this 173-year-old institution. Briana accomplished this in five steps, which you may emulate to balance your approach to leadership, learning, strategy, design, and engagement. Notice that while these steps do not align sequentially with the steps in this chapter, they are present and each has a multiplier effect on DE&I transformation.

1. **Becoming a Trusted Advisor and Dialogue Facilitator**
   Briana first drew immediate attention to the way the traditional leadership structure unintentionally left people of different races, classes, genders, and sexual orientations disenfranchised. She was careful not to have leaders develop a dependence on her expertise but helped develop sustainable cultural competence among leadership that included higher-order acts of empathy, inclusion, and critical reflection. Part of this meant helping everyone in the organization manage a common paradox that stifles most DE&I efforts: sometimes those in charge of DE&I efforts develop an understandable sense of learned helplessness when they cannot garner the sincere attention of leaders on their first, second, third, or fourth try. Instead, Briana flipped this approach inside-out. Rather than approaching leaders as an expert who must be listened to, Briana started her journey by listening to employees, planting seeds, asking stimulating questions, praising their insights, making connections, and ultimately setting leaders on the track for building the case for DE&I from within.

2. **Championing a Shared Leadership Team Structure**
   With the trust of leadership and employees, Briana helped to move close to 2/3 of leadership decision-making, agency, representation, recognition, and access to those at the bottom of the organization chart, and simultaneously replacing them with systems that would lift minority employees into and beyond supervisory roles. By focusing awareness on the dimension of "What if?," Briana influenced the development of

three forms of leadership equilibrium demonstrated in this before and after depiction. This new structure produced five powerful outcomes for DE&I. First, it eliminated silos so inclusive teams must work together to produce shared outcomes. Second, it provided a leadership development model in which members of the Organization Development (OD) team were groomed to move into management and finally leadership positions. Third, it simplified and focused dialogue topics that relate to specific performance outcomes. Fourth, it provided vivid examples of how DE&I and business outcomes are not mutually exclusive but rely on each other. Fifth, and most important to Briana's efforts, it included a new OD capacity that systematically intervenes at the cross section of culture and performance.

Next, Briana worked with all leaders to develop the vision for this inclusive structure, which was *to cultivate and support free, full, and iterative dialogue around the alignment of vision, strategy, culture, and performance.* Ground rules for dialogue between these teams followed a formula, which aligned with the P.R.I.M.E. methodology, namely, enter communication with an open mindset, share divergent perspectives, reflect critically utilizing the shared framework, engage inclusively, appreciate individual differences, and relate empathically. To make these teams not only diverse but also inclusive and equitable, the expressed goals were to develop a nonhierarchical feedback culture; a forum for cocreated knowledge; and a collaborative learning and wisdom sharing mentality.

3. **Priming Dialogue in Self-Directed Teams**
   Kurt Lewin (1947, 5–41) once said that teams are the primary unit of change in organizations because they produce a social balance. Much of Briana's success comes from decentralizing and embedding DE&I efforts in several self-directed teams, committees, and councils. She first created an overarching DE&I Council. She also introduced, trained, and coached diverse sets of employees in a process called "GE Workout," which breaks down structure and authority that hampers or disrupts organizational DE&I and performance. Briana championed the development of Employee Resource Groups (ERGs) with an open invitation to members of the organization, followed by instruction on the process of ERG formation, and providing resources on legal implications. To balance power, rather than directing ERGs centrally through HR, they are all self-directed.

4. **Embedding DE&I in the Mission and Long-Term Strategy**

Because of Briana's ability to inspire and organize systematic change, she was called upon to help lead the development of MNHS's new long-term strategic plan. Being embedded in this process, which is often a feat unto itself for HR, left an unmistakable footprint because Briana led others to reimagine MNHS's public value proposition through its existing vision statement. This repositioned the historical society from simply being another place where artifacts are preserved and shared, to one that teaches all its stakeholders (including employees) a process of historical inquiry to steward greater critical reflection, inclusion, and empathy. MNHS is now transforming its traditional "museum authority" over history, by sharing that authority with local communities throughout MN, and ensuring that all history is treated with equal respect, dignity, and visibility. In this way, the DE&I strategy now transcends the organization.

5. **Transforming the Employee Experience**

Briana has also actively sought, developed, and institutionalized safeguards for DE&I that would permeate every phase of the employee life cycle (attraction, onboarding, development, rewards, and retention, mentoring, career trajectory, and retirement). Briana also transformed the Learning & Development arm of HR into a Transformative Learning and Development architecture. This assimilated DE&I through five pillars: Onboarding, Intercultural Competence, Transformational Learning, Employee Engagement, and Career Development. This approach cultivates self-directed learning, community learning, collaborative learning with diverse external stakeholders, cross-cultural learning, and a host of evidence-based cultural competency interventions. Transformative Learning was no longer a simple matter of support but had become an expectation of all employees.

Key Questions about the Chapter

1. You won't move this mountain on your own – a gentle and balanced approach, which invites everyone into embracing disorientation, dialogue, and experimentation holds greater potential for successful DE&I efforts. Why is this the case?
2. Even your greatest efforts at teaching employees about cultural competencies and unconscious bias will struggle to "stick," unless you directly,

skillfully, and patiently engage in dialogue around preexisting anxieties, assumptions, attachments, and awareness. The 3 As play a substantial role in the way DE&I efforts balance learning, leadership, strategy, design, and engagement. Can you provide an example to illustrate this principle?

3. Continuously assess and transform the way you balance leadership using the *Balanced DE&I Leadership Assessment*. Could you try one out for yourself and an organization with which you are familiar?

4. Despite an employee's best intentions, without cultivating mindful awareness, they are likely to act upon stubborn habits of mind that inadvertently hamper DE&I efforts. Mindfulness practice is essential to Transformative Learning. Could you describe how you might demonstrate "mindfulness practice?"

5. The way we question and answer ourselves from within largely determines how much we own DE&I change. Use the *4 Ifs Guide* to guide questions that advance and sustain this inner growth. Could you write out an example?

6. Don't assume your employees are prepared or unprepared to transform their inner lives around DE&I. Could you assess and reassess openness and willingness to change using the *Transformative Learning Agility Assessment*?

7. Prime your employees for transformative development by asking leaders and employees to adopt the P.R.I.M.E. approach, which introduces conditions that must be maintained for genuine dialogue, including Permeability, Reflectiveness, Inclusion, Measured Approach, and Emotional capability. How might you do that? Describe a step-by-step approach.

Works Consulted

Amaro, Ajahn. 2021. "The I-Making, Mine-Making Mind." *Mindfulness* 12, no. 7 (January): 1839–1844. doi:10.1007/s12671-020-01579-0.

Bandura, Albert.1988. "Self-Efficacy Conception of Anxiety." *Anxiety Research* 1, no. 2 (January): 77–98. doi:10.1080/10615808808248222.

Brendel, William, Israa Samarin, and Farhan Sadique. 2021. "Open-Source OD: A Platform for Creating Novel Innovation and Inclusion Applications." *Organization Development Review*, 53 (5) (December).

Brockner, Joel. 1992. "The Escalation of Commitment to a Failing Course of Action: Toward Theoretical Progress." *The Academy of Management Review* 17, no. 1 (January): 39. doi:10.2307/258647.

Cooper, Terri, and Eliza Horn. 2019. "State of Inclusion Survey, the Bias Barrier: Allyships, Inclusion, and Everyday Behaviors." *Deloitte Development.* Accessed June 22, 2021. https://www2.deloitte.com/content/dam/Deloitte/us/Documents/about-deloitte/inclusion-survey-research-the-bias-barrier.pdf

Cranton, Patricia, and Edward W. Taylor. 2011. "Transformative Learning." In *The Routledge International Handbook of Learning.* Edited by Peter Jarvis and Mary Watts, 214–223. Routledge.

de Jong, Peter J., and Maartje Vroling. 2014. "Better Safe Than Sorry: Threat-confirming Reasoning Bias in Anxiety Disorders." In *Emotion and Reasoning.* Edited by Isabelle Blanchette, 22–43. Psychology Press.

Elias, Dean. 1997. "Transforming Learning into Action: A Case Study." *Revision* 20, no. 1 (Summer): 20–28.

Fennessey, Ruth F. 1962. "Experiences in Groups and Other Papers. W. R. Bion." *Social Service Review* 36, no. 4 (December): 470–471. doi:10.1086/641348.

Glassdoor.com. 2021 "Find the Job That Fits Your Life." Accessed March 31, 2021. https://www.glassdoor.com/index.htm.

Hilbig, Benjamin E. 2009. "Sad, Thus True: Negativity Bias in Judgments of Truth." *Journal of Experimental Social Psychology* 45, no. 4 (July): 983–986. doi:10.1016/j.jesp.2009.04.012.

Kabat-Zinn, Jon. 2003. "Mindfulness-based Interventions in Context: Past, Present, and Future." *Clinical Psychology: Science and Practice* 10, no. 2 (Summer): 144–156.

Kent, Jacinta. 2021. "Scapegoating and the 'Angry Black Woman.'" *Group Analysis* 54, no. 3 (February): 1–18. doi:10.1177/0533316421992300.

Kirkland, Rick, and Iris Bohnet. n.d. "Focusing on what works for workplace diversity." *McKinsey & Company Featured Insights.* Accessed June 22, 2021. https://www.mckinsey.com/featured-insights/gender-equality/focusing-on-what-works-for-workplace-diversity

Lewin, Kurt. 1947 "Frontiers in Group Dynamics." *Human Relations* 1, no. 1: 5–41.

Maack, Danielle J., Erin Buchanan, and John Young. 2014. "Development and Psychometric Investigation of an Inventory to Assess Fight, Flight, and Freeze Tendencies: The Fight, Flight, Freeze Questionnaire." *Cognitive Behaviour Therapy* 44, no. 2 (November): 117–127. doi:10.1080/16506073.2014.972443

Mezirow, Jack. 2000. *Learning as Transformation.* San Francisco, CA: Jossey Bass.

Miller, Jane, and Amy Adkins. 2016. "Reality and Perception: Why Men Are Paid More" *Gallup Workplace.* Retrieved June 22, 2021. https://www.gallup.com/workplace/236345/reality-perception-why-men-paid.aspx

Müller-Pinzler, Laura Czekalla, Nora., Mayer, Annalina V., Stolz, David S., Gazzola, Valeria, Keysers,Christian., Paulus, Frieder M., and Krach, Sören. 2019. "Negativity-Bias in Forming Beliefs About Own Abilities." *Scientific Reports* 9, no. 1 (October): 1–15. doi:10.1038/s41598-019-50821-w

Newkirk, Pamela. 2019. *Diversity, Inc.: The Failed Promise of a Billion-Dollar Business.* London: Hachette UK.

Nickerson, Raymond S. 1998. "Confirmation Bias: A Ubiquitous Phenomenon in Many Guises." *Review of General Psychology* 2, no. 2 (June): 175–220. doi:10.1037/1089-2680.2.2.175.

Oswald, Margit E., and Stefan Grosjean. 2004. "Confirmation bias." In *Cognitive Illusions: A Handbook on Fallacies and Biases in Thinking, Judgment and Memory.* Edited by Rüdiger F Pohl, 79–96. Psychology Press. doi:10.4324/9780203720615

Parkinson, Brian, and Gwenda Simons. 2012. "Worry Spreads: Interpersonal Transfer of Problem-Related Anxiety." *Cognition & Emotion* 26, no. 3 (April): 462–479. doi:10.1080/02699931.2011.651101.

Ross, Howard J. 2020. *Everyday Bias: Identifying and Navigating Unconscious Judgments in Our Daily Lives.* Rowman & Littlefield.

Spielberger, Charles D., ed. 2013. *Anxiety and Behavior.* New York: Academic Press.

Transformative Learning Institute. 2021. "Free Resources." Retrieved on June 22, 2021 from https://www.transformativelearning.institute/resources

Van Gordon, William, Edo Shonin, Sofiane Diouri, Javier Garcia-Campayo, Yasuhiro Kotera, and Mark D. Griffiths. 2018. "Ontological Addiction Theory: Attachment to Me, Mine, and I." *Journal of Behavioral Addictions* 7, no. 4 (June): 892–896. doi:10.1556/2006.7.2018.45.

Wasserman, Ilene, Plácida V. Gallegos, and Bernardo M. Ferdman. 2008. "Dancing with Resistance." In *Diversity Resistance in Organizations,* Edited by K.M. Thomas, 175–200. Milton Park, Oxfordshire: Taylor & Francis Group.

Chapter 2

Step 1: Defining Your Organization's Culture

Phillip L. Ealy

Contents

Case Study

In 2020, the U.S. Army post, Fort Hood, in Killeen, Texas, experienced at least 28 soldiers' deaths that were not from combat actions (Rempfer 2020). These deaths were accidents, suicides, and homicides. The unusually high number and manner of deaths prompted an investigation. A Fort Hood independent review committee was formed to examine the culture and climate of the military post (Cohen and Browne 2020). The committee found that there was ineffective implementation of a U.S. Army Sexual Harassment/

DOI: 10.4324/9781003184935-5

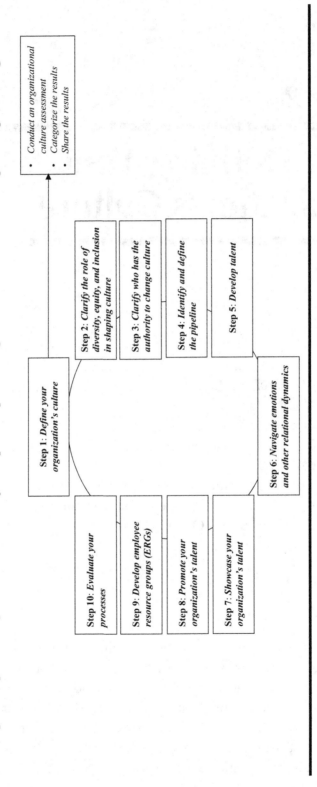

Frontmatter Figure 2.1   The diversity, equity, and inclusion (DE&I) roadmap model.

Assault Response and Prevention (SHARP) program. The committee also determined that female soldiers lacked confidence in the program and feared retaliation, resulting in underreporting of sexual harassment and assault cases (Cohen and Browne 2020; The Guardian 2020). Many leaders were fired from their positions, and repairing the culture became a top priority. There are many lessons to be learned here. Three of these lessons are below.

First, there can be pockets of the organization that can have a culture different from or even counter to the culture of the overall organization. This could be because the written policies or values outlined by leaders are not practiced by those within the organization. The U.S. Army does not condone sexual harassment or sexual assaults. Many policies and punishments are outlined in documents, symbols, speech, and other aspects of the culture. However, this unit, a subset of the larger organization, had allowed the behaviors of sexual harassment to continue to fester, grow, and eventually manifest. An organization's culture requires consistent monitoring and maintenance. If culture is ignored, the culture may not be the same as outlined in written documents.

Second, the same culture can mean different things to different people. How could some soldiers feel a part of the team when they were being harassed and assaulted? In the same culture, many thrived, while others were marginalized and faced obstacles to success. The perception of the effectiveness of the organization's culture is different depending on who is asked. A farmer may feel the farm life is great, while one of the children may prefer city life. The impact of culture on those who are diverse from those in the leadership may differ greatly from those who are more like the leadership. Chapter 3 discusses that issue in more detail.

Third, culture can change. Culture changes when people come and go from the organization, as new information is available, or for other reasons. Underlying truths help shape and drive our culture. For instance, when the world was flat. Fishermen would only go but so far fearing falling off the face of the earth. As more information was gathered, the fundamental truth was changed to the world was round. This had a direct change to how people sailed and traded goods. An organization's culture will change, but it is up to the organization if the change is intentional or happens unintentionally as in this story of Fort Hood. More on changing organizational culture can be found in Chapter 4.

Organizations may need to change their culture to increase diversity, equity, and inclusion (DE&I). This chapter will outline the importance of organizational culture regarding DE&I, help organizations define culture, and lay out steps to define and understand the organization's culture.

What Does the Research Say?

DE&I must be part of the organization's DNA as opposed to being a singular program to target a singular group. Therefore, many DE&I efforts fail, because they are trying to solve symptoms instead of the root issue. Think of equity and social justice. Equity attempts to correct wrongs imparted by the system, whereas social justice attempts to correct the system itself. Equity is DE&I programs. For example, a program to close the pay gap. However, without solving why the pay gap started, the gap will reemerge again. The steps in this book are akin to social justice, changing the entire system to prevent pay gaps from occurring in the first place. Three areas are key in increasing DE&I within an organization. These include organizational culture, talent management, and networking. The steps in this book cover these three areas. Because no specific program or magic pill will increase DE&I, the system must change (Figure 2.1).

Culture influences everything we do: our language, beliefs, actions, what we eat, our entire lives. It is no different in an organization; culture influences how we hire, how we develop talent, if we have mentorship or sponsorship programs, feedback systems, or if we support networking. To

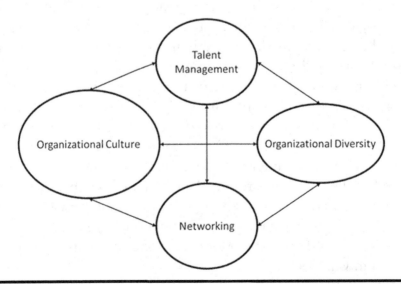

Figure 2.1   Ealy Conceptual Framework for Organizational Diversity.

embrace DE&I, a culture that accepts and supports diversity must be present. Edgar Schein has been considered by many as a leader in organizational culture. He defines culture as follows:

> The culture of a group can be defined as the accumulated shared learning of that group as it solves its problems of external adaptation and internal integration; which has worked well enough to be considered valid and, therefore, to be taught to new members as the correct way to perceive, think, feel, and behave about those problems. This accumulated learning is a pattern or system of beliefs, values, and behavioral norms that come to be taken for granted as basic assumptions and eventually drop out of awareness.
>
> **(Schein 2016, Chapter 1, p. 6)**

Two important takeaways are (1) culture is shared learning and (2) it influences how to perceive, think, feel, and behave. Culture is learned and therefore, as illustrated in the story, can change as new factors are shared with the organization. For example, most cultures embrace airplanes to travel long distances in a short time. This behavior was learned based on the advancements in flight since the Wright brothers' maiden flight. In early 2001, people could walk around freely in airports, even escort friends, colleagues, and loved ones to the boarding gate. When planes were hijacked in September 2001 and flown into the World Trade Center in New York City, people in the United States had a shared learning experience that more stringent security was needed to avoid tragedies like this. This leads to takeaway number 2. Perception, thoughts, feelings, and behaviors toward airport security changed. No longer were people allowed to escort loved ones to the gate.

Schein (2016) outlines three levels of culture: artifacts; espoused beliefs and values; and basic underlying assumptions. Artifacts are those symbols or totems that represent your organization. Espoused beliefs are the recorded culture of the organization. Basic underlying assumptions are the unwritten truths of the organization. It is imperative to understand these three areas to define what the culture is of an organization. Imagine an unwritten truth that immigration is bad for business. This truth is now shared within the organization. It will affect perception, thoughts, feelings, and behavior. When hiring, immigrants will not be favored in the candidate pool. Potential mentors will not want to mentor those with immigrant status for a likelihood it would adversely affect the mentor.

Johnson and Scholes' Cultural Web Model is a popular model used by business to evaluate and change organization culture. This model outlines six elements that affect culture: stories and myths; symbols; power structures; organization structures; control systems; and ritual and routines (Leadership Centre 2021). Thinking about Schein's work and the Johnson and Scholes' model, culture can be described into three categories.

What Are Your Symbols and Totems?

Johnson and Scholes outline symbols and Schein speaks of artifacts. These are placed in the category of symbols and totems. What are the symbols and totems that represent the organization? These are more than just the external branding such as the Nike swoosh, the Mercedes-Benz star, LG Electronics (Jeong-do Management) Life's Good branding, or the Dangote Group's eagle. The symbols and totems also include the images on the walls of the building and the websites. They include statues, architecture, and monuments the organization has erected on organizational property such as the Sydney Opera House in Australia or the Christ the Redeemer statue in Rio de Janeiro, Brazil. These symbols and totems have meaning and mean different things to different people. In the United States, the confederate battle flag can have the meaning of rebelling against an overreaching government. While to others, this flag can mean oppression, slavery, and racism. It takes time and care to establish meaning to organizational symbols. These symbols and totems may have a different meaning to others. Identify what symbols and totems represent to the organization and what they mean to those who see them. A way is to have people close their eyes and think of the organization. Then ask what images immediately come to mind and what do those images mean to them.

What Is Your Recorded Culture?

Recorded culture is everything sanctioned by the organization that someone can read, watch, and hear. These include policies, procedures, memos, emails, videos, blogs, podcasts, position papers, and much more. This would include Schein's espoused beliefs and values and Johnson and Scholes' power structures, control systems, and organizational structures. Recorded culture sends messages and shapes the actions of individuals. If an organization located in Israel states, they believe in the birthright of Jews in Israel, what does that say to Palestinians whose family was born on the same land for generations? Changing the statement to say that the organization believes in the birthright of all people born in Israel has a very different meaning. Ensuring the organization is sending the intended message is important. Ask those in the organization to identify the most influential or prominent documents (or messages they can produce, e.g., videos, podcasts) within the organization and what they mean to them. This will help to understand what the recorded culture means to those in the organization.

What Are Your Unwritten Truths?

An organization can have the right symbology and the right written messages. But if Malik, Omar, Muhammad, and Xavier keep getting promoted, while Sabrina, Bridgette, Suzanne, and Jennifer do not, then is there something deeper going on? Johnson and Scholes describe stories and myths and rituals and routines. Schein mentions basic underlying assumptions. Your unwritten truths are your daily habits, patterns, and norms. What does it mean for the leadership team to ask a junior member to go play golf? For some, it could mean they just want to play golf. For others, it could be an invitation to be groomed for higher positions and less about the golf itself. Know what members in the organization see as unwritten truths in the organization.

Again, understanding that culture is shared learning and influences how to perceive, think, feel, and behave. We must also know how various people in the organization view the organization's culture. As in the story of Fort Hood, the culture can be seen differently by those in the organization.

Putting into Practice

Step 1: Conduct an organizational culture assessment

There are many organizational culture tools and surveys available. There are also culture audits available that can determine how different stakeholders regard the culture within the organization. It is important to ensure these tools account for symbols and totems, recorded culture, and unwritten truths. You can also develop your own assessment. Capture data from as many people (preferably everyone) within the organization.

Step 2: Categorize the results

See if there are discrepancies between the viewpoints of the culture of various members of the organization. They may be people who fit in multiple categories.

How Does the Leadership See the Culture?

How does the leadership see the symbols, recorded culture, and unwritten culture? As in our Fort Hood story, the Army leadership intended one culture; however, a subordinate unit displayed a different culture. But who are the leaders? Leadership could be the C-suite, an executive board, board of trustees, the managers, or even just the singular boss. There can also be varying levels of leadership that can drive a separate cultural identity. It is up to the organization to determine who the leader is in the organization.

How Does the Organization as a Whole See the Culture?

Next, capture how the entire organization (or at least all that participated) sees the organization's culture. The more dominant group(s) in the organization will heavily influence the overall results. Understanding how people in the organization see themselves will allow leaders to know if the ideal organizational culture matches the actual culture.

How Do Minorities in the Organization See the Culture?

Minorities in your organization are simply those who do not make up a majority demographic. For instance, if the majority of those in your organization have a college degree, those without would be a minority group. Many minority groups are relatively easy to figure out. For example, if 85% of those in the organization are natives of the country and 15% are foreigners or immigrants, then foreigners or immigrants would be a minority group. If 90% of the organization is able-bodied individuals and 10% were disabled individuals, then disabled individuals are a minority group. Get the minority view of the organization's culture. For example, an organization may have a new health initiative to have everyone take the stairs. The 90% of the organization that is able-bodied may be happy with the new initiative. But the 10% who are disabled may think this is a horrible idea. There was no malice involved with the new health initiative idea; however, it can have a very negative impact on a minority population. Getting the viewpoint of how minority groups in your organization view the organization's culture is critical.

Step 3: Share the results

Transparency is a friend to DE&I. Sharing results can open eyes to how various groups view the organization's culture. The results can also help to create a sense of urgency. Creating a sense of urgency is step 1 in Kotter's (2014) 8-Step Process for Leading Change. This will also allow you to see potential areas of concern and recruit people to help in future steps outlined in the chapter.

Use the tool to make notes on how you want to accomplish the steps in this chapter. These steps will help in identifying and defining your organization's culture.

CHAPTER 2 TOOL: A WORKSHEET ABOUT DATA COLLECTION METHODS

Data Collection	
Question	*Place your answers here*
1. How will you collect the data?	*(for example, individual surveys, focus groups)*
2. What question(s) will you ask to identify symbols/totems and their meaning?	
3. What question(s) will you ask to identify recorded culture and its meaning?	
4. What question(s) will you ask to identify unwritten culture and its meaning?	
5. How will you determine leadership?	
6. How will you determine minority groups?	
Results	
Question	*Place your results here*
1. How does the leadership see the organization's culture?	
2. How does the majority of the organization see the organization's culture?	
3. How does the _____ (minority group) see the organization's culture? (Repeat this question for each minority group identified.)	

There is a tool, appearing in Appendix E, that tracks with the step-by-step approach toward implementation described in this chapter. If you complete that tool and the others in chapters following this one, you will have the foundation for a proposal to your organization's management for installing an effective DE&I effort.

Discussion Questions

1. How can discrepancies in organizational culture present problems for DE&I?
2. When have you reached saturation in identifying your organization's minority groups?
3. How will you present your findings to leadership and the rest of the organization?

Works Consulted

Cohen, Zachary, and Browne, Ryan. 2020. "Army Punishes 14 Senior Officers After Murder and Other Deaths at Fort Hood." *CNN*, December 8, 2020, https://www.cnn.com/2020/12/08/ politics/ fort-hood- investigation/index.html

Kotter, John. 2014. *Accelerate: Building Strategic Agility for a Faster-moving World.* Brighton, MA: Harvard Business Review Press.

Leadership Centre. "Cultural Web." Accessed May 20, 2021. https://www.leadership-centre.org.uk/artofchangemaking/theory/cultural-web/

Rempfer, Kyle. 2020. "Fort Hood Soldier Arrested on Murder Warrant in Year-old Case." *Army Times*, November 4, 2020, https://www.armytimes.com/news/your-army/2020/11/04/fort-hood-soldier-arrested-on-murder-warrant-in-year-old-case/

Schein, Edgar. 2016. *Organizational Culture and Leadership* (5th ed.). Hoboken, NJ: Wiley. https://www.wiley.com/en-us/Organizational+Culture+and+Leadership%2C+5th+ Edition-p-9781119212041

The Guardian. 2020. "US Army Fires Fort Hood Officers and Orders Policy Shift Following 25 Deaths." *The Guardian*, December 9, 2020, https://www.the-guardian.com/us-news/2020/dec/ 09/fort-hood-army-base-officers-fired-deaths-sexual-assault

Chapter 3

Step 2: Clarifying the Role of Diversity, Equity, and Inclusion in Shaping Culture

Norm J. Jones

Contents

Case Study

Ingrid was beyond excited. She'd finally made it to the C-Suite after seven grueling years of slowly ascending the analyst ladder, moving into middle, and then upper management and now joining the most senior leaders of the McGregor Group, Savannah's oldest boutique management consulting

DOI: 10.4324/9781003184935-6

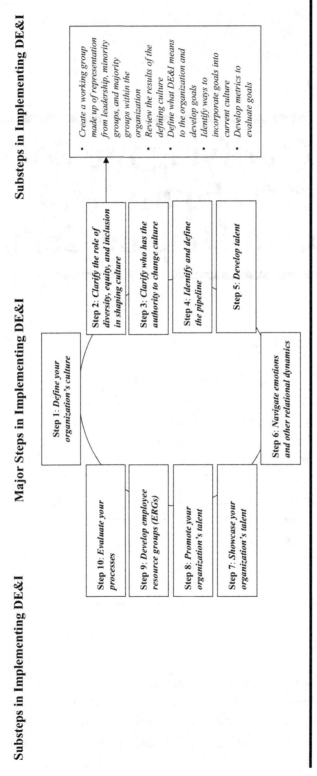

Frontmatter Figure 3.1   The diversity, equity, and inclusion (DE&I) roadmap model.

firm. She was a new CFO with new ideas. The firm was known for its classic yet contemporary approach to client engagements and its philanthropic disposition within one of Savannah's oldest communities. Recently, the firm almost doubled in size when it launched a new department of Community Outreach, primarily charged with distributing mini-grants to blighted neighborhoods desiring to work with local municipalities to improve community policing and school truancy.

Ingrid had big plans to right-size the firm's central budget such that departments were positioned to devote more resources to community development. She remembered sound bites the local news station had chosen from one of her most recent press conferences: "McGregor is proud to be part of the Hillsdale community, one of Savannah's oldest and culturally rich neighborhoods. It is our responsibility to invest in this community just as this community has invested in us."

Little did Ingrid know that just three weeks into her tenure as CFO, the managing partner, Phil Loller, would walk into her office and announce his plan to hire a Chief Diversity Officer (CDO):

> We need someone dedicated to this work daily. We're getting pressure from inside and outside the firm. I know it's not your job to handle diversity matters but you've done so much to help us understand it, I'd like you to run the search. I'm announcing to the rest of the team later today. Can I count on you?

Ingrid was stunned. Where was this coming from? Was it about the recent rash of stories about police brutality? Was it because she was the only person of color in senior management? Or maybe someone filed a discrimination claim. She'd barely made a dent in the first 90 days! How was she going to launch and lead a national search for a CDO? One thing was for sure – she would not say no.

Richard Vargas came highly recommended by almost every member of the Neiman Group's executive search team. He was bright, ambitious, conscientious, adaptable, and, seemingly, a quick study! He would need to be because his charge was monstrous. "We've worked hard to build a strong culture here at McGregor," Phil exclaimed.

> But when it comes to diversity we're not doing enough. I think we've been asleep at the wheel. We need new programs and

initiatives. We need a vision for attracting a more diverse work-force; we need everybody trained in unconscious bias and each department needs a diversity plan. We need a statement on anti-racism that we can share with the community so they know we stand with them ... all of us ... black, white, yellow, and green.

Richard tried to suspend his judgment. "People aren't yellow," he thought to himself. "And if you're green, something is very wrong?" Phil continued, "McGregor is a community within a community, and *every* community member matters!"

So many words. So much work. So little time and unless there were typos in the budget – so little money. Determined to tackle the task and meet the challenge, Richard set out to create a plan. He was McGregor's first CDO. All eyes were on him to create the change McGregor desperately needed. If he heard the word "culture" once a day, he heard it a million.

Richard knew a lot about culture. He'd taken entire classes on the sub-ject. But one thing struck him as odd: everyone at McGregor seemed to talk about the culture they wanted *him* to create as if (1) there wasn't already a culture before he arrived and (2) he could somehow magically create a cul-ture on his own. Richard remembered the Chimamanda Adichie quote that used to hang on the lobby wall at his former place of employment: "Culture does not make people. People make culture."

Based on the leadership prospectus provided by the search firm, within the first few months, Richard would be expected to review and assess poli-cies, practices, organizational structures, and partner with HR to create a new rewards system more intentionally focused on one of McGregor's three core values: celebrating diversity. The other two were community investment and leveraging people power.

Richard hunkered down in his office late on Friday and by Sunday he'd mapped out a planned approach to better understand McGregor's policies, practices, organizational structure, and reward system. He wanted the firm's workforce to appreciate his structured approach. In a brief memo to Phil, he introduced his plans by positing: "Neither diversity, equity, or inclusion is a feeling, but rather a science." He knew his success was largely dependent on a climate that would allow for change and the space for both experienced and emergent leaders to steward that change in their context. He found him-self ruminating on Adichie's words: "Culture does not make people. People make culture."

What Does the Research Say about Culture?

"Our cultures are part of our identity. Cultures contain stories" (Page 2007). This thought is mainly offered about individuals and their familial/environmental ties. But the same is true in organizations – especially as it relates to the stories well tell about our experiences with each other and the organization. Organizational culture, among other elements, involves a firm understanding of policy, practice, and organizational structure. With DE&I work, many organizations first have to reject the impulse to socialize their DE&I efforts as something outside of the organization's core values or the strategic realm. Often, critical stakeholders do not expect DE&I leaders to engage with policy, practice, or organizational structure unless legal and compliance issues be resolved. What often happens is the creation of new initiatives and programs that may well sit outside of what the organization understands as its core work. This is partially why Damon Williams, in his foregrounding book, *Strategic Diversity Leadership*, urges DE&I leaders to connect their efforts, no matter how grand or small, to an organization's strategic plan (Williams 2013, 14).

Policy and Politics

Organizational policy is key to understanding culture because it creates the conditions by which an organization's members understand what governs behavior. In a more negative but practical sense, policies (unlike practices) formally bind members by way of possible consequences if the policies are violated. Organizational policy and DE&I rarely are uttered in the same sentence. Given the heft that policy holds, it is an irony that the two would not connect in the minds of leaders. Policies can prescribe, prohibit, and even promote behaviors that situate members in a particular organizational context and that context often plays a key role in shaping culture. Leaders play a key role in shaping culture as well.

Key Definitions of Diversity, Equity, and Inclusion

To better understand the role of DE&I in shaping culture, one must define diversity, inclusion, and equity, respectively. Although the literature and field often refer to "DE&I", the order of the letters matters with organizational culture. Without subjects, the difference is difficult to quantify and even harder to grasp as concerning composition. Inclusion is the domain in which many of the salient features of culture reside. How do organizations behave because of the diversity they have amassed? And finally, equity is not about individual people but more so about constructing policies, practices, structures, and protocols that reflect an organization's disposition toward diversity and inclusion. For this chapter, I submit these definitions:

Diversity: For our purposes, "diversity" refers to the demographic composition of a community, a constituency within a larger community, a state, a nation, etc. Diversity as a goal for communities may refer to the heterogeneity of members from different groups or identities and active efforts to ensure people from historically underrepresented groups. It does not and cannot apply to an individual. An individual cannot be diverse, despite the increasingly popular use of the term to refer to individuals of color. The backgrounds and identities of an organizational community, taken together, constitute diversity. Because of the positive benefits of compositional diversity for learning, discovery, and problem-solving, organizations often identify goals of increasing the diversity of their members in backgrounds, identities, and perspectives.

Inclusion refers to the culture of an organizational community and how much people from all groups are welcomed and valued for who they are. Often, the organizational goal is to ensure that neither background nor identity stands in the way of belonging and success and that everyone can play a role in shaping the environment, not as individuals stripped of their identities, but as people whose cultures and perspectives make the organization better.

Equity refers to fairness in policies, procedures, and practices. The organizational goal is typically to ensure equal access to the programs, services, support, and opportunities appropriate to a constituency, role, or work.

The General Landscape of DE&I

Diversity, equity, and inclusion have been part of the Western landscape for some time. The nomenclature has shifted over decades and even centuries. That people are, in some ways, socialized to see differences and make judgments about what makes something or someone different is age-old. I refer to a "Western landscape" because that may be considered the most salient points of diversity, equity, and inclusion in the United States, which is different in many other countries.

The workplace benefits from a shared language, a way to garner shared meaning and understanding about what particular words mean. When organizations are attentive to this, they've taken important steps to cultivate a healthier workplace culture.

The strategic nature of DE&I work requires practitioners to gain immediate knowledge of organizational culture. One does not create this culture but steps into a culture that is created over time and continues to evolve. The work of the practitioner, therefore, is to figure out what is needed to gain a level of understanding that informs necessary paths for DE&I goal development and realization.

Squaring Definitions

Part of such sense-making involves the squaring of definitions and concepts. Fundamental definitions of DE&I and organizational culture are key to reconciling one's role as an internal Organization Development practitioner focused on DE&I work. Table 3.1 illustrates possible connections between DE&I definitions and important culture concepts set forth by Edgar Schein, a leading theorist around organizational culture.

The Macro-Frame of Organizational Culture

In a general sense, Schein defines *culture* in the following way:

> *Culture* is what a group learns over time as that group solves its problems of survival in an external environment and its problems of internal integration. Such learning is simultaneously a behavioral, cognitive, and emotional process. Extrapolating further from a functionalist anthropological view, the deepest level of culture will be the cognitive in that the perceptions, language, and thought processes that a group comes to share will be the ultimate causal determinant of feelings, attitudes, espoused values, and overt behavior.

As Schein continues:

> If the organization has had shared experiences, there will also be a total organizational culture. Within any unit, the tendency for integration and consistency will be assumed to be present, but coexisting units or a larger system can have cultures that are independent

and even in conflict with each other. Culture can now be defined as (a) a pattern of basic assumptions, (b) invented, discovered, or developed by a group, (c) as it learns to cope with its problems of external adaptation and internal integration, (d) that has worked well enough to be considered valid and, therefore, (e) is to be taught to new members as the (f) correct way to perceive, think, and feel about those problems.

Schein (1998) believes that antecedents of a *consistent* culture rely upon five variables:

Table 3.1   Squaring Culture and Diversity, Equity, and Inclusion

Internal culture consistency	Diversity	Equity	Inclusion
Stability of the group	Addresses the extent to which demographic composition of the group add the stability of group dynamic	Group may interpret its stability by comparing itself to other homogenous groups within the organization (e.g., employee resource groups analyzing budget allocations)	Group may assess the degree to which its members are engaged in organizational life across a variety of variables
Length of time the group has existed	Demographic composition of the group may connect with its collective tenure relative to the overall organization	Variable access to organizational opportunity is marked by structural inequality in the larger culture	Group may take stock of how long it takes for certain individuals and/or groups to become fully integrated into the day-to-day life of the organization
Intensity of the group learning experiences	Demographic composition of the group may define its own learning separate and apart from that of the organization	Groups may interpret efficacy based on opportunities for professional growth and pathways for promotion	Group may take stock of learning opportunities that either include or exclude marginalized and underrepresented groups in training and development designs

1. The stability of the group
2. The time the group has existed
3. The intensity of the group's experiences of learning
4. The mechanisms by which the learning has taken place
5. The strength and clarity of the assumptions held by the founders and leaders of the group.

Schein speaks of the fundamental challenges of defining organizational culture as a by-product of the ambiguity of "organization" as an actual concept (Schein 1988). Despite this ambiguity, if we think about the key elements of Schein's more narrowed definition organized across five elements, we can draw important linkages between conceptions of culture and diversity, equity, and inclusion. Table 3.1 outlines these linkages.

Culture in Context

Despite one's specific diversity role, as an Organization Development practitioner, the ability to not only understand but actively engage with organizational culture and subcultures is key to navigating client systems. Edgar Schein posits that "the simplest way of thinking about culture is to liken it to personality and character in the individual" (Rothwell et al. 2010). Some believe that organizational personality prevails over organizational identity, including diversity characteristics.

Countless surveys illustrate the difficulties associated with transforming culture. Neville and Schneider (2021, 2) harken back to Schneider's attraction–selection–attrition (ASA) framework to describe the basis for an organization's culture, which is typically established by the organization's founding members (Neville and Schneider, 2021). Organizations cultures simply reflect the values, personalities, and traits of those who have chosen (and been chosen) to work there. This amplifies Adichie's words: "People make culture."

What Neville and Schneider (2021) call "the homogeneity of personality" (4) against a backdrop of a mosaic diversity (demographic analysis, diversity programming, strategic planning focused on equity and inclusion goals) prohibits many from appreciating the salience of organizational personality. This personality is largely where culture lives and usually personality is connected to a unit within an organization – yielding *multiple* personalities in the aggregate.

Putting into Practice

Step 1: Create a working group made up of representation from leadership, minority groups, and majority groups within the organization (as you defined in the previous chapter).

Creating a representative working group will provide opportunity for diverse thoughts and viewpoints for analyzing results or developing policies and procedures. Again, don't think of diversity as only a race or gender issue. Think through how different levels of the organization (e.g., managers, frontline supervisors, line workers, division heads) will be represented.

Step 2: Review the results of the defining culture from the previous chapter.

Use the working group to review and analyze the results of defining your culture. To build toward the culture the organization wants, you must first understand what the culture you have is. Knowing (Chapter 2) and understanding (this chapter) are different. Someone may know what a smartphone is, but understanding all of its functionality is something different.

Step 3: Define what DE&I means to the organization and develop goals.

A recurring theme you should identify is that DE&I can mean something different to everyone you ask. You will suffer confusion, frustration, and never achieve desired results without clearly defining what DE&I means to the organization and developing goals. Again, use the working group for this step. Later chapters will discuss recruitment, talent development, and promotions. It is okay to peek ahead to generate ideas on areas you want to develop goals to improve DE&I within your organization.

Step 4: Identify ways to incorporate goals into current culture (e.g., mission, vision, values).

Another theme you should identify from this book is that DE&I should be a part of the culture (hence three chapters dedicated to culture). Your organizations mission, vision, and values should reflect your thoughts on diversity. If your organization doesn't have a mission, vision, or values, you may have issues bigger than you know. Brainstorm how else you can make DE&I as you define it part of your culture or DNA.

Step 5: Develop metrics to evaluate goals.

How will you know your efforts are working? Developing metrics will allow you to measure your progress along the way. This will allow you to know what is working and what needs more attention. See Chapter 11 for more information on evaluation.

There is a tool, appearing in Appendix E, that tracks with the step-by-step approach toward implementation described in this chapter. If you complete that tool and the others in chapters following this one, you will have the foundation for a proposal to your organization's management for installing an effective DE&I effort.

Key Questions about the Chapter

1. Search on Google about corporate culture change. Then describe, based on what you find, how to create a corporate culture change that supports DE&I.
2. This chapter quotes Tom Peters when he wrote that "as a rule of thumb, involve everyone in everything" (Peters and Waterman 1982). What might that quote mean when applied to DE&I? Explain.
3. How much input is needed from different stakeholder groups when formulating a DE&I program? When changing the corporate culture to support DE&I?

Works Consulted

Hubbard, E.E., 1997. *Measuring Diversity Results.* Volume 1, Petaluma, CA: Global Insights Publishing.

Neville, L., Schneider, B., 2021. "Why Is It So Hard to Change a Culture? It's The People." *Organization Development Review*, 53:1, 41–46.

Page, S., 2007. *The Difference: How the Power of Diversity Creates Better Groups, Firms, Schools and Societies.* Princeton, NJ: Princeton University Press.

Quartz, 2016. "Three Ways Leaders Should Shape Culture." Accessed on May 10 2021. https://qz.com/839382/three-ways-leaders-should-shape-culture/

Roberts, L.M., Wooten, L.P., Davidson, M.N., 2016. *Positive Organizing in a Global Society: Understanding and Engaging Differences for Capacity Building and Inclusion.* New York. Routledge.

Schein, E.H., "Organizational Culture." *MIT Sloan Management Review*, 8:13, 3–4.

Stevenson, H. "Paradox: A Gestalt Theory of Change." *Gestalt Review*, 22:2, 5–22.

Chapter 4

Step 3: Clarifying Who Has the Authority to Change Culture

S. Ron Banerjee

Contents

A Case Study of Failed Cultural Change Leadership

Company A is a financial services firm. Company A executives reviewed their year-end data from the previous year. They were not satisfied with the previous year's results, so they decided to be more competitive and also decided that a significant change initiative should be undertaken. Company A provides financial services to individuals and businesses in Central

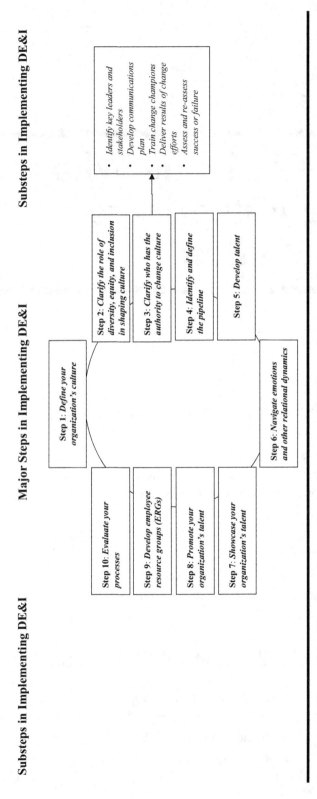

Substeps in Implementing DE&I **Major Steps in Implementing DE&I** **Substeps in Implementing DE&I**

Step 1: *Define your organization's culture*

Step 2: *Clarify the role of diversity, equity, and inclusion in shaping culture*

Step 3: *Clarify who has the authority to change culture*

Step 4: *Identify and define the pipeline*

Step 5: *Develop talent*

Step 6: *Navigate emotions and other relational dynamics*

Step 7: *Showcase your organization's talent*

Step 8: *Promote your organization's talent*

Step 9: *Develop employee resource groups (ERGs)*

Step 10: *Evaluate your processes*

- *Identify key leaders and stakeholders*
- *Develop communications plan*
- *Train change champions*
- *Deliver results of change efforts*
- *Assess and re-assess success or failure*

Frontmatter Figure 4.1   The diversity, equity, and inclusion (DE&I) roadmap model.

Pennsylvania. Company A's workplace is fast-paced, highly competitive, and subject to high scrutiny due to the heavy levels of mandatory regulatory compliance. Company A began focusing on the financial services needs of the small town, rural communities they served. For Company A, control is focused at the top in what has been called a highly integrated, "good old boy" network, leading the organization to rapid growth through mergers and purchases of other similar community-focused banks and brokerages. However, what started as a community focus at a local level has now blossomed into a regional financial services powerhouse. Several years prior, Company A top executives had attempted to introduce the concept of self-managed workgroups and teams much as other banking and financial organizations had been doing as their mechanism to achieving organizational change.

Clan-hierarchy-type organizations are typical of financial services and banking companies. However, the biggest challenge was whether the new management approach would overcome the challenges of the "command and control"-type culture that had prevailed for the previous decade under the original Company A ownership. The C-level executives were becoming frustrated at the prospect of the organization losing its competitiveness and could not understand how other regional financial services groups could build scale and increase their profitability and market reach?

Finally, the CEO commissioned assessments to carefully analyze their culture to understand what would be necessary to alter their fundamental culture. It was soon discovered that although the cultural change was planned and initiated from the top, the change was ad hoc, and the middle and frontline managers had little support from above and struggled with helping their workforce groups cope with change.

The shortfall for the change initiative was determined to stem from the shift in cultural belief from the small-town, community-based emphasis to profitability, growth, and greater regional reach focus being emphasized by top leadership. The leadership had failed to understand their organization's new vision and mission while also being negligent toward building the change-coping capacity of their employees. Ultimately, Company A missed the mark on providing dedicated resources to build consistency across departments and divisions in managing the change. System-wide change needed to be built incrementally by adding to current working policies and procedures while promoting collaborative opportunities between those most affected and by empowering stakeholders to generate and manage change within their levels and workgroups with high trust and autonomy without relying on central control or interference from the top. Company A leaders developed a new change roadmap and articulated the considerations by all employees and change influencers for its use. Company A leaders delivered a roadmap that was consistently applied in various iterations tailored to each tier for successful cultural change/shift, i.e., at the personal/individual level, at the team or group levels, and the organization's team or group levels system-wide level.

In previous chapters, authors have discussed DE&I within the context of the components of organizational change, what comprises an organization's culture, and how change must be effectuated at different levels of the organization. It is unnecessary to relitigate those definitions and concepts. Other texts and authors have approached change from the technical/process perspective. This chapter draws on understanding the role of leaders within their organizational system and the best practices for leaders to affect and influence cultures to achieve transformative change. This chapter intends to assist organization leaders in understanding that effective and efficient change occurs when those with the authority to explore, direct, and manage change are highly engaged and visible. Identifying those critical characteristics in oneself and other individuals within the organization who are strategically beneficial to the change initiative is essential to leading or supporting cultural change. Change leaders with these capabilities are mission-critical when creating a culture and tradition of inclusivity. This chapter is dedicated to identifying and developing how organization leaders can execute or adapt as the sociotechnical change mechanism to transformational change. The premise is that we can foster and identify these characteristics as change leaders and as the primary stakeholders who are the catalysts at various organization levels for cultural change. Strategically positioning those stakeholders implementing those traits provides the spark for a contagious, inclusive mindset that leads to genuine, generative, transformative cultural change.

What Does the Research Say?

Not surprisingly, the world is in a state of flux as individuals and organizations work to build more inclusive environments in all aspects of life. Large and small organizations continue to focus and prioritize DE&I strategies. Although DE&I interest appears to be widespread, each organization has a unique set of motivations for creating and sustaining DE&I program success.

It is that unique set of motivations that are the foundation and launchpad for transformation. It is up to the organization's leader to use their specific skill set to make that transformation palatable and acceptable system-wide.

Today's leaders are being held accountable for not just talking about diversity, equity, inclusion, and belonging, but taking action. Today's businesses are being held to a higher standard to build cultures of inclusivity. Profitability is no longer the sole concern of C-level executives as their company missions, visions, and values reflect the demand for cultural change. Although that may be the case, in 2015 McKinsey Research revealed that "companies in the top quartile for diversity financially outperform those in the bottom quartile" (Hunt et al. 2015). Organizations that do not address DE&I guarantee an assured route toward irrelevancy.

Organization leaders must serve a higher purpose, having a clear inclusivity vision while establishing diversity and belonging cultures. Leaders must demonstrate today's equity values while performing tangible, meaningful actions that foster DE&I cultures. Now, organization leaders must serve a higher purpose of building, nurturing, and promoting organizational cultures founded on a clear set of values reflecting inclusive actions that benefit the world. Organizations are looking for leaders with deep expertise and leadership in people operations. Organizations continue to search for leaders who can guide companies and organizations toward high growth while achieving a best-in-class employee experience through a culture of inclusivity and belonging (Cox and Blake 1991). Today's organization leaders must be thought leaders, coaches, talent managers, learning and development professionals, and performance managers while navigating their organizations within the context of diversity, equity, inclusion, and belonging. Today's DE&I leaders provide strategic direction and expertise while demonstrating best practices in their people functions.

The challenge to leaders today when dealing with cultural change is especially noticeable when the organization is experiencing growth. A variety of contexts are the backdrop as cultures blend. A leader must understand that new hires joining the organization and the broad and diverse existing employee population contribute to culture change systems. The introduction of new organization members through mergers and acquisitions, outsourcing, strategic partnerships, and organizations going through physical/geographical expansion blends multiple generations in the organization's workplace.

To this effect, leaders develop a better understanding of the characteristics of a successful diversity, equity, and inclusion leader for successful introduction into their competency portfolios to ultimately become a DE&I leader, a champion for inclusivity. Situated atop the power matrix, an organization's senior leaders are positioned to mold organization vision, strategies, organizational design, and culture while generating performance benefits from diversity. Due to this influential position at the apex of power, leaders must recognize who can be the catalyst for cultural change or develop into one.

Over time, it has become more apparent that a leader must pay attention to culture, various populations affected by change, and effective leadership during change practices which are difference makers between a successful, transformative change and a failure. "Individual perceptions about how the cultural change process is handled and the direction in which the culture is moved is integral in the success of cultural change initiatives" (Stefanowski 2018). And communication occurs, including frequency and clarity, and how transparent leaders are regarding the change process are all equally important to cultural change success. Communication is pivotal regarding how leaders and stakeholders are viewed and the leader who is the "face of the cultural change" (Kavanagh and Ashkanasy 2006).

Leaders need to be competent and trained in transforming organizations to ensure that individuals accept the changes prompted by a merger. A broad array of data establishes that a genuinely diverse workforce drives innovation. A diverse workforce does not just have a workforce with a broad range of cultures and backgrounds together. Diversity is also created by compiling an array of "lived experiences, perspectives, thinking styles and abilities" (Marie A. Bernard 2020). Recent research reinforces and connects diversity and organizations with cultures of acceptance to company financial performance. Data suggests that how organizations develop better inclusion strategies and integrate them into their organizational culture becomes an essential enabler for growth and leads to a more potent competitive edge (Hunt et al. 2018). Organizations are developing many programs and policies to increase diversity of leaders, faculty, staff, and learners in higher education (Fuentes-Afflick 2018). Many CEOs and business thought leaders are now considering diversity to be the source of improved degrees of creativity and innovation, warranting increasing leadership interest in making diversity, equity, inclusion, and belonging a keystone strategic priority (Groysberg and Connoly 2013). Although diversity initiative implementation is perhaps at an all-time high, spurred by increased demand for social justice and better treatment of the underserved, several empirical investigations uncover the obstacles associated with these DE&I initiatives and organizational culture change. Dover et al. (2020) suggest that one of the testing points regarding the effectiveness of diversity and cultural change leadership pertains to often "unintended signals" that diversity and equity initiatives send, namely, through the miscommunication of (1) fairness signals, (2) inclusion signals, and (3) competence signals (Figure 4.1).

Putting into Practice

Step 1: Identify key leaders and stakeholders

As the case study earlier in this chapter exposed, for cultural change to take root and be sustainable, the organization leader should understand who makes up the system and who will be affected by the cultural change and to what degree. Without understanding the stakeholders and the "What's in it for them" people side of cultural change, the overall transformation could be derailed from the beginning as change resistance, mistrust, or lack of clarity regarding the cultural change could be prevalent. Therefore, time identifying who will be using the roadmap and who will be affected by the change strategy is time well spent preparing for initiating cultural change.

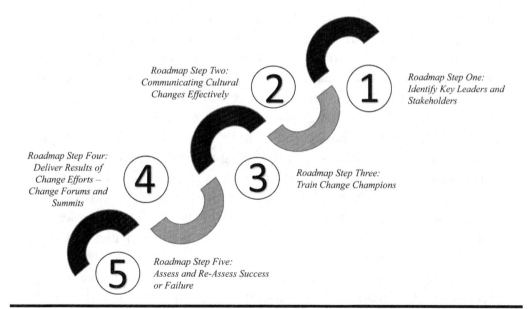

Figure 4.1   Roadmap to cultural change – Original author creation © S. Ron Banerjee 2021.

In an interview with world-renowned process consultation guru Ed Schein, he reminded me that all change begins with the first conversation with stakeholders to build level two relationships. This follows the notion that conversations, from the get-go, are a form of sociotechnical intervention. Using those conversations to build relationships, the following are examples of who will be joining in those conversations, and following the cultural change roadmap created by the organization leader, revealing how the road-map must be tailored to each:

1. *You as the Change Leader* – The person leading the cultural change must have a clear, sensible roadmap that has outlined steps easy for the change leader to understand. This roadmap version should be logical and not so complex that the leader herself gets lost in the details and soon loses direction and focus.
2. *Stakeholders and Change Catalysts* – The most intelligent way to create an adaptative organization is by starting with highly agile employees who positively change who you as the change leader connect to executive or leadership direction regarding the cultural shift. The people involved in the cultural change must reference what is expected of them and when they are to act. This roadmap audience/segment is significant as stake-holders are on the front lines of the change effort. They typically need the roadmap to define their roles while also providing a resource that affirms what has been completed and actions yet to be taken.
3. *Change Sponsor(s)* – Although you may be the leader tasked with trans-forming the organization's culture, the Change Sponsor is the individual who is ultimately accountable for completing the cultural change trans-formation and ensuring that the changes are benefiting the organiza-tion as intended. The change sponsor roadmap is the comprehensive guide to the cultural change and includes vital information regarding the different interventions utilized during the cultural change process. This "master plan" describes deliverables to be shared with organiza-tion leaders and stakeholders describing change progress and success milestones. The change sponsor roadmap is used to identify roles for change and indicates when and to whom responsibilities or tasks should be delegated.
4. *Quality Managers and Change Auditors* – The final group that might receive the roadmap are those tasked with auditing the change effort and understanding the changes at various stages to confirm successful completion and cultural transformation.

By honing their inclusivity skills, organization leaders can significantly affect policy implications and education in their respective organizational cultures. Organization leadership must make all levels of decision-making in organizational environments barrier-free, offering complete, effective participation to all social categories. By planning and developing increased engagement opportunities for the underserved populations by adopting equitable and inclusive workforce development policies, a leader can reflect her commitment to supporting organization members to improve inclusion and foster cultures of equity and fairness. Leaders can foster bias-free, strategic mechanism creation and implementation to establish frameworks and enforceable gender and diversity equity policies while championing cultures of equitable empowerment.

Step 2: Develop communications plan

As the cultural change leader, it is mission-critical to recognize and communicate with all participants and stakeholders regarding the cultural change process. Leaders must articulate the goals of the new culture to be established, the roles and expectations of individuals impacted by the cultural change, and affirm how important the individuals are to the success of the change process. This is an opportunity for the cultural change leader to establish trust and rapport with the organization's stakeholders, articulating how important they and their acceptance of the culture change are to its success. Thorough, regular communication, therefore, must be a cultural change leader's commitment from moment one. The communication plan must convey the metrics for which culture change success will be measured – failing to acknowledge that the ultimate power to change lies in the larger organization's individuals dooms the change initiative to fail. Each person's ability to process change is hardwired into who they are. Different psychometric tools are available to measure how individuals respond to change situations (Banerjee 2021).

A cultural change leader can use one technique known as the "Be On the Look Out (BOLO)" technique. This is a communication strategy that a leader uses through several communication modes to communicate early to inform stakeholders throughout the organization's structure. The BOLO technique explains expectations, responsibilities, and potential impacts. Early communication is needed to indicate that the change process was about to occur. It was essential for stakeholders. They received the communication to "be on the lookout" for things related to the forthcoming change initiative.

Communication strategies are integrated by the change leader directly into how the organization wants to accomplish the change. However, there must be a balance between communicating with a purpose and communicating just for communicating.

Communicating without purpose and detail could fuel change resistance as stakeholders could use words like "inundated" or "overload" or "death by memo." Successful cultural change depends on how the information being shared relates to the stakeholder audience receiving the information. The cultural change leader must tailor communication to a particular audience. By communicating with all stakeholders regarding the anticipated benefits of the cultural change, communication plans often stumble when organizations focus on the proposed changes and benefit the organization but inadvertently fail to communicate how the cultural change benefits the stakeholder. In the case of Company A, how the person receiving the communication would benefit from the new culture of growth and greater scope of their services was painfully omitted.

By being inclusive in communication, it prevents any particular constituency from being or feeling left out. Unfortunately, when stakeholders feel overlooked, those forgotten or omitted stakeholders inevitably become a source for rumor and partial truths regarding the past's cultural change efforts, which can become disruptive. It was equally problematic when communications dumbfounded stakeholders with unnecessary and extraneous details that had nothing to do with the stakeholder or the stakeholder's position (Banerjee 2021). Cultural change leaders must integrate a strategy where personalization to the change initiative establishes connectivity between the organization and an individual stakeholder's commitment to change. By eliciting personalized feedback through targeted, deliberate opportunities for individual engagement, the cultural change leader creates a foundation of collaboration and cooperation from the beginning.

Step 3: Train change champions

There are four structures or approaches that an organization navigates when dealing with a large-scale change initiative (Banerjee n.d.; Banerjee 2021). Changing culture is a systemic progression of mini-changes that ultimately results in the cultural transformation system-wide. These four structures should also be considered when leading cultural change. The organization often shifts between each throughout the cultural change effort. The change leader might find that the structure or process to successfully adopting the cultural change is one way initially, but it quickly morphs into another approach. The awareness of this constant interaction between different change structures allows the change leader to remain agile and responsive to contextual and situation adjustment requirements. The following table is a description of each structure and how each is used when leading a cultural change:

1. *The Shadow Organization* – This is where the change effort requires an organization to create a separate organization chart of various specialized teams, i.e., training and development, physical plant, where the team engages the change effort based on the milestones required, but only those that are focused on their specialization. An essential characteristic is these specialized teams still operate within their existing, respective overall workgroups or divisions targeting the change milestones that the organization requires of their specific areas (Banerjee n.d.; Banerjee 2021). The shadow organization structure for cultural change is often used in DE&I work as often organizations establish a separate internal entity to focus on the development and the administration of DE&I programs. Often, leaders find an increased level of confidence in creating a shadow organization because of specifically establishing the group using individuals who either self-identify as change catalysts or those who have been recognized as change leaders. This structure is also often in a direct hierarchal relationship with the shadow organization Chair reporting to the Chief Diversity Officer position if one exists or in its absence, the Chief Executive Officer, Managing Director, or President of the organization depending on organizational structure.

2. *The Embedded Effort* – The responsibilities of required change are built into the employees' job descriptions. As part of the change effort, embedding the responsibilities of change into the job descriptions mandates attention to any change effort as part of job performance. Change-related performance is added as the list of KPIs to be assessed as part of overall job performance. The premise here is that by mandating change responsibilities at the individual level, no additional organization structures are necessary to effectuate change (Banerjee n.d.; Banerjee 2021). Often, the Embedded Effort structure leads to a revision of performance and productivity requirements to reflect specific DE&I–related components. These specific DE&I requirements are integrated into performance reviews and play an integral role in promotions and bases for financial raises. The delivery mechanism within the organization

that uses an Embedded Effort is in a steering committee comprised of known individuals identified as change catalysts, change supporters. Specifically, DE&I advocates are usually assembled by the Chief Diversity Officer/Diversity Leader.

3. *The Dream Team* – This change structure can also be called the star approach. The change consultant works with the organization to identify superstars from within the organization. Once these stars are identified, a change task force is created comprised of these stars. The sole purpose of this task force is to generate a proposal for change implementation based on the stars' opinions and observations, which are ultimately presented to the C-level executives for disposition. It is a known fact in talent management circles that an organization's "stars" are as much as 20% more productive than the average rank and file employee. This change structure builds on high level of engagement and performance (Banerjee n.d.; Banerjee 2021). Like the Embedded Effort, the Dream Team leverages known supporters and those influencers in whom the Chief Diversity Officer/Diversity Leader has the most confidence to promote, facilitate, and deliver programming, specifically for the DE&I policy. Often the Dream Team Lead is given a high level of autonomy and trust; however, she still reports regularly to the C-Suite executives regularly. Successful Dream Team efforts are also designed to include various backgrounds to appeal to many organization segments. The foundational principle of incorporating the Dream Team superstars in the change is their valuable contributions to developing the DE&I program structures themselves while eliciting the support and compliance of their subordinates and peers.

4. *Institutionalized Structured Change* – This change structure is when the organization chart is modified to create specific departments that handle a change aspect. For example, organizations are increasingly establishing departments that focus exclusively on diversity- and inclusion-related change. Other departments might manage change affecting product quality or safety. The creation of separate change-focused departments augments the organization as a recognized part of the overall organization. These change silos only focus on the parts of the large-scale change that impact those within their silo's boundary (Banerjee n.d.; Banerjee 2021). Unlike the previous three structures, the Institutionalized Structured Change is a dedicated channel deliberated, formed, and run by the Chief Diversity Officer. The formal department dedicated to the DE&I effort is where all change programming is

brainstormed, developed, and delivered to the department stakeholders. This is generated internally through typical research processes such as surveys and interviews of stakeholders. However, an integral part of a successful DE&I department is also maintaining regular external research to identify DE&I innovation and opportunities emerging in the world around the organization. With a specific department tasked with only DE&I–related programming, leaders are provided with a set mechanism to deliver DE&I–related content in the most relevant manner, using internally and externally generated insights for program updates and the basis for future innovation.

Author's Note: One form of Institutionalized Structured Change is forming employee resource groups (ERG) designed explicitly to be the DE&I source for the organization. As ERG's have been discussed in a previous chapter as a mechanism for change, ERG's continue to increase in popularity as an organization structure for DE&I cultural impact.

Step 4: Deliver results of change efforts (e.g., change forums and summits)

A leader plans for cultural change, creating events where change status and findings can be shared throughout the culture change initiative. These events are necessary to generate recommendations and opportunities to calibrate and recalibrate different change interventions delivered as part of the change process. These events are also utilized to inform stakeholder engagement opportunities, such as communication planning or training plan development. This is critical because aligning the results and sharing the status of the change initiative periodically and deliberately is essential, especially when maintaining the correct tone regarding change planning and execution with stakeholders. These sessions can be large-scale group sessions or can be executed at more local levels. The danger in making these events too small, however intimate, does not necessarily help describe how the local cultural change fits in with or follows other constituencies' change efforts. Misalignment will create confusion and anxiety among stakeholders. As a leader, here are a few hints toward making forums and summits effective:

1. Involve representatives/change champions from the local levels. This accomplishes building a higher level of engagement at the front line. Given the change leader's presence, this visibility and local change

catalysts show unity and strength in the purpose and commitment of the senior leader.

2. Forums and summits are good opportunities for facilitated discussions to discuss change impacts at a very granular, precise level. This gives the additional opportunity for those affected by the change to discuss various probing questions collectively and prompt discussions regarding ongoing interventions or concluded interventions and their value or lack thereof.

3. An alternative to the approach mentioned above, the following approach is driven by the cultural change leaders themselves, who might go into depth regarding other communication plans, training, and further engagement interventions. This is also mission-critical to managing expectations of change participants system-wide.

4. Regardless of the approach chosen or developing a hybrid of the above, one should be cautious of any change in formats or approaches from one event to another. Any inconsistency can make the event participants anxious regarding the change effort, but it might create uncertainty for others who lead future forums or summits. Uncertainty can lead to inconsistency in messaging and undermine the process. Consistency and continuity recognition are critical considerations when the cultural change process is still emerging.

5. Utilize technology to deliver high-quality, engaging presentations that make the cultural change exciting and remind attendees that the "What's in it for me" is still imperative to the organization. Those affected are valued by the organization.

6. Scheduling multiple forums, summits, or other gatherings throughout the change process is a good idea as each event informs the masses regarding the change roadmap and plans. These events can create added value for senior leadership and change sponsors. The events draw attendee attention to leader visibility and a chance to identify obstacles to change or change resistance in its early stages to remedy the situation before it harms the overall change strategy later.

7. Stakeholder requirements and expectations can vary significantly throughout the cultural change process. These events create occasions to manage expectations, promoting priorities and organization needs while connecting them to the greater good.

Step 5: Assess and reassess success or failure

As leaders work through the change process, the roadmap leads to the final step, the chance to reveal gaps that have emerged between the desired cultural change and the level of change being exhibited. Sharing assessments through the previous forums allows the leader to convey details regarding those interventions that have either succeeded or have yet to be delivered and support the workforce's continual education and engagement. To create a cultural adjustment or build sustainable cultural change, establishing which interventions are working and which are not allows the leader to identify and reward individuals. It creates an opportunity to recognize and praise different positive responses, attitudes, and behaviors while embedding other sociotechnical mechanisms to convey the desired culture. It is also an opportunity to highlight the new generative, collective way of doing things. By assessing how close the parts of the organization system are to accomplishing strategic objectives, goals, and challenges, the leadership can elicit vital feedback. Feedback is used to create personal narratives linking the benefits of cultural change to the positive impact of the changes on the individual level.

There is a tool, appearing in Appendix E, that tracks with the step-by-step approach toward implementation described in this chapter. If you complete that tool and the others in chapters following this one, you will have the foundation for a proposal to your organization's management for installing an effective DE&I effort.

Chapter Questions

1. As a cultural change leader, what has the data shown as the most critical characteristic of leading cultural change?
2. What is the purpose of the communication strategy as part of the cultural change leader's roadmap?
3. Name the four change structures that a culture change leader must know when considering introducing cultural change to their organization?

Works Consulted

"An Open Letter to the World: We Should Care About Human Capital." n.d. World Bank. Accessed May 9, 2021. https://www.worldbank.org/en/news/opinion /2018/10/11/an-open-letter-to-the-world-we-should-care-about-human-capital.

Banerjee, S. Ron. 2021. "Large Scale Interventions." In *Organization-development Interventions: Executing Effective Organizational Change*, edited by William J.

Rothwell, Sohel M. Imroz, and Behnam Bakhshandeh, 1st ed. Boca Raton, FL: CRC Press/Taylor & Francis Group.

Banerjee, Soumitra. n.d. "How to Structure Large Scale Change Efforts: Forum." *12Manage.Com* (blog). Accessed August 11, 2020. https://www.12manage.com/forum.asp?TB=kotter_change&S=29.

Bernard, Marie A. 2020. "A Case for Diversity Driven by Data | SWD at NIH." *Scientific Workforce Diversity* (blog). October 27, 2020. https://diversity.nih.gov/blog/2020-10-27-case-diversity-driven-data.

Cox, Taylor H., and Stacy Blake. 1991. "Managing Cultural Diversity: Implications for Organizational Competitiveness." *Academy of Management Perspectives* 5 (3): 45–56. https://doi.org/10.5465/ame.1991.4274465.

Dover, Tessa L., Cheryl R. Kaiser, and Brenda Major. 2020. "Mixed Signals: The Unintended Effects of Diversity Initiatives." *Social Issues and Policy Review* 14 (1): 152–81. https://doi.org/10.1111/sipr.12059.

Fuentes-Afflick, Elena. 2018. "Promoting Inclusion in Academic Medicine." *JAMA Network Open* 1 (4): e181010. https://doi.org/10.1001/jamanetworkopen.2018.1010.

Groysberg, Boris, and Katherine Connoly. 2013. "Great Leaders Who Make the Mix Work." *Harvard Business Review* 91 (9): 68–76.

Hunt, Vivian, Sara Prince, and Dennis Layton. 2015. "Why Diversity Matters | McKinsey." *McKinsey Insights*. 2015. https://www.mckinsey.com/business-functions/organization/our-insights/why-diversity-matters.

Hunt, Vivian, Lareina Yee, Sara Prince, and Sundiatu Dixon-Fyle. 2018. "Delivering Growth through Diversity in the Workplace | McKinsey." *Delivering through Diversity*. 2018. https://www.mckinsey.com/business-functions/organization/our-insights/delivering-through-diversity.

Kang, Sonia K., and Sarah Kaplan. 2019. "Working toward Gender Diversity and Inclusion in Medicine: Myths and Solutions." *The Lancet* 393 (10171): 579–86.

Kavanagh, Marie H., and Neal M. Ashkanasy. 2006. "The Impact of Leadership and Change Management Strategy on Organizational Culture and Individual Acceptance of Change during a Merger." *British Journal of Management* 17 (S1): S81–103. https://doi.org/10.1111/j.1467-8551.2006.00480.x.

Little, Jason. 2014. *Lean Change Management: Innovative Practices for Managing Organizational Change*. Middletown, DE: Happy Melly Express.

O'Donovan, Gabrielle. 2018. *Making Organizational Change Stick: How to Create a Culture of Partnership between Project and Change Management*. London ; New York: Routledge, Taylor & Francis Group.

Stefanowski, Robert. 2018. *Material Adverse Change: Lessons from Failed M&As*. Hoboken, NJ: Wiley.

Chapter 5

Step 4: Identifying and Defining the Pipeline

Catherine Haynes

Contents

DOI: 10.4324/9781003184935-8

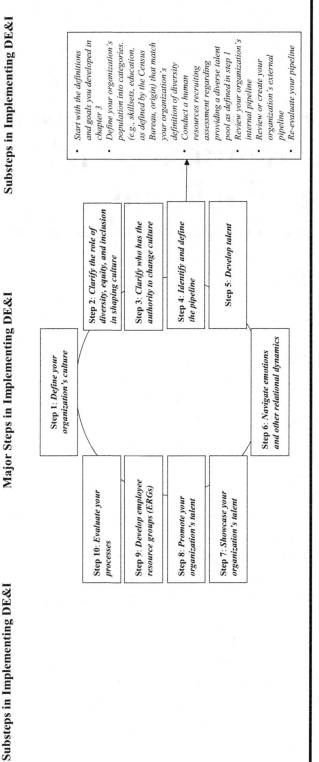

Frontmatter Figure 5.1   The diversity, equity, and inclusion (DE&I) roadmap model.

The Background Story

Much activity is happening regarding gender, race, ethnicity, social justice, and corporate responsibility in many countries, cities, towns, and neighborhoods. These activities are captured by nightly television news crews, everyday individual social media posts, in print, and on mobile devices. As these different situations spread to different organizations, it can be devastating. But organizations that are proactive and fair to employees can survive these issues. The top management has completed an assessment and now wants your organization to be more diverse, equitable, and inclusive. Some would argue that a diverse workforce is necessary for more than just survival, equity is the right thing to do, and that it must be woven throughout the organizations' culture, boardroom, and strategic mission. The organization wants you to hire more diverse talent. The question is how are you going to get a more diverse organization through recruiting? What steps should you take to achieve this goal? Where will you get diverse talent? How can you keep the talent you already have? In this chapter, we will discuss these questions and many more. This chapter provides you with some tools and information to create a diverse pipeline to meet organizational strategic goals.

In the early years of Title VII, the EECO and EEO, companies used training to merge and teach employees to get along. According to Amand and Winters (2008), after the landmark legislation was passed, organizations were on a fast track to train all employees. Organizations knew that non-compliance with the law would lead to fines and penalties from the federal government. But that was many years ago. One lesson learned from such pressurized training is that it was exceedingly difficult for the participants to separate themselves from the training sessions. Participants often left diversity training sessions with few positive emotions. Today's organizations realize that hiring more diverse individuals is better for business and that diverse individuals bring new life experiences to work. Hiring diverse individuals should not be done solely for legal compliance. Diversity and inclusion issues are expressed values in many businesses' core elements, websites, logos, job descriptions, and employee evaluations.

The U.S. Bureau of Labor Statistics (BLS) is the fact-finding division of the U.S. Department of Labor that provides a wide range of economic data about the economy. The BLS provides the public with web-based statistical data on the U.S. population, including a variety of data access tools and the online version of the *Occupational Outlook Handbook*. As a DE&I professional, you can access this data to help identify the underrepresented groups your company can focus on hiring. The great thing about using the BLS site is that you can narrowly search by zip codes or geographic area. While you are preparing the company's equity pipeline framework, the data from the BLS will be most useful. Subscription or access to their newsletter will give you email update about a wide variety of data points that can be useful to your organization.

According to the U.S. Bureau of Labor Statistics (BLS) website, the labor force characteristics are broken down into four large groups by race and ethnicity – Whites, Blacks, Asians, and Hispanics.

- Whites make up most of the labor force.
- Higher education generally leads to employment that pays more.
- Hispanics and Blacks have earnings considerably lower than Whites and Asians.
- Unemployed Asians and Blacks are unemployed longer.
- More Black and Hispanic families are maintained by women without a spouse.

Contact information for the U.S. Bureau of Labor Statistics is at https://www .bls.gov/bls/demographics.htm as of June 27, 2021.

To build a successful pipeline you should have targeted groups. Data from the U.S. Census Bureau is the best way to get to know who is out there. If you have been using your pipeline, you know the participants. Through the data from the Census Bureau, you can create an extensive action plan to expand your pipeline. One great attribute of the data is that the interpretation is up to the user. Research conducted by the Census Bureau is extensive.

They use several methods to collect data on any research, including surveys in ten languages, Braille, large print, and American Sign Language. Here is the information on why you should use data from the U.S. Census Bureau:

- It is the leading source of statistical information.
- Counts the entire U.S. population every ten years.
- The website data is up to date.
- Their tools are free and easy to use.
- Publication library includes a variety of human-interest data in several languages.
- Conducts meaningful surveys about women, veterans, and young adults.

What the Research (Law) Says

The laws make it illegal to discriminate against an employee or a job applicant because of that person's race, color, religion, sex (including pregnancy, transgender status, and sexual orientation), national origin, age (40 or older), disability, or genetic information. This includes all phases of work situations such as hiring, promotions, sexual harassment, harassment, training, wages, benefits, and dismissals.

The Equal Employment Opportunity Commission (EEOC) is the federal agency that advances opportunity in the workplace by enforcing compliance with federal laws. Most middle and top-level managers know of discrimination based on the law and Title VII of the Civil Rights Act of 1964. Some large organizations have specialized departments to ensure federal compliance with these laws, while other organizations place the enforcement, compliance, and reporting responsibilities on the human resources department.

You need to know what services the EEOC can provide your organization. For example, for companies that employ 15 or more individuals, there are some mandatory reporting and compliance requirements. The EEOC provides training conferences, workshops, and network opportunities to human resources professionals. I urge you to check the commission's website for the latest information on future events. The website for the commission is https://www.eeoc.gov/legislative-affairs. The EEOC has several regional offices. The legislative office headquarters is in Washington, DC. The EEOC also has a great media presence on LinkedIn, Facebook, and Twitter. The commission's specific information is listed at the end of this chapter.

National Diversity and Leadership Conference

The National Diversity Council (NDC) is a great nonprofit organization that connects public, private, and nonprofit organizations to share best practices to benefit diverse communities and workplaces. For the past 16 years, the National Diversity and Leadership Council has held a national conference that provides professionals and organizations the tools and resources to remain competitive in a global economy. During the conference, attendees are encouraged to network and share their best practices in diversity and inclusion. The NDC continuously promotes a positive atmosphere for organizations to expand their awareness of diversity through a variety of conferences, programs, and symposiums. The NDC provides great opportunities for organizations to learn from some of the top corporate leaders who value equity, diversity, and uniqueness. NDC also embraces the principles of equity through corporations, communities, and youth. The NDC is an excellent resource and advocacy for the value of inclusion and diversity (Table 5.1).

List of Agencies

Census Bureau Headquarters
U.S. Census Bureau
4600 Silver Hill Road
Washington, DC 20233
Call Center: 301-763-INFO (4636) or 800-923-8282
TDD: TTY 1-800-877-8339

EEOC Headquarters
U.S. Equal Employment Opportunity Commission
131 M Street, NE
Washington, D.C. 20507
Telephone: (202) 921-3191
Fax: (202) 663-4900
Email: legis@eeoc.gov

National Diversity Council
NDC Headquarters
1301 Regents Park Dr., Suite 210
Houston, Texas 77058
Local Texas Number: (281) 975-0626
http://www.nationaldiversitycouncil.org

U.S. Bureau of Labor Statistics
Postal Square Building
2 Massachusetts Avenue NE
Washington, DC 20212-0001
Telephone:1-202-691-5200
Federal Relay Service:1-800-877-8339
www.bls.gov

Table 5.1   A Tool to Create or Improve Equity in Your Organization

Directions: Use this worksheet as a tool to create or improve your organization's framework for an equity pipeline. For each step listed in the left column below, describe in the right column what steps your organization should do to create a framework. This tool should be modified as necessary to fit your organization's strategic goals.	
What steps are needed to create or improve equity in your organizations?	**What steps should your organization take to create or improve equity?**
1. Define the organization diversity strategic plan	
2. Advise current employees on changes	
3. Evaluate employer brand to attract diverse candidates	
4. Personalize organization's equal opportunity hiring statement	
5. Review existing policies and benefits through a diversity lens	
6. Compose more inclusive job descriptions	
7. Advertise jobs through diverse networks	
8. Implement blind resumes reviews	
9. Create diverse interview panels	
10. Other resources	
11. Review and evaluate your efforts	

Putting into Practice

Step 1: Start with the definitions and goals you developed in Chapter 3

This is important because the organization's specific meaning of diversity, equity, and inclusion and its commitment to accomplishing this goal is the cornerstone of your diverse pipeline. Everyone in the organization must know, understand, and share that meaning. Once the leadership of your organization communicates that meaning to all the stakeholders, it should be part of the strategic plan. You can now use this strategic plan to create a diverse pipeline and move forward with your project goals. But you will not be going through this process alone. There are government agencies and other organizations that provide the information you can leverage in this effort. You will also have the tools and checklists from this publication to assist you with creating a diverse workforce through a diverse pipeline or recruiting.

Step 2: Define your organization's population into categories (e.g., skill sets, education, as defined by the Census Bureau, origin) that match your organization's definition of diversity

The next step in the process is to define employees in your organization based on their self-reported categories. The report need not include a name, but it must include race, ethnicity, gender, and any other category as stated in the strategic plan (e.g., skill sets, education). Although there are many ways to achieve organizational equity besides race, ethnicity, and gender, organization development professionals should implement guidelines to effectively build a pipeline to attract potential candidates. It is not against the law, nor it is unethical for human resources to have demographical information on all employees. However, some information such as race, ethnicity, and gender are self-reported.

There are government organizations and agencies that assist in creating a diverse workforce. The United States Census Bureau is one agency that provides a wealth of free demographic information. One function of the bureau provides categories of the people who reside in the United States. Thus, population categories are not defined by individual organizations but by the U.S. Census Bureau. In this effort, everyone has the same definitions and categories making reporting consistent. Remember these specific definitions are described specifically for the United States. You might have to modify these categories to suit groups in your specific country or region to meet your organization's strategic goals. Below is a partial list of groups as described and identified for the United States by the Census Bureau:

- White
- Black or African American
- American Indian or Alaska Native
- Asian
- Native Hawaiian or Pacific Islander
- Hispanic or Latino
- Two or more races

The U.S. Census Bureau website provides the public with a tool called QuickFacts. It is a very easy-to-use application that provides tables, charts, and maps of frequently requested statistics from numerous Census Bureau censuses, surveys, and programs. Profiles are available for the country, the entire United States plus the District of Columbia, and Puerto Rico and all counties, cities, and towns with a population of 5,000 or more. This information helps you focus on the population when planning your recruitment strategy.

The U.S. Census Bureau has several regional offices. The headquarters is in Washington, DC. The agency maintains an online presence on Facebook, LinkedIn, Twitter, and YouTube. As of June 27, 2021, the agency can also be reached at https://www.census.gov.

Step 3: Conduct a human resources recruiting assessment regarding providing a diverse talent pool as defined in step 1

Conducting a good HR assessment would expose areas that recruitment is working well and conversely highlight areas that can be improved. To have a diverse pipeline, organizational development practitioners must look for potential candidates inside and outside the organization. A pipeline with qualified candidates is essential for growth. A diverse organization is inclusive of cultures, sparks innovation, and is a place where employees feel accepted and valued. As part of reviewing the pipeline, it is critical to ensure employees and potential candidates view the organization in its best light. At the end of this assessment step, you will have identified sources that are working well, those that have great potential, and the ones not working.

Step 4: Review your organization's internal pipeline

At the beginning of the step, you will use the assessment results to continue using the pipelines working well, stop using the pipelines not working, and improve on the pipelines that have great potential to attract diverse candidates. Promotion from within is a popular phrase on company websites. For job seekers, that means if they get hired, they can work their way up in the organization. Organizations advertising promotions from within should honor that commitment when opportunities arise within the company. This concept of hiring from within is a great start for your internal pipeline.

Using your internal pipeline is great for several reasons. Internal candidates already know the ins and outs of the organization. Their onboarding takes less time, and internal candidates are considered loyal. According to research by Society for Human Resource Management (SHRM), internal candidates are more productive in the short term than new hires.

Internal candidates also have drawbacks. The most prevalent one is that they are more resistant to change and therefore may not be the right fit if the company is heading in a different direction. Your internal pipeline should include all sources of talent. These sources should include, but are not limited to, succession planning, promotions, mentoring, rehires, and employee referrals.

Improving your internal pipelines creates a more inclusive and diverse culture. Here are ways to improve your internal pipelines while promoting diversity in your organization.

1. Demonstrate the organization's commitment to diversity, equity, and inclusion.
2. Modernize your job posting on company websites.
3. Write more inclusive job descriptions.
4. Understand why internal candidates are seeking this position.
5. Offer meaningful diversity training.
6. Inform employees of organizational goals.
7. Openly ask employees for diverse referrals.
8. Create better incentives for the employee referral program.

Step 5: Review or create your organization's external pipeline

This step focuses on the external areas to get new employees. There are many ways to access great new candidates to achieve organizational diversity. But organizational diversity is more than just checking the box or making sure you have just a few different individuals. An external pipeline allows the organization to access candidates diverse in ideas, culture, creativity, backgrounds, sexual orientation, heritage, education, and life experience. In this step, you will use the assessment of the organization's hiring practices improving your external pipeline. You can use the resources of a professional organization for recruiting diverse candidates. Most of these organizations have job boards that be great resources for your organization. Some areas of the pipeline are listed below. Please modify this list as you see fit based on your organization's needs. This list is by no means ranked or inclusive but can serve as a resource:

1. Minority Alumni Associations
2. Historic Black Colleges and Universities
3. LGBT Meeting Professionals Association
4. Women for hire
5. Diversity working
6. Hire purpose
7. Professional organizations serving underrepresented populations
8. National Association of Asian Americans
9. Local community organizations
10. Public, private, and nonprofit job centers

Your diverse pipeline strategies should include some unnoticed and untapped talent groups to encourage the underrepresented to apply for positions in your organization. There are several ways an organization can be diverse. Hiring for a diverse workforce includes recruiting minorities, welfare to work, older workers, Americans with disabilities, individuals on the autism spectrum or other neurodiverse workers, individuals with criminal records, single parents, and former military members.

Acquiring new diverse talent is challenging, but the wider your organization spreads the recruiting net, the more diverse the individuals you will get. National and international circumstances can make the recruiting process more difficult. The Society for Human Resource Management (SHRM) indicated that organizations are using different methods to attract new talent. Here are ways you can improve organization efforts to attract and hire new diverse external talent. Please modify this list for your organization and location.

1. Reflect on the candidate you want to hire and go where they are.
2. Include key phrases such as remote work or remote jobs to job boards.
3. Use several online recruiting services.
4. Review benefit packages to include more inclusive options such as child care, flexible hours, and student loan repayment.
5. Be open to candidates from other industries.
6. Recruit further than local.
7. Encourage diverse individuals to apply for your jobs.
8. Openly mention your organization's commitment to diversity, equity, and inclusion.
9. Include hiring managers in the recruiting process.
10. Create scholarships and internships for underrepresented groups (Table 5.2).

Table 5.2   A Tool to Implement Internal and External Equity Pipelines

Directions: Use this worksheet as a tool to implement your organization's framework for an internal and external equity pipeline. For each step listed in the left column below, describe in the right column what steps your organization should do to create a framework. This tool can be modified as necessary to fit your organization's strategic goals.		
What steps should be taken to implement internal and external pipelines		**What steps would you take to implement your organization's internal and external pipelines?**
1.	Succession planning	
2.	Promotions	
3.	Mentoring	
4.	Rehires	
5.	Employee referrals	
6.	Public, private, and nonprofit job centers	
7.	Minority Alumni Associations	
8.	Historic Black Colleges	
9.	Professional organizations serving underrepresented populations	
10.	Local community organizations	
11.	Additional resources	
12.	Review and evaluate your efforts	

Step 6: Reevaluate your pipeline

Periodically reevaluate your internal and external pipelines as you implement updates to your recruiting and hiring process.

There is a tool, appearing in Appendix E, that tracks the step-by-step approach toward implementation described in this chapter. If you complete that tool and the others in chapters following this one, you will have the foundation for a proposal to your organization's management for installing an effective DE&I effort.

Key Questions about the Chapter

1. Did the leadership define diversity to all stakeholders?
2. What steps can I take to make the workplace more inclusive for everyone?
3. What are my organizations' diversity strategic goals?
4. How can I improve my pipeline to attract more diverse applicants?
5. What are my internal and external sources for recruitment?

Works Consulted

Anand, Rohini, and Mary-Frances Winters. "A Retrospective View of Corporate Diversity Training from 1964 to the Present." *Academy of Management Learning & Education* 7, no. 3 (2008): 356–372.

Chapter 6

Step 5: Developing Talent

Michele McBride

Contents

Case Study: Cummins Inc.

Diversity and inclusion are critical to our ability to innovate, to win in the marketplace, and to create our sustainable success. They are about recognizing and valuing our differences and using those differences to solve the challenges in the world today.

–Tom Linebarger
Chief Executive Officer, Cummins Inc.

DOI: 10.4324/9781003184935-9

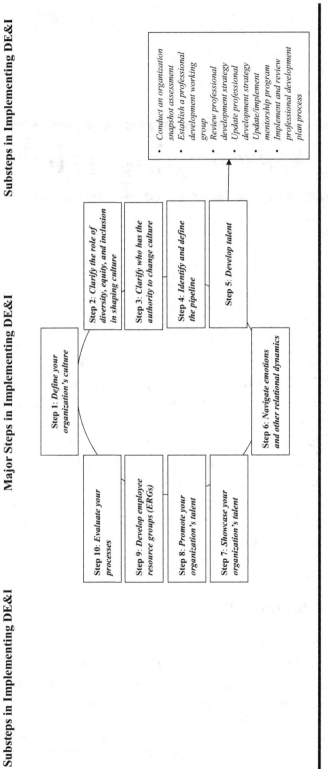

Frontmatter Figure 6.1   The diversity, equity, and inclusion (DE&I) roadmap model.

Cummins was started in the early 1900s as a family-owned business. Clessie Cummins was a mechanic to the wealthy Irwin family. W.G Irwin provided the capital to start Cummins Inc. when Clessie developed his diesel engine in Irwin's garage. The company had a rocky beginning, and it took almost two decades for Cummins to turn a profit. Each time the company almost closed, Irwin's wife would plead with him to keep the company open because of the jobs it provided for the community.

In 1934, J. Irwin Miller, the grandnephew of the founder, joined the company. Miller used his position to bring his own beliefs and passions about diversity forward and to help create the corporation's identity. When Miller joined the firm, he persuaded Cummins to hire otherwise marginalized groups, including women and black employees. From company reports, Miller empowered disadvantaged workers. At this point in American history, that was radical. In the early 1960s, Miller was an activist throughout the American civil rights movement, and in 1963 he shared in a statement to the stockholders, "The Company stands in favor of Civil Rights."

Based on memos written, it was important to Miller to not only hire non-white workers but to do so at the executive management level. One memo to upper management from 1963 reads:

> To extend leadership in this community, I should like for each of
> you gentlemen to make a vigorous effort to hire qualified Negroes
> in the next few months. To be meaningful, such employment
> will have to be in positions outside the menial services for which
> Negroes are usually employed.

While Miller was an early leader of diversity for Cummins, his legacy lived on in another important Cummins leader. Tim Solso was also a forward-thinking leader, who in the early 1990s championed LGBTQ rights, and in the early 2000s, adopted a domestic partner benefits policy to provide benefits to the life partners of Cummins's workers. That was a radical decision based on the time. Leaders like Miller and Solso made it their priority to bring DE&I conversations outside of the boardroom and into the public. Solso published the following in the local Columbus newspaper after the decision was announced:

> Change can be difficult for any organization to accept. For
> some, this new policy felt like a departure from the traditions of
> Cummins. In fact, just the opposite is true. This policy embodies

the principles of J. Irwin Miller; principles upon which this company was founded – such as inclusion, tolerance, responsiveness, and the pursuit of excellence.

Today, Cummins employees come from different backgrounds, and diversity, equity, and inclusion are business imperatives. One of the core mission statements of the business is to hire, retain, and develop employees to reach their full potential. Cummins is committed to creating a workforce population with representation similar to the markets in which they operated; and to leverage their influence to promote diversity and inclusion in the communities in which they operate (Reed 2017).

The Cummins Corporation is a solid example of what it means to be founded on the principles of diversity, equity, and inclusion. From early in the company's history, the business leaders strived to have a diverse and inclusive workforce. However, for some of you, your organizations are not starting from the same solid foundation. You might have had no formal diversity, equity, and inclusion training; however, that doesn't mean you can't use your position to influence the future of your company and the talent that makes up your company.

Many organization leaders have recognized the moral and ethical obligation for ensuring that their companies are diverse and gender-balanced. However, many conversations on these topics happen behind closed doors with a small group of organizational leaders. This happens for a variety of reasons. Unless your organization is purposeful with purveying those ideas and insights out to the workforce, the ideas might end up the esoteric knowledge of a few rather than the common wisdom of many.

Organization Development (OD) and change management (CM) help people who lead organizations to identify and plan how to deal with both intentional and unintentional changes (Rothwell 2009). Organization Development is a long-term strategy that can solve complex, deep, and meaningful opportunities for change identified by organization leaders. OD is not a short-term fix. There are no gimmicks or silver bullets. OD is a systematic change effort that builds upon itself to change beliefs, attitudes, and the structure of organizations. It works best when the leaders at the top support the change efforts. A key tenet to OD is that it emphasizes employee involvement in assessing the current state of a company and giving the responsibility to workers for creating and evaluating the results. It is facilitated change, which means it draws on the ideas of workers and managers and then turns them into action plans. In that respect, it differs from some change efforts that start in the heads of leaders and then try to cram that wisdom down the throats of everyone else.

I can't think of anything more important than to create long-term, meaningful, and systematic change with DE&I talent development efforts. Edward Jones (1986) offered this advice: "Corporations cannot manage attitudes, but they can manage behavior with accountability, rewards, and punishment, as in all other important areas of concern. What gets measured in business gets done; what is not measured is ignored.". A key goal in this change effort should be to lessen the anxiety, assumptions, and attachments and bring about awareness. What might it look like for you, as the leader of your company's DE&I efforts, to have an army of stakeholders behind you, all feeling like they have ownership as the outcome of your DE&I change effort? How much faster might you be able to implement long-term, meaningful change in talent development processes? How would these changes help your recruiting and retention efforts?

In the previous chapters, you learned the role of diversity, equity, and inclusion in shaping culture. You then explored with the authority to change the culture. In the previous chapter, you learned how to identify and define your pipeline of talent coming into your organization. In this chapter, we will explore developing the talent inside your organization, and we will cover these concepts:

1. What does the research say?
2. Putting into practice
3. Creating your DE&I talent development strategy using OD
4. Mentors and professional development plans
5. Evaluation tool

What Does the Research Say?

It is well documented that training activities have a positive impact on the performance of individuals and teams. An article by Tobon and Luna-Nemecio (2020) discusses talent and a new concept based on "socioformation." If we think about the people in our organizations as talent, we will want to do what we can to develop and nurture the talent in them. Tobon & Luna-Nemecio argue "that humanity is currently undergoing a series of crises that affect its consolidation as a species" and that it is important that we look for actions that will help resolve these crises for civilization to achieve sustainable social development (p. 22). Some problems for which we will need to find solutions include collaborative work, quality of life, work–life balance, and personal fulfillment. Even while we are experiencing a high degree of change and evolution of work, we must keep the *human* experience of work at the center. If we start with the people who make up our organizations in mind, then our challenge is to find ways to successfully apply skills, insight, energy, and commitment to make our organizations better (Bolman & Deal 1984). You have already learned ways to increase diversity in your workplace. What we will talk about now is once you have a pipeline of talent that is diverse, how do you activate their talent and ensure all of your employees are getting a fair shot at opportunities?

In July 2020, LinkedIn surveyed 1,500 human resources specialists. Half of those specialists reported that they expected their recruitment budgets to decrease in 2021, while two out of three expected their training and development budgets to grow or stay the same. Many of these organizations reported that they planned to upskill existing employees to meet emerging business needs (Galt 2021). This is good news for employees who have been with their companies and are established in their positions. Any time an organization will invest in their employees will most likely have a positive return on investment, and it is the premise of what we will talk about in this chapter. But before we can talk about developing employees, we must first understand why it is important to you. Getting clear on why this is important to you will be a key motivator for you as you move forward with this process because it will not be easy. You will hit obstacles, naysayers, and roadblocks. Understanding your big why and the reason this work is important to you cannot be understated.

Employers who see their employees as whole people will soon have loyal people. Let's slow down now and do a quick visioning exercise. You might find it helpful to grab a pen and a piece of paper for this part as you think through these questions. Why is developing a diverse workforce important to you personally? Why is it important for the people you lead? What would it look like for you had you reduced turnover in your company? What might it look like for you if you had happy, thriving employees celebrating their 10th or 20th anniversary with your organization? What type of traction would you be able to gain? Allow yourself to think about that for a moment. Why is this important to you? When you think about what you could achieve over the next ten years with a happy, thriving, and diverse workforce, what excites you the most? Take some time with this. You can use the following prompt to help you capture your ideas (Table 6.1).

Table 6.1 Big Why Thinking Prompt

Directions: Take a few minutes and reflect on the following questions. This exercise will work best if you allow your answers to come to you freely simply write down the first things that come to mind.

Why is developing a diverse workforce important to you personally?

Why is developing a diverse workforce important for the people that you lead?

What would it look like for you if you had reduced turnover in your company?

What might it look like for you if you had happy, thriving employees who were celebrating their 10th or 20th anniversary with your organization? What type of traction would you be able to gain? Allow yourself to think about that for a moment. Why is this important to you?

When you think about what you could achieve over the next ten years with a happy, thriving, and diverse workforce, what excites you the most?

According to Van Rossem (2019), motivators show up differently depending on the generation you were born in. Generations consist of different birth cohorts who share the same and unique understanding due to their shared experience in a similar sociohistorical context they were born and lived in (Pilcher, 1994). When we think about the generations who work, they have broken down into the following birth cohorts according to Pew Research Center: Baby Boomers (1946–1964), Generation X (1965–1980), Millennials (1981–1997), and Gen Z (1997–2020). Baby Boomers perceive social contacts as a source of work motivation; Generation X highly values training and autonomy; Millennials value career development possibilities and training; Gen Z values diversity, personalization, and creativity.

According to Raisiene, different leadership traits and attributes are valued within certain generations, and applying different management practices to different generations could lead to higher performance in employees. For example, big picture orientation is valued by older generations, while younger generations value day-to-day focus. Baby Boomers dislike authoritarian management styles, while younger generations want to work with leaders who will mentor and coach them. Understanding who you are working with will help you maximize the employee's potential.

Not considered in the descriptions above are race, gender, or socioeconomic status. We know that ethical viewpoints are created by combining race, gender, age, religion, professional experience, class, whether someone was raised by a single parent or a two-parent household, if they were raised in an urban or rural area, their education, access to resources, learning style, sexual orientation, disability, country of origin, etc. (Shapiro, 2011.) This unique blend of what makes a person unique also translates into what they believe to be ethical. Why is ethics important to this piece of the conversation? Understanding your makeup will help you understand where you may have unconscious bias, which may affect your decision-making and ultimately the decisions you make for your organization and how you develop talent.

Ethics is defined by the Oxford Dictionary as the moral principles that govern a person's behavior or the conducting of an activity. Consider the following scenario:

> *A father and his son are in a car accident. The father dies at the scene and the son, badly injured, is rushed to the hospital. In the operating room, the surgeon looks at the boy and says, "I can't operate on this boy. He is my son."*

Wait. What?

If your immediate reaction was confusion, that's because automatic unconscious associations caused you to think "male" when reading the word "surgeon." This is an example of how stereotypes work. In the riddle above, the surgeon is a woman or the boy's mother.

Don't be too hard on yourself if you got stuck. Your brain can play tricks on you, so we must do purposeful work to ensure that our brains and our unconscious stereotypes and biases aren't affecting our decision-making abilities when growing our organizations and the talent inside of our organizations. Taking stock in your own beliefs and behaviors will allow you to be a better leader for the people you lead. The next step? What might it look like if you gave that question to your key executives? What would you discover?

Putting into Practice

Step 1: Conduct an organization snapshot assessment

For those of us who practice OD, the assessment and feedback stage is vitally important to the health of the organizations we consult. It helps an organization decide where to change, how to change, and is used to design change initiatives. The assessment and feedback loop is how organizations manage their way to success.

A key assessment you will want to complete is your *Organization Snapshot Assessment*, or the demographic summary of your organization that includes the number of employees; how many full-time, part-time, and contract laborers you have, and whether they fill staff/worker or executive-level positions; the age; race; gender; salary; and training allotment you have spent on each type of employee. When creating your organization snapshot, one thing you will want to do is identify the key stakeholders for whom this assessment is important and ask for them to engage in this process with you. This could include executives, HR professionals, operations managers, and directors of finance. You will want to select these people based on your unique work environment. Remember the Edward Jones quote? "What gets measured in business gets done, what is not measured is ignored."

Best practices for creating your organizational snapshot:

1. Do it! Some of these questions might seem remedial, and the answers might surprise you. The below list is just the starting point. You can add to the list based on what your team decides is important for your organization.
2. Gather this information in a format you can easily adjust. Excel or Google Sheets might be a solution if you are part of a smaller organization and you don't have this data organized. Gathering and recording the information this way will allow you to adjust the data to answer different questions and see different trends. See Figure 6.1 for an example.
3. If you are a large organization and have this information easily accessible, have your department heads verify the information. Even the best organizations can have outdated information in their reporting systems.

Employee Name/Number	Part Time, Full Time or Contract	Age?	Race?	Gender?	Contract Labor, Staff or	Salary	Hourly Wage	Amount spent on employee training last	Cost to hire employee

Figure 6.1   Organizational Snapshot

4. If you work for an organization that has not gathered this information, you can start today by creating a system in your hiring process to include the capturing of this information.

Organizational Snapshot Questions:

1. How many people do I employ?
2. How many of my employees are full-time/part-time/contract labor?
3. What does my organization look like in terms of age, race, and gender?
4. What department does this person belong to?
5. What does this look like in the staff/worker ranks versus the leadership ranks?
6. How much do I spend on salaries each year?
7. How much do I spend on hourly workers each year?
8. How much do I spend on contract labor each year?
9. What are the wages of my organization based on race?
10. What is your current training budget?
11. How much of my current training budget was spent on executives?
12. How much of my current training budget was spent on staff/worker ranks?
13. What is your current hiring budget?

Step 2: Establish a professional development working group

Now that you understand why this DE&I change effort is important to you, and you have gathered important feedback on your organization, it is time to create your talent development strategy. You will need to select who you will include in this change effort. Who will come along this journey with you to offer support, guidance, ideas, and insights from a perspective that differs from your own? You might include key executives who will implement the change effort, administrators, newly hired employees, long-standing employees, contractors, and HR professionals. This group should be diverse in terms of race, gender, age, and experience level. This is not a comprehensive list, and you have plenty of latitude with who you include. The important thing is to bring in many perspectives.

Once you have identified your potential leadership team, invite them to be part of this change effort. This is usually best if done in person and then followed up with an email outlining why they were chosen and what your desired outcomes of this intervention will be. Share with them the goal, why it's important to you, and why you selected them to participate. Helping them understand that you see them as a valuable contributor and asking for their input.

Step 3: Review professional development strategy

Before your first meeting, you will want to organize yourself to lead a powerful discussion. You will not be presenting facts. Instead, you will be facilitating a conversation that will allow everyone's ideas and insights to be heard. You will use this insight to guide your decision-making process.

Two weeks before your first meeting, you will want to send an introductory email that outlines the key objectives of your launch meeting. You will want to ask everyone to complete the *Big Why Exercise*. They will not turn this in to you or anyone else. It is just for them, so tell them that! Make sure they know that you will be discussing it, so ask them to give it plenty of time and thought. You will also want to share anything relevant to talent development processes you have in place. This could include a copy of your onboarding program, a description of your current mentorship programs, any forms that your managers or employees use related to talent development, including performance review forms or professional development plans. You might share a copy of this book and have them read the first five chapters. Just saying! Finally, encourage them to write down their thoughts on how your DE&I talent development efforts could be improved.

The first meeting is to be in person. During this first meeting, you will want to set the stage for having purposeful conversations! Some supplies you might have on hand include a flip chart, sharpies, post-it notes, snacks, and water. Make sure the room is big enough that everyone can be facing each other, and not facing the front of the room with you standing there. This is a conversation, not a presentation. If you can host this meeting in a place with natural light and views of nature, you are even better off yet!

On the day of the meeting, make sure you are the first person in the room. As people arrive, greet them and thank them for being there! It works best if everyone is standing up at the beginning! Introduce people to each other as they arrive. If you work for a smaller organization and everyone knows each other, you could consider sharing why you chose the person to be part of this change effort. If you work for a larger organization, have name tags handy, so it eases any awkwardness that might be present.

Once everyone arrives at the meeting, give them a few minutes to mill around and talk to one another. You might encourage everyone to chat with everyone else in the room before you get started. You could do this by including an icebreaker or get to know you exercise. This will help your attendees have psychology safety, and get their voices in the room!

No more than 5 minutes after your published start time, ask everyone to get seated and comfortable, and start the meeting.

Here is a sample meeting agenda you could use:

October 19, 2021: DE&I Talent Development Launch Committee Meeting
10:05 am: Welcome everyone to the meeting and share why this change effort is important to you personally. Be as vulnerable as you can. Explain briefly the goal of the DE&I Talent Development Committee and how long you expect this change effort to take place. Thank everyone for being there.

10:10 am: Have everyone introduce themselves and share why they agreed to be part of this change effort. Ask each person to share what they feel comfortable sharing from the *Big Why Exercise.*

10:30 am: Share key statistics you found in your *Organization Snapshot Assessment* and ask everyone to share their feedback on what they are seeing. Capture their aha's on the flip chart. If you feel more comfortable, you could ask for a volunteer to do this for you. After you write down what the person shared, asked them to verify that you properly captured the essence of what they were saying.

11:05 am: Review your talent development strategies and ask for preliminary feedback. What are we doing well, and what is important that we keep? What is important that we improve right away? Capture their ideas on the flip chart. If you feel more comfortable, you could ask for a volunteer to do this for you. After you write down what the person shared, ask them to verify that you properly captured the essence of what they were saying.

11:45 am: Based on the themes that emerge from the meeting, form task force groups that will do certain tasks that are related to this change effort. Assign due dates no more than two weeks out. Plan your next meeting.

Noon: Bring in lunch and have a casual lunch before everyone going back to their normal day. (Don't skip this part … this is where the good stuff comes out.)

Step 4: Update professional development strategy

After your initial meeting, you will want to take some time to distill down what you heard and what you captured on the flip charts and in your notes. What did you learn? How can you take the ideas of your team and organize them in such a way that you can implement some of what you heard? What surprised you? What were important traditions that everyone wanted to keep? You will most likely have a two-week gap period where you are allowing the people on your task force to work through their assigned projects. Don't waste this time! Use it to do additional research and formulate how you can implement what you heard. You will also want to prepare for your next meeting by documenting what you captured on the flip charts. Depending on how the meeting goes, it might be best to do this in written format or spreadsheet format. Either way, capture this while it is fresh and make sure it is sent in a follow-up email to your team.

Taking an Organization Development approach to change management will lead you through a cycle of assessment and feedback where you will manage your way to success. You have asked key people in your organization to step up and assist you in gaining perspective. A natural by-product of this will be buy-in from those individuals. Your key objective now will be to keep your team focused and provide timely feedback so that you can implement your initiatives. It will be important to include your leadership team when you share changes being made and giving them credit for their hard work. Remember, your team will be a very diverse group, so this should help your entire organization feel as though their voice was represented!

Once you gain perspective on what is working well in your organization, and where you need to immediately improve, you will want to make sure that a few key systems are in place, which we will cover in the next section. Some of these might have been identified in your first meeting, which would be great! Below is a sample agenda to use for all of your follow-up meetings. Your supplies list from your first meeting will stay the same.

November 1, 2021: DE&I Talent Development Committee Meeting

10:05 am: Welcome everyone to the meeting. Open the meeting by sharing a Mission Moment. These could be celebrations where you or one of your committee members has seen someone in your organization demonstrate your new DE&I talent development processes.

10:15 am: Space for voicing concerns or struggles. This will be a place for your leaders to share any concerns or struggles they are facing with their tasks and provide solutions they have considered employing. Encourage committee members to offer insight or feedback.

10:25 am: Introduce a new system/process/idea in which you are seeking feedback. Include DE&I research. Have an open conversation and encourage feedback. Capture their ideas and feedback on the flip chart. If you feel more comfortable, you could ask for a volunteer to do this for you. After you write down what the person shared, ask them to verify that you properly captured the essence of what they were saying.

10:55 am: Create action items and the meeting is adjourned.

Step 5: Update/implement a mentorship program

After your initial assessment is completed with your team, one key system you will want to review and improve is your employee onboarding and mentorship programs. You must be purposeful to devise programs and systems that will expand individual employee comfort zones. Your employees will bond with people most like them. This part of our human nature makes it more difficult for people new to your organization to feel like they belong inside of your organization. Instead, they feel like they must change to fit in and be accepted, to move up into higher-level positions. Let's state the obvious: if your organization is made up of mostly white people, it's going to be even more difficult for people of color to feel like they fit in, let alone belong. And don't give me the old, "I don't see color" line. YOU SHOULD! We should celebrate and accept all races, colors, creeds, and sexes because that's what it means to create an inclusive work environment.

What I am touching on here is the difference between someone feeling like they belong somewhere versus feeling like they fit it. People who fit in don't feel comfortable to be their whole self. They change certain parts of themselves to conform to their environment. Read that again. To create a diverse, equitable, and inclusive work environment, we have to create organizations so that our employees feel safe to be who they are. Their whole wonderful, beautiful self.

In his book *Everyday Bias: Identifying and Navigating Unconscious Judgments in Our Daily Lives*, Howard Ross outlines in the appendix the top ten ways to identify and navigate bias in talent management. Ross shares that most people decide within the first three to four months whether they see their new job as a short-term or long-term position. Because of this, it's important to ensure that your onboarding process is set up so that your new hire has the highest probability of getting a fair chance to succeed. A tip that Ross shared provided a cultural and logistical orientation. Organizations have unwritten rules. Clarify unwritten and unspoken cultural rules. You can do this by assigning a coach or mentor to your new employee. This helps develop the talent in two individuals!

Thomas (2001) shared that despite the best intentions, many organizations continue to fail to achieve racial balance within their executive teams. Some have a revolving door of talented minorities, recruiting the best only to see them leave, frustrated, and angry. Thomas completed a three-year research project, where he studied the career trajectories of minority and white professionals at three major U.S. companies. A key finding in his research is that professionals of color who plateaued in middle management received mentoring that was instructional; it helped them develop better skills. Minority executives who broke through middle management, however, had mentors that not only instructed them on how to develop better skills, but they also consulted them and helped them to build confidence, credibility, and competence. These executives had someone who cared about their emotional well-being, talked to them about their own experiences, and helped their mentees to expand their network of relationships broke through the middle ranks into the executive ranks.

Because race and racism can pose obstacles for people of color, mentors of minorities will need to approach mentoring differently than they do with their white counterparts (Thomas 2001, p. 104). To do this, you must consider two things. First, mentors must be trained to provide both instructional and emotional support to the people they are mentoring. Second, as soon as your company can afford it, you should invest in professional training for your mentors. Often, mentors are selected because they have succeeded in their roles but don't have formal training on how to develop people. Investing in training your mentor population can have long-term ripple effects for your organization.

If this topic is tickling your brain and you would like to get a clear snapshot of how you are doing, I have created the following assessment, which should indicate to you how your employees feel they fit in versus belong. If you use this survey, I suggest keeping it anonymous and creating a way for them to turn in the surveys that help to maintain anonymity.

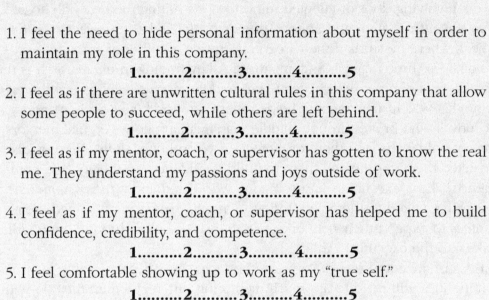

CHAPTER 6 TOOL: "FITTING IN" VERSUS "BELONGING" ASSESSMENT

Directions: Use this assessment to determine how much you feel you "fit in" versus how much you feel "a sense of belonging." There are no "right" or "wrong" answers. On a scale of 1 (representing never) to 5 (representing always), answer the following questions. When finished, add up your score and calculate the mean (score divided by 5 = mean). Then share this assessment with others in your group to prompt discussion.

1. I feel the need to hide personal information about myself in order to maintain my role in this company.

   1..........2..........3..........4..........5

2. I feel as if there are unwritten cultural rules in this company that allow some people to succeed, while others are left behind.

   1..........2..........3..........4..........5

3. I feel as if my mentor, coach, or supervisor has gotten to know the real me. They understand my passions and joys outside of work.

   1..........2..........3..........4..........5

4. I feel as if my mentor, coach, or supervisor has helped me to build confidence, credibility, and competence.

   1..........2..........3..........4..........5

5. I feel comfortable showing up to work as my "true self."

   1..........2..........3..........4..........5

Step 6: Implement and review Professional Development Plan process

After you have reviewed your mentor system, the next step will be to assess and get feedback on your Professional Development Plan process. A few things to remember when creating a Professional Development Plan. First, it's important that if you have your employees create professional development plans and that you have a system to check in with them on their plans! You will want this to mean something, so there will need to be

Personal Information		Career Role Anticipated			
Name email supervisior Plan Last Updated: 3/23/2021 **Milestones:** Hire Date: Promotion Date:					

Mentors					
Name Why did you chose this mentor? What are they helping you with right now? Name Why did you chose this mentor? What are they helping you with right now? Name Why did you chose this mentor? What are they helping you with right now?					

Professional Development Courses and Books

Type	Name	Date	Scope
Book			
Class			
Seminar			
Spec. Project			

Work/Business Accomplishments

1 Year Goals	2 Year Goals

3 Year Goals	4-5 Year Goals

Figure 6.2   Sample Professional Development Plan.

buy-in not only from the employee but from their direct supervisor. But, wait. They have a mentor! I would advise you to proceed with caution. The mentor's role in this process could be to help them create their plan, but the actual review of the plan should be done outside of that relationship.

Create something that your employees can count on happening at a regular cadence. This could mean yearly or biannually. Whatever you decide is right, as long as you do it!

A second thing to note when helping an employee to develop professionally is to not discount outside of work experience. Hewlett (2005) shared that many minority professionals, especially women of color, have deeply substantive outside of work lives. Because they have "made it," women of color are often called upon to be mentors to young people in their communities. They play high-profile volunteer roles in their towns, schools, and churches, and are a fertile source of continued personal growth. These arenas are where they are honing their leadership skills, time management skills, and cultural capital! Don't discount this work, your next budding leader might be right there in your organization, getting groomed for their next step in a different area of their life.

As with the other systems of DE&I that we have reviewed, this will be a process you will review with your DE&I Talent Development Committee. It might not be surprising to you, but carve out extra time for the initial meeting to review your current process. In many organizations, there may be an array of experiences and insights that your committee will want to share with you regarding their own personal experience and how they believe your organization can do this better. You will want to prepare by gathering all information you have on hand regarding your Professional Development Plan system. This might include examples of templates, how the plans are recorded, who reviews the plans, who approves the plans, and how often the plans are completed. You might find it beneficial to prep your committee beforehand by sending out all information, and asking for everyone to come prepared to the meeting to share their insights and perspectives.

After you go through the assessment and feedback stage with your committee, you will want to ensure that a training system is put into place for existing employees and supervisors. You will also want to ensure that your onboarding process is updated to include this new process.

If this is new to you, figure 6.2 outlines a sample Professional Development Plan to get started!

There is a tool, appearing in Appendix E, that tracks the step-by-step approach toward implementation described in this chapter. If you complete that tool and the others in chapters following this one, you will have the foundation for a proposal to your organization's management for installing an effective DE&I effort.

Key Questions about the Chapter

1. The chapter notes that "employers who see their employees as whole people will soon have loyal people." Describe what that means and how employers can "see their employees as whole people."
2. Go to a web browser and research the "70-20-10" rule. Describe what that "rule" means and how it might apply to DE&I.
3. How should a Professional Development Plan (PDP), sometimes called an Individual Development Plan (IDP), help to guide development? What does it have to do with DE&I?

Works Consulted

Galt, Virginia. 2021, February 5. "The Pandemic Has Shone a Spotlight on Internal Hiring and Talent Development: OPINION." *Globe & Mail* [Toronto, Canada], B10. Gale in Context: Global Issues (accessed February 14, 2021). https://link.gale.com/apps/doc/A650776942/GIC?u=psucic&sid=GIC&xid=1e48f0b3

Hewlett, Sylvia Ann, Carolyn Buck Luce, and Cornel West. 2005. "Leadership in Your Midst: Tapping the Hidden Strengths of Minority Executives." Harvard Business Review, November 1, 2005. https://hbr.org/2005/11/leadership-in-your-midst-tapping-the-hidden-strengths-of-minority-executives.

Jones, Edward W. Jr. 1986. "Black Managers: The Dream Deferred." Harvard Business Review, May 1, 1986. https://hbr.org/1986/05/black-managers-the-dream-deferred.

Pilcher, J. 1994. Mannheim's Sociology of Generations: An Undervalued Legacy. *The British Journal of Sociology*, 45(3), 481–495. https://doi.org/10.2307/591659

Reed, Heidi. 2017. "Corporations as Agents of Social Change: A Case Study of Diversity at Cummins Inc." *Business History* 59(6), 821–843.

Rothwell, William, Jacqueline Stavros, Roland Sullivan, and Arielle Sullivan. 2009 Practicing Organization Development: A Guide for Leading Change: A Third Edition. Electronic resource. 1st edition. Pfeiffer,https://go.oreilly.com/pennsylvania-state-university/library/view/-/9780470523926/?ar.

Shapiro, J. P. and J. A. Stefkovich 2011. Multiple ethical paradigms and the preparation of educational leaders in a diverse and complex era. Ethical leadership and decision making in education (pp. 3–27). Routledge.

Thomas, David A. 2001. "Mentoring Minorities." *Health Progress (Saint Louis, Mo.)* 82(4), 62.

Tobon, S., and J. Luna-Nemecio 2021. Proposal for a new talent concept based on socioformation. *Educational Philosophy and Theory, 53*(1), 21–33.

Van Rossem, A. 2019. Introducing a cognitive approach in research about generational differences: the case of motivation. *The International Journal of Human Resource Management*, 1–41. https://doi.org/10.1080/09585192.2019.1616592.

Chapter 7

Step 6: Navigating Emotions and Other Relational Dynamics

Marie Carasco

Contents

DOI: 10.4324/9781003184935-10

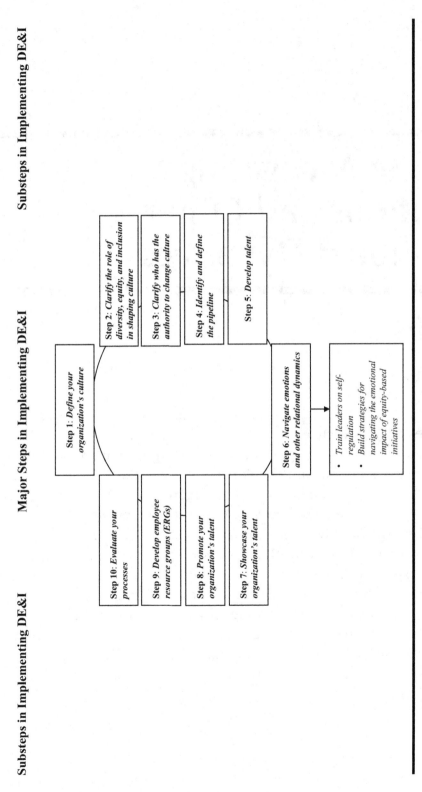

Frontmatter Figure 7.1 The diversity, equity, and inclusion (DE&I) roadmap model.

Story

Tiawo, a seasoned organization development (OD) practitioner specializing in culture transformation, was contracted by a private academic institution to help the school operationalize its diversity and inclusion goals recently added to the strategic plan in the wake of rising racial tensions around the United States. Like many other black-owned consulting firms, Tiawo experienced high demand for his services to support organizations that desired to take actions that would allow them to be more inclusive and equitable workplaces.

The following will describe steps Tiawo took to help navigate the emotional and relational dynamics that emerge when supporting equity-based change initiatives. It will highlight the eight steps in one of the most well-known models employed by organization development practitioners, namely the Action Research Model.

Step 1: Entry – After several months of planning and data analysis, the leadership team concluded that the University should increase recruitment efforts for students and faculty. The numbers indicated that students of color represented less than 3% over the overall student body, and faculty of color was roughly 2%. The data also showed that both students and faculty of color left the university, with most students transferring after one year. Those observations were discussed with the university president, provost, academic deans, and the board of trustees, all of whom developed a strategic plan they hoped would create a more inclusive and equitable institution.

Step 2: Start-up – Tiawo was invited to attend a faculty senate meeting as an observer on a day when the senate would vote on the approaches to increasing diverse representation in future faculty. One proposed measure was an introduction of a diversity statement as part of the hiring process for academic teaching positions. Generally, a diversity statement asks the applicant to reflect on experiences or future commitment to advance diversity, equity, and inclusion. The statement can include questions around what diversity means to the applicant and its importance, and the influence of diversity on teaching, advising, and student engagement. Before the meeting, Tiawo was provided with a copy of the proposal and the draft elements of what the statement directions would look like. Overall, he believed the university was heading in the right direction with this initial draft and he was curious to hear the feedback of the faculty on the senate, who represented various departments across the university. This group would allow him to gain critical insight into some sentiments held toward equity work at this institution.

Step 3: Assessment and feedback – Although the faculty senate meeting was only one source of data for Tiawo at that point in his engagement with the university, it proved to be tremendously helpful. When the proposal to include a diversity statement was presented, most of the faculty objected to its inclusion, citing several reasons, including that hiring committees can determine who is committed to diversity or not, the diversity statement will add to the workload of the hiring committees, introducing the diversity statement itself being "the flavor of the month" to mirror other more liberal institutions, and finally not understanding at all what diversity is and why they have to do it. Most of those in attendance were visibly agitated, and those who shared their objections to the diversity statement did so with anger and frustration which created palpable tension in the room. Only a few faculty of color bravely asserted the importance of diversity work at the institution, while the presenter of the diversity statement relented and said that the diversity statement itself wasn't something that the senate had to agree to. Since Tiawo was only present to observe, he did not intervene to address the shifting relational dynamics. Instead he gathered the data from the meeting while setting aside his feelings until he had a moment to decompress later in the day.

Step 4: Action planning – Tiawo reviewed the institution's strategic plan goals connected to diversity and determined that achieving those goals would be an uphill battle if the sentiments expressed during the senate meeting were echoed across the university. There appeared to be a gap in an understanding of and appreciation for equity work and he was concerned that his presence during the facilitated session would be met with hostility. Tiawo's preparation to manage the emotions of others and his responses began long before he contracted to support this institution's diversity objectives. Over many years of engaging in deliberate personal development, he had honed the skills to both manage conflict and engage in self-regulation.

Step 5: Intervention – After the faculty senate meeting, Tiawo debriefed his initial observations with the academic leadership team. Most of that team supported faculty who expressed anger about a diversity statement. Tiawo was surprised that the academic leadership was defending the faculty opposing the diversity statement, and he experienced a momentary sense of hopelessness as he listened. He noted this feeling and instead focused on the "here and now" as it was being presented to him. This debrief would also serve as another crucial data point for Tiawo's work going forward.

After the debrief, Tiawo was mentally exhausted and opted to have a solo lunch away from the campus at a local restaurant. After ordering his meal, he took the time to check-in with himself using the *Quad Check* approach pioneered by the Hoffman Process. The Quad Check allows an individual to restore balance and harmony to the self by going through four aspects of self, hence the quad, short for quadrinity. While taking deep breaths, Tiawo checked in with the current state of his emotions, intellect, physical state, and spiritual nature. This exercise gave Tiawo personal space to express what he experienced earlier and to prepare for other challenges he would face later in the day. Increasing his awareness of the impact and influence of what transpired earlier in the day, Tiawo was in a much better position to manage his emotional responses, hold back his judgments, and support the relational dynamics presented by others.

Step 6: Evaluation – By the time his lunch arrived, Tiawo is breathing easily. His emotional self was frustrated with the leadership team's response, and he needed to accept the reality of those responses to be objective with this engagement; his intellect was pessimistic that the diversity goals would happen without some fiat approach and he knew he needed to look for opportunities to build on positive responses to gain some traction; his physical self was balanced and he wanted that to continue, and finally his spiritual self hoped that he could stand on his experience and face the challenges coming. (See Table 7.1 in Appendix E for strategies to manage practitioner and client relational dynamics.)

Step 7: Adoption – After lunch, Tiawo returned to campus prepared to manage his own emotions, but also ready to engage in facilitated discussions he anticipated could be hostile. Leaning on his training in conflict management, he was prepared to see people react emotionally, physiologically, and behaviorally, but assured himself those reactions are normal. He was also prepared to serve as a mediator to help those with opposing views hear each other by using active listening, asking open-ended questions, exploring interests, reality testing, all while focusing on the goals and interests of the client and not his own desired outcomes for this institution.

Step 8: Separation – Although he was prepared to receive hostility during his facilitated sessions, Tiawo was pleasantly surprised that most of his interactions in this client system were positive despite increasing resistance toward the diversity goals growing across the organization. The data gathered during the planning phase supported the need for change, but that need was yet to be internalized by most stakeholders across the university. One initial action plan determined by the academic leadership team for the next academic year provided education on the importance of diversity at the institution. Tiawo would aid in empowering the team in determining what and how of making that happen.

What Does the Research Say?

Use of Self and Self-Regulation in Managing Feelings at Work

In applied behavioral science which studies human behavior, the concept *of using self* is understood to be impactful in the effectiveness of an intervention. Using self in mental health fields combines practitioner skill-based training with aspects of an individual's heritage, belief systems, experiences, and personality integrated into an authentic self, better able to engage clients (Dewane 2006). In OD, which can be defined as a planned and sustained effort to apply behavioral science for system improvement, using reflexive, self-analytic methods (Schmuck and Miles 1971), use of self is part of OD's early value statements. "Writing in 1969, Warren Bennis proposed that OD practitioners (change agents) share a set of normative goals based on their humanistic/democratic philosophy" (French and Bell 1999, 65). The first of his normative goals was an improvement in interpersonal competence (French and Bell 1999), an essential attribute to facilitating change. The Action Research Model in OD, expanded from Kurt Lewin's model, captured phases of entry into an organization, contracting, data collection, analysis, feedback, action planning, intervention evaluation, and exit. In her 2014 model entitled *The "What" and "How" of OD: Action Research and Use of Self*, Rainey places use of self in the center of the six action research steps, where using self is defined as "acting on feelings, observations, and thoughts to advance the work of the client" (Jones and Rainey 2014, 107). And according to Carter and Gestalt OSD (2019), "[c]entering yourself is how you connect yourself to your most integrated and significant inner core to support mobilizing your energy to engage yourself and others" (24).

Since "OD is the application of behavioral science knowledge, practices, and skills in ongoing systems in collaboration with systems members" (French and Bell 1999, 97), practitioners use of themselves to engage and lead interventions is not only fundamental but occurs despite the explicit awareness of the practice. Yet with the proliferation of change management consulting, and practitioner educational programs that yield millions of dollars, there is little emphasis on how to become skilled at use of self, nor is there significant insight into the experiences that lead to mastery or at the very least mitigation of pitfalls. Given that significant financial investments are made by individuals seeking coaching or counseling, organizations seeking support for enterprise transformations, and the impact an applied behavioral science practitioner can have on a client and organization system, it behooves stakeholders to understand the experiences that lead to effective use of self for the efficacy of the field.

Managing Emotions in Practitioners

Self-regulation is prevalent in the applied behavioral science literature. We find it represented as using self, inclusive of organization development competencies, and as an imperative in the mental health field. In recent years, there has been a revived interest in these topics noted through insights from doctoral dissertations and practitioner research studies. Duhl (1987) informs us that using self serves to "safeguard and promote the autonomy of each person's fluid interconnection with others" (73). There are several theoretical approaches to self-regulation that are primarily drawn from social and personality psychology (Strauman 2017). Foundational to the subject are *control theory, self-control resources and willpower, intentions and behavioral inaction, and regulatory focus* (Strauman 2017). Tangney, Baumeister, and Boone (2004) assert that the human capacity to exert self-control is arguably one of the most powerful and beneficial adaptations of the human psyche.

> Self-regulation refers to the self exerting control over itself. In particular, self-regulation consists of deliberate efforts by the self to alter its states and responses, including behavior, thoughts, impulses or appetites, emotions, and task performance. The concept of self-regulation is close to the colloquial terms *self-control* and *self-discipline,* and many social psychologists use the terms interchangeably.
>
> **(Baumeister 2007, 841)**

Self-regulation is a pivotal aspect of facilitating successful interventions in organization development, especially those related to DE&I.

Self-Management Competencies in Organization Development

Seashore, Shawver, Thompson, and Mattare (2004) highlight that

> among the many competencies required of OD practitioners (in
> 2004 the OD Network lists 141, and the OD Institute defines 139),
> the Use of Self as an instrument is considered by many to be at
> the core...[and there is a need for] engaging in consulting with a
> clear self-concept, an understanding of why we do the things we
> do and do not do, and an appreciation of the values that guide
> our behavior.
>
> **(45)**

According to the book *Practicing Organization Development: A Guide for Consultants*, there are key competencies that an internal OD practitioner should have. These competencies include knowledge of professional theories, techniques, human values, self-awareness, and performance skills. The internal OD practitioner should have high collaboration, credibility, resourcefulness, initiative, maintain detachment, and self-mastery through personal development. This concept of self-mastery is directly connected to self-regulation and using self.

Use of Self in the Field of Organization Development

According to Seashore et al. (2004), the use of self in OD serves as a link between our potential and the world of change and begins with an understanding of who we are and the perceptions we hold of the world. With this foundation in mind, Keister and Paranjpey (2012) expound on the impact of the practitioner when they state:

> the purpose of use of self is to be able to execute a role, in this
> case, the role of the OD consultant, effectively, for others and the
> organizational system, without personal interference (bias, blindness, avoidance, etc.) and with enough consciousness to have clear
> intentionality and choice.
>
> **(87)**

Cheung-Judge (2001) provides practical insight into "the how" of developing self as an instrument akin to statements made by the mental health disciplines noted by Lum (2002) and Dewane (2006), respectively, who proposed five operational uses of self-based on the social work literature: (a) use of personality, (b) use of belief system, (c) use of relational dynamics, (d) use of anxiety, and (e) use of self-disclosure. Cheung-Judge asserts that

> in practice, owning the self means devoting time and energy to learning about who we are, and how issues of family history, gender, race, and sexuality affect self-perception. It means also identifying and exploring the values by which we live our lives, as well as developing our intellectual, emotional, physical, and spiritual capacities.

(44)

The OD field's foundational emphasis on using self seeks to require the practitioner to uncover and address areas of vulnerability and understand and value individual traits that would allow conscious intentionality in the ways the practitioner shows up in a client system without disrupting or interfering with the needs of that system. This is most similar to mental health practitioners that are also charged with skillfully navigating the use of self with their patients.

In 2018, Dr. David W. Jamieson, Professor at the University of St. Thomas, and Dr. Mee-Yan Cheung-Judge, Director of Quality-Equality Consultancy, embarked on a global study on using self.

> This research project is a first in our field to engage a wide-ranging, diverse global sample of respondents to create new understanding, knowledge, theory, and practice in the core concept of Use of Self. So that more innovative and effective development programs can be designed to support practitioners' continuous development journey – regardless of what stage of OD career they are in.

(Global Use of Self Research Project-2018)

They designed a 137-item survey based on a literature search that identified five clusters. The project sought input on (1) personal characteristics and values; (2) self-work and development practices; (3) use and consistency of various actions in practice; or (4) accuracy in describing your behavior patterns. The study was performed with 704 respondents from 25 countries who had at least five years of OD experience. In their first-level analysis, Cheung-Judge and Jamieson (2018) explained how five factors contribute to our understanding of the concept of using self, of which I will focus on factor 4 which highlights the importance of self-management in the uncertain, dynamic situation:

> [A]s ODPs will never know what may come around the corner … So practicing their presence regardless of the emerging situation, managing their emotions, holding back their judgment … is an important aspect in supporting the clients to do their work.
>
> **(28–29)**

> Without a deliberate understanding by the OD practitioner that he or she is an instrument that must be leveraged and managed during an engagement, there is an increased likelihood that the consultant's interests and goals will become the focus and compass guiding the OD effort and outcomes.

Supporting Employee Emotions

Historically, the workplace has not been known as a safe space for expressing emotions. "Workers [often] suppress their emotion and express positive emotion to meet work demands" (Jung et al. 2018, 367). Sadly, this behavior is connected to the concept of emotional labor associated with the physical symptoms of occupational stress (367). "At any given time, 20% of employees have personal problems that impact their job. According to the National Institute of Mental Health, 30% of all absenteeism and 66% of all terminations are related to employees' personal problems" (Carchietta 2015, 132). What's more, Ashkanasy et al. (2002) state: "employees may bottle up feelings of frustration and resentment, often resulting in angry outbursts. These feelings result, in part, from the constant requirement to monitor one's negative emotions, and to express positive ones" (322). If these feelings of frustration are unmanaged, they can lead to emotional exhaustion and burnout.

To address this, in general, many organizations have included a referral service to support employees experiencing emotionally triggering events as part of the health benefits. "Employee assistance programs (EAPs) are the most well-known, utilized, and studied workplace mental health resource"

(Lam et al. 2012, 1395). These external vendors provide confidential, short-term personal and job-related counseling and are often preferred by employees who would rather self-select mental health resources instead of more noticeable health resources (Lam et al. 2012). Functionally, "vendors operate centralized call centers for 24-hour access and intake" (Frey et al. 2018, 2). However, the impact of stay-at-home orders due to the COVID-19 pandemic, increased protests due to the murder of George Floyd, and racially motivated assaults on the AAPI community in 2020 have compelled organizations to go beyond EAP programs and embrace ways of directly supporting emotions and mental health concerns in the workplace. These approaches include round tables, town halls, and facilitated discussions where employees can openly share personal stories and express the impact of specific events. Organizations are also providing mental health or wellness days as part of paid time off to allow employees time for rejuvenation when the need arises. A small percentage of employers have mental health counselors on staff available to talk with employees during the workday.

The Emotional Impact of Equity-Based Initiatives

Quoting the work of Sara Ahmed, Mark (2017) states: "a diversity worker can be someone appointed by institutions with an explicit aim of transforming and diversifying them, or a diversity worker might be someone who does not inhabit the norms of an institution" (219). The team members charged with managing equity-based initiatives frequently experience *emotional labor* "the term used to describe situations where employees, especially those in client contact service occupations, are required to display emotions that may differ from the emotions they actually feel" (Ashkanasy et al. 2002, 317). OD professionals engaged in equity-based change initiatives like many other OD efforts will experience emotional labor because "diversity in teams triggers emotion management for all of its members" (Imose and Finkelstein 2018, 719). A study on diversity and emotional labor by Kim et al. (2013) found that age and racial diversity influenced emotion regulation (Imose and Finkelstein 2018, 726).

Earlier in this chapter, we established that use of self and self-regulation are important aspects of doing OD work, without supportive mechanisms to manage the weight of one's emotions and the emotions of others, "[e]motional labor can be particularly detrimental to the employee performing the labor and can take its toll both psychologically and physically" (Ashkanasy et al. 2002, 321). According to Imose and Finkelstein (2018), there are "[t]wo emotional labor strategies, surface acting, and deep acting.

Deep acting is a preemptive form of emotional labor in which the actor intentionally regulates the factors that stimulate emotions before an emotion has been experienced" (722). For example, preparing for a difficult meeting by focusing on the good feelings that came from visiting with friends the night before. "On the contrary, surface acting is a response-focused strategy in which the actor only manipulates their emotional expression ... Surface acting tends to be regarded as a more harmful emotional labor strategy while deep acting is considered more beneficial" (722). It is the author's opinion that most practitioners engaged in equity-based change initiatives engage in surface acting rather than deep acting, which is more akin to self-regulation.

Putting into Practice

Step 1: Train leaders on self-regulation

> The importance of understanding how self-regulation works (and how it can go wrong) becomes apparent when one considers the array of human suffering that can be linked to difficulties with effectively pursuing goals and directing behavior ... [Moreover] the psychological processes that self-regulation comprises can be studied across time and situation (Type 1) or as temporally and situationally constrained (Type 2).
>
> **(Strauman 2017, 3)**

It would be advisable for researchers to also study the negative sides of self-regulation and self-control, "in particular, theories about overcontrol have held that high levels of self-control contribute to pathologies such as obsession and compulsion" (Tangney et al. 2004, 25). Given these assertions, there is an opportunity to uncover what constitutes an optimal balance in self-regulation, and to fill the gap identified by Tangney et al. (2004) to develop theoretically informed, reliable, and valid measures of self-control.

With the understanding of some of the core elements needed to foster the use of self as an instrument including elements of self-awareness, self-knowledge, and self-differentiation, agency, self-efficacy, and an integrated presence, there remains an opportunity to provide insight into the experience of developing self-regulation from the perspective of applied behavior scientists and build on the work of Rupert (2006) who interviewed seven social workers about their experience of self and described using self and the ways clinicians were self-aware. One interesting finding from Rupert was that "the clinicians in that study did not refer to ways in which their self might impact negatively on practice, as previous countertransference literature might indicate" (114).

Step 2: Build strategies for navigating the emotional impact of equity-based initiatives

OD practitioners supporting equity-based change initiatives need a variety of coping strategies in their toolbox. The Professional Self-Care Scale (PSCS; Dorociak et al. 2017) is a validated 5-domain, 21-item instrument that excellently references the activities and actions that can be taken by OD practitioners engaged in equity-based change efforts. They include:

■ Professional Support – professional relationships
■ Professional Development – professional knowledge
■ Life Support – activities or people comforting
■ Cognitive Awareness – monitoring of feelings and reactions to clients
■ Daily Balance – taking a break during the day

A tool in Table 7.1 will outline detailed strategies to manage practitioner and client relational dynamics.

Key Questions about the Chapter

1. Why is it important for an OD practitioner to uncover and address areas of vulnerability and to understand and value individual traits that would allow conscious intentionality?
2. What is the connection to personal values and use of self?
3. What are the two emotional labor strategies?
4. Which emotional labor strategy is most connected to using self and why?
5. Which emotional labor strategy is viewed as detrimental and why?
6. Using one of the five categories highlighted in Table 7.1, come up with at least two activities you can use as a strategy to provide professional self-care when engaged in equity-based organization development work?

Table 7.1 Strategies to Manage Practitioner and Client Relational Dynamics

Directions: Use the following five professional self-care strategies to guide your daily, week, monthly and annual activities to navigate challenging emotions and other relational dynamics in equity-based Organization Development engagements.			
Professional self-care strategies for organization development practitioners engaged in equity-based work			
Category	*Description*	*Frequency*	*Activities*
Daily balance	Take a break	Daily	1. Make and guard your time to disconnect from work for things like lunch, stretching, walks, journaling, or a cognitive awareness activity 2. Use coaching as a leadership style and ask questions of your team and colleagues that will allow them to come to their own solutions/conclusions 3. Limit your involvement in multiple emotionally draining projects
Cognitive awareness	Monitor your feelings	Daily	1. Engage in prayer, meditation, quad checks, deep breathing, and alike to connect to your feelings and spiritual practice 2. Where appropriate, name your feelings and or the impact that others are having on your feelings
Life support	Find comfort	Weekly or More	1. Engage in activities that bring you joy and peace of mind 2. Repeat affirmations that inspire you 3. Spend time with people who are empathetic to your concerns 4. See a therapist to share the things your loved ones might not understand
Professional support	Connect with colleagues	Weekly or more	1. Connect with colleagues who share an interest in work similar to yours 2. Join a professional association or group that meets regularly
Professional development	Hone your craft	Annually or less	1. Identify the kinks in your professional armor and address them 2. Attend professional conferences 3. Participate in an interpersonal dynamics experience (i.e., The Hoffman Process, Tavistock Institute Group Relations Program Group, T-Group/Human Interactions Lab) 4. Take a vacation that allow for no engage with any work-related or stress-inducing activities

Works Consulted

Ashkanasy, Neal M., Charmine E.J. Härtel, and Catherine S. Daus. 2002. "Diversity and Emotion: The New Frontiers in Organizational Behavior Research". *Journal of Management* 28 (3): 307–338.

Baumeister, Roy F. 2007. "Self-Regulation". In *Encyclopedia of Social Psychology*, edited by Roy F. Baumeister and Kathleen D. Vohs, 841–845. Thousand Oaks, CA: SAGE Publications.

Carchietta, Gail A. 2015. "Five Steps to Increasing Utilization of Your Employee Assistance Program". *Workplace Health & Safety* 63 (3): 132–132.

Carter, John D., and GestaltOSD Center. 2019. *Use of Self and Self-Mastery: Making a Difference with Your Presence*. Aitkin: River Place Press.

Cheung-Judge, Mee-Yan. 2001. "The Self as an Instrument: A Corner-stone for the Future of OD". *OD Practitioner* 33 (3): 11–16.

Cheung-Judge, Mee-Yan, and David W. Jamieson. 2018. "Providing Deeper Understanding of the Concept of Use of Self in OD Practice". *OD Practitioner* 50 (4): 22–32.

Dewane, Claudia J. 2006. "Use of Self: A Primer Revisited". *Clinical Social Work Journal* 34 (04): 543–558.

Dorociak, Katherine E., Patricia. A. Rupert, Fred. B. Bryant, and Evan Zahniser. 2017. "Development of a Self-Care Assessment for Psychologists". *Journal of Counseling Psychology* 64 (3): 325. https://doi.org/10.1037/cou0000206

Duhl, Bunny. 1987. "Uses of Self in Integrated Contextual Systems Therapy". *Journal of Psychotherapy and the Family* 3 (2): 71–84.

French, Wendell, and Cecil Bell. 1999. *Organization Development: Behavioral Science Interventions for Organization Improvement*. Upper Saddle River: Prentice-Hall.

Frey, Jodi Jacobson, John Pompe, David Sharar, Rachel Imboden, and Lauren Bloom. 2018. "Experiences of Internal and Hybrid Employee Assistance Program Managers: Factors Associated with Successful, at-Risk, and Eliminated Programs". *Journal of Workplace Behavioral Health* 33 (1): 1–23.

Imose, Ruth A., and Lisa M. Finkelstein. 2018. "A Multilevel Theoretical Framework Integrating Diversity and Emotional Labor". *Group & Organization Management* 43 (5): 718–751.

Jones, Brenda B., and Mary Ann Rainey. 2014. "Use of Self as an OD Practitioner". In *The NTL Handbook of Organization Development and Change: Principles, Practices, and Perspectives*, edited by Brenda B. Jones and Michael Brazzel, 105–126. San Francisco, CA: NTL Institute.

Jung, Kyungyong, Dae Hwan Kim, and Ji Young Ryu. 2018. "Relationship Between Concealment of Emotions at Work and Musculoskeletal Symptoms: Results from the Third Korean Working Conditions Survey". *Industrial Health* 56 (5): 367–372.

Keister, Angie, and Neelima Paranjpey. 2012. "Self as Instrument: Dual Consulting Identities the Evaluator and the Designer". *Organization Development Journal* 30 (2): 85–97.

Kim, Eugene, Devasheesh P. Bhave, and Theresa M. Glomb. 2013. "Emotion Regulation in Workgroups: The roles of Demographic Diversity and Relational Work Context". *Personnel Psychology*, 66: 613–644.

Lam, Raymond W., Debra Wolinsky, Cynthia Kinsella, Cindy Woo, Paula M. Cayley, and Anne B. Walker. 2012. "The Prevalence and Impact of Depression in Self-Referred Clients Attending an Employee Assistance Program". *Journal of Occupational and Environmental Medicine* 54 (11): 1395–1399.

Lum, Wendy. 2002. "The Use of Self of the Therapist". *Contemporary Family Therapy* 24 (1): 181–197.

Mark, James S. 2017. "Feeling the Problem: Working through Diversity Work". *Transformations: The Journal of Inclusive Scholarship and Pedagogy* 27 (2): 217–228.

Seashore, Charles N., Mary M. Shawver, Greg Thompson, and Marty Mattare. 2004. "Doing Good by Knowing Who You Are: The Instrumental Self as an Agent of Change". *OD Practitioner*, 36 (3): 55–60.

Schmuck, Richard A., and Matthew B. Miles. 1971. *Organization Development in Schools*. New Delhi, India: National Press Books.

Strauman, Timothy J. 2017. "Self-regulation Theory". In *The SAGE Encyclopedia of Abnormal and Clinical Psychology*, edited by Amy Wenzel, 2–4. Thousand Oaks, CA: SAGE Publications.

Tangney, June P., Roy F. Baumeister, and Angie Luzio Boone. 2004. "High Self-control Predicts Good Adjustment, Less Pathology, Better Grades, and Interpersonal Success". *Journal of Personality*, 72: 271–322.

Tolbert, Mary Ann Rainey., and Jonno Hanafin. 2006. "Use of Self in OD Consulting: What Matters Is Presence". In *The NTL Handbook of Organization Development and Change: Principles, Practices, and Perspectives*, edited by Brenda B. Jones and Michael Brazzel, 69–82. San Francisco, CA: Pfeiffer.

University of St. Thomas. Accessed May 3, 2021. https://stthomas.az1.qualtrics.com/jfe/form/SV_d5AQM2T0g49fmIt

Chapter 8

Step 7: Showcasing Your Organization's Talent

Marie Carasco

Contents

Within every organization there are talented employees. Depending on the role, reporting structure, and culture dynamics, some talented employees can receive more opportunities for recognition, rewards, development, and promotion than others. Equitable approaches to showcasing talent require deliberate consideration and planning regarding the best avenues to increase an individual's visibility to generate interest in, and opportunities

DOI: 10.4324/9781003184935-11

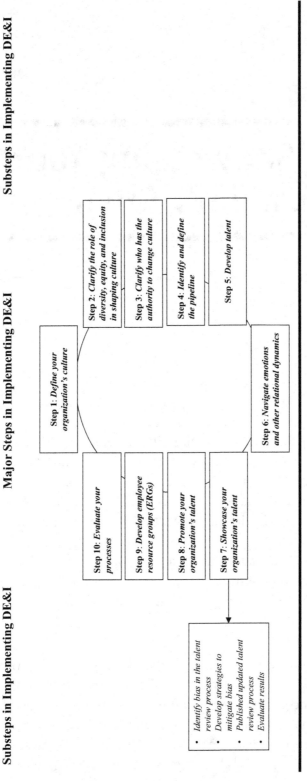

Frontmatter Figure 8.1   The diversity, equity, and inclusion (DE&I) roadmap model.

for, meaningful collaboration and stretch opportunities. These opportunities should not only allow workers to highlight their skills but could also facilitate the development of new ones, particularly knowledge and capabilities needed by an organization to meet strategic objectives. In countries where there are legal requirements around the ways to manage career opportunities of protected groups, the process of showcasing talent is taken seriously but is not without bias.

Case Study

Angelica, a Supply Chain Manager for an energy company based in Europe, had worked for the company over the last two years. Her performance was good. She believed that she could have a long and satisfying career with the organization. Toward the end of her second year with the company, Angelica approached her team's HR Business Partner to share the news she was pregnant and wanted to understand how to plan for her maternity leave and subsequent return to work.

The following will describe some steps taken to highlight the talent that would serve as Angelica's replacement based on Kurt Lewin's Action Research Model, a foundational model used by practitioners as a guiding frame of reference in an organization development (OD) effort:

Step 1: Entry – By sharing her pregnancy news with the Human Resources team, Angelica initiated an element of the company's succession management strategy related to leadership continuity in her role during her maternity leave, and considerations for her return. Angelica was entitled to 52 weeks of statutory maternity leave, and although she did not have to take the full 52 weeks, she had to take no less than two weeks' leave after her baby was born. The earliest she could begin her leave was 11 weeks before the expected week of childbirth, but generally, her leave would start the day after the birth of the baby if it arrived early. These baseline parameters set the wheels in motion to select Angelica's replacement.

Step 2: Start-up – As part of the talent management and succession planning process for the supply chain function, Angelica's role was flagged as a critical one given her portfolio of contracts and her leadership of a team across the European Geo-market. Her personnel file provided a starting point to understand the scope of her work, current projects, and objectives, past performance, and highlighted her career aspirations. Angelica's personnel file also reflected managerial comments and development areas. This file was shared with her immediate manager to serve as the foundation to discuss who might fill her role over the next year.

Step 3: Assessment and feedback – Angelica's manager Geoff used her personnel file and knowledge of the strategic business objectives for the supply chain team in Europe to shape his thinking around who would be best suited to cover Angelica's role during her maternity leave. Meetings were held between Geoff and Angelica; meetings were also held among the supply chain leadership team and Human Resources. Leadership discussions considered several scenarios, including expanding or contracting the role, promoting one of Angelica's subordinates, presenting the role as a short-term assignment or a lateral move to someone in a similar job in another region, and even splitting the role into two jobs.

Step 4: Action planning – After determining that the role would be offered as a lateral opportunity to someone in a similar job from another region, Geoff clearly understood what he was looking for in Angelica's replacement. Given the succession planning process had identified individuals within the company who are both "ready now" (possessing the skills need to do the job immediately) and those that would be "ready in the future" (needing some additional development), Geoff used the organization's Human Resource Information System (HRIS) to filter only ready now candidates willing to move. The results yielded two white males (one married, one single) and one black female candidate (single). After reading the personnel files of the three candidates, Geoff chose the single white male who he deemed would have the most flexibility to travel across the geo-market, and whose personnel file indicated an interest in growing in this area of specialization. He believed that the married male candidate would eventually express concerns about travel and that the black female candidate would not be comfortable leading an all-white team. Geoff shared his selection with his boss and the HR team to begin coordination of the internal offer.

Step 5: Intervention – The best intervention for mitigating bias with Geoff's selection process is in having the process occur openly while maintaining levels of confidentiality. For example, as Geoff talks through his choices, it would have been beneficial to work with an HR team member that could ask probing questions and serve as an advocate for candidates that may be overlooked. See Table 8.1 in Appendix E for OD actions to take to develop more equitable talent reviews.

Step 6: Evaluation – To ensure an equitable selection process, leverage the key elements of the role as the foundation for selection. Ask questions such as: does this candidate have the experience needed to do the role? How can this person's past performance inform future performance? Then have a second tier of nice-to-have elements that are not required but would be helpful for the role. Stop and interrogate that list. Finally, if anything falls outside of those two buckets, dig into what is behind this element being added and eliminate unnecessary barriers.

Step 7: Adoption – Candidate selection for internal transfers and promotion should be treated with the same rigor and seriousness as new hires. By creating policies and practices that capture the same commitments to nondiscrimination, the company can provide the first line of accountability to ensure diverse internal talent is highlighted.

Step 8: Separation – As Angelica prepared to take her maternity leave, she was increasingly concerned that she wouldn't have a job when she returned. Since her replacement came from another region, she worried that he wouldn't be too keen on leaving that role after only one year. After speaking with Human Resources, Angelica was assured that based on the law and depending on the leave days taken, she had the right to return to her job or something similar if it were impossible to have her old role. In her absence, the HR team remained in touch with Angelica's manager to discuss possibilities for her return and devised a plan for her return to work. By the time Angelica returned from maternity leave, the supply chain business had expanded and her previous role had grown into a larger scope for which she was not ready. She was given a similar role to the one she had before her maternity leave, with the same pay, but a smaller team.

Although the organization had several tools and mechanisms in place to allow leaders to identify candidates within the company, there were several implicit biases held by Geoff that hindered him from highlighting diverse talent to replace Angelica. These included conformity bias and race-based assumptions. This chapter will cover some of the bias checks that can be integrated into the talent review process, a common approach used for talent advancement in organizations.

Table 8.1 Design Thinking Phases and OD Actions to Create More Equitable Talent Reviews

Directions: Based on the five phases in design thinking – an inclusive process to develop or refine content grounded in the user experience. Review this table to increase your awareness of key areas to give focused attention as you leverage OD practices for transformational change in approaches to talent reviews. First, evaluate the general considerations section; then if you can commit to each consideration, move to the corresponding specific actions.

Phase	General considerations to inform actions	Specific actions
1 Empathize	This is the phase of planning and performing preliminary research to understand the current state. **Planning and Preparation** • Is your organization willing to make the talent review process a fully transparent one? • What is the issue being addressed for change? • How will the awareness of the change initiative be shared? By whom? and how frequently? (Website, newsletters, townhalls, etc.) • What are the desired outcomes? How will you know you reached it? What are the measures to evaluate attainment of the desired outcomes? • Who are the key stakeholders (those impacted by the change) within and external to the organization? What roles will they play? Who might try to get in the way of the change? • Determine the type of data needed • Who will be doing the data collection? How will it be shared and with whom? • What are the risks involved in this change initiative and how might they be mitigated? **Preliminary Research and Data Collection** • Use quantitative and qualitative approaches (observation, interviews, surveys, focus groups) • Encourage storytelling • Look for inconsistencies • Give attention to nonverbal cues	• Develop a communications plan from the leadership team that will create a sense of urgency for the change and highlight historical challenges with current talent review process • Include an emphasis on transparency and interest in employee involvement in creating an inclusive process • Perform a talent audit and generate reports on the current state of diverse representation across levels in the organization. Identify trends • Observe the current talent review process • Perform interviews, focus groups with stakeholder groups across all levels in the organization for feedback on the current talent review process and elicit suggestions on changes • Summarize key findings by finding themes and share with stakeholders • Communicate next steps

(Continued)

Table 8.1   (Continued) Design Thinking Phases and OD Actions to Create More Equitable Talent Reviews

	Phase	*General considerations to inform actions*	*Specific actions*
2	Define	Grounded in the preliminary research and data collection, this phase allows for a better understanding of the challenges connected to making the change. • Unpack your findings • Reframe the challenge/issue based on the data and insights collected • Preserve the sentiments expressed including strong emotions and insights • Communicate findings and potential action plan with all stakeholder groups	• Use the key findings and stakeholder suggestions from phase one as part of a preliminary action plan • Share preliminary action plan with stakeholder groups and obtain feedback
3	Ideate	Based on the feedback shared by stakeholder groups, brainstorm additional solutions, changes, and opportunities. • Consider what could be and how to get there • Use the content from this phase to prototype/experiment/pilot a new approach	• Across stakeholder groups, create a list of unrestricted creative ideas of changes to the talent review process • Allow the most outlandish ideas to be shared
4	Prototype	This phase will facilitate the development of a pilot or experimental approach to explore based on the prior phase. • Determine which ideas from the prior phase will offer either quick wins and/or lasting impact to experiment with • Scenario planning or role-playing talent reviews are a good way to preserve employee confidentiality as you test new approaches	• Develop a survey to obtain feedback on which ideas to pilot, then select the highest-ranking responses to take actions on first in refining the talent review process • Create a scenario/role play based on the survey answers
5	Test	Create an experience that authentically represents a test or pilot of your new proposed approach to talent reviews from the previous phase: • Look for insights, positive and challenging experiences with the new approaches to the talent review • Embrace the notion that you might have to go back to the ideate and prototype phases • Only integrate/embed a new approach when there is agreement	• Identify stakeholders to engage in the testing of the new approach • Observe the process • Ask for feedback from the participants in the pilot • Go back to phases 3 and 4 as many times as needed until the organization and collective stakeholders are satisfied with the new process • Integrate the new process with actual employee data

What Does the Research Say?

Talent Management

> [T]here are at least three different ways of interpreting [talent management (TM)] in practice: (1) TM is often used simply as a new term for common HR practices (old wine in new bottles), (2) it can allude to succession-planning practices, or (3) it can refer more generically to the management of talented employees.

(Ariss et al. 2014, 173)

In this chapter, we focus on the definition of talent management that involves "designing and implementing an integrated set of processes, programs, and cultural norms to attract, develop, deploy, and retain talent to achieve strategic business objectives" (Rothwell et al. 2016, 421). To optimize success, the organization "must recognize the need for proactive talent management and have a systematic way of accomplishing that activity" (Berger and Berger 2004, 3). The process requires differentiation among employees in an organization and a narrowed focus on those that are essential in supporting the success of the organization (Rothwell et al. 2016). These employee groups comprise key talent, including technical experts, high-potentials, high-value, and senior leaders.

Succession Planning

Rothwell (2015) states succession planning and management (SP&M) "is perhaps best understood as an effort designed to ensure the continued effective performance of an organization, division, department, or workgroup by providing for the development, replacement, and strategic application of key people" (6). Rothwell describes the essential components of a succession planning program:

■ Establish a clear purpose for why the program is needed.
■ Determine measurable objectives over a specified time frame.
■ Understand the key competencies needed for success in the present/ .
  now.
■ Articulate how key competencies will be measured.
■ Understand the key competencies needed for success in the future.

- Define standards on how the organization will assess promotion potential.
- Outline strategies on how to narrow/mitigate any development gaps for future role/levels.
- Measure and evaluate the overall succession program and individual elements.

Rothwell says that organizations with effective succession planning and management programs "must have a means by which to replace key job incumbents as vacancies occur in their positions. Promotion from within is a time-honored and crucially important, albeit traditional, way to do that" (Rothwell 2015, 255). "A robust succession management strategy provides a roadmap for succession and leadership continuity. It further guides development activities of identified successors, serves to anticipate and manage issues of career ambition and avoids transition problems and premature promotions" (Stadler 2011, 266). Talent reviews are an essential part of the succession planning and management process.

General Approaches to Highlighting Talent

When an organization has a strong alignment of talent management with core business processes, there is a clear understanding of ways of effectively identifying, developing, managing, and deploying talent to meet current and future business needs. Of critical importance is the area of talent assessment and alignment which facilitates the development of action plans that address retention risks, talent gaps, and opportunities for development as part of a robust and viable succession plan. With those key elements in place, many organizations use that information to categorize the talent pool and based on their talent designations, definitions, and actions using a variety of core talent, high-potentials, emerging leaders, domain experts, technical experts, and an at-risk group. When it comes to ways of highlighting the talent, the most promising talent is often presented with differentiated opportunities for growth and visibility and choices for development can include formal and informal learning programs, training, mentoring, coaching, job rotations, stretch assignments, international assignments, short-term assignments, and joining or leading various project teams (Fernandez-Araoz et al. 2011). These activities allow individuals to gain new skills, connect with an expanded network, build a positive reputation, and more importantly, get on the radar screens of key decision-makers in the organization. However, talent review meetings are the most common opportunities for employee visibility with senior leaders making strategic business decisions connected to talent. Talent reviews are discussed in the next section.

Talent Reviews: The Key Lever

A talent review process is "the regular cycle of evaluating a company's leaders consistently and systematically. … The Power of talent reviews lies in their consistent, disciplined execution" (Effron and Ort 2010, 76). These meetings provide "an opportunity to bring together key decision-makers to discuss how to manage the development of talented people in an organization. It is a critical culmination of any succession planning or talent management process" (Rothwell 2015, 271). During the talent review meetings, participants understand the talent they have, "identify the talent [they] are missing, and create plans to address both" (Effron and Ort 2010, 75). Without this process "many times an organization may not be aware of a talented employee who could fill an open or future position" (Sims 2010, 25). "[A] talent review, usually executed within the context of a talent strategy, is a rigorous competency-based assessment of employees, to identify high-potential employees and future leaders, determine bench strength at a particular level, identify talent gaps, organizational vulnerabilities and risks" (Stadler 2011, 266). Brandemuehl (2009) emphasizes that talent reviews and succession planning are important during times of economic crisis because it allows organizations

> to make better business decisions in the current economic climate by driving targeted leadership development investments with maximum ROI; [facilitating] timely and relevant assessment of its leadership talent to staff key positions in newly restructured organizations; [and determine] assessment of learning agility as a key leadership characteristic required for leading effectively in uncertain times.

(17)

Talent review meetings are highly confidential and can focus on identifying talent pools, flagging high-potential talent, highlighting talent at risk, and determining successors. Most often senior leadership holds talent review meetings at least once per year – and ideally once per quarter. The talent selected for discussion in these meetings depends on the processes in place

in the organization. Sometimes, division heads must do initial talent identification in collaboration with a HR team member before those efforts are
presented to the senior leaders. The HR team is key in providing access to
confidential talent information, including performance appraisals, key contributions, and the profiles of successors. The presentation of this information can vary from printed to electronic profile summaries that can include
photos, key accomplishments, and education. The selection of employees
to be part of talent reviews is often foundationally based on performance.
Based on the business needs, subsequent discussions are typically on an
employee's key contributions, expertise, short- and long-term development
needs, and promotion potential. Stadler (2011) gives additional insight into
the process of talent reviews which involves various techniques and tools
including:

> [A]ssessment center methodology (simulations), a range of standard-
> ized psychometric measures. … A talent map [to] help organiza-
> tions to analyze data and match talent to talent pools or succession
> plans. A talent map is the visual output of a talent review. A
> nine-box performance/potential matrix [to] allow for a time-based
> snapshot of the relative distribution of talent across a given organi-
> zational level or target group.

(267)

With all the tools applied and the process completed, without the follow-
up of "in-depth conversations with employees to discuss their development
plans, then you have quite simply wasted everyone's time" (Burt 2005, 40).
Succession planning comes with additional risks, particularly for leadership
positions. According to "Leadership Succession Risks and What HR Can Do
about Them" (2020), these risks include:

> Vacancies cause time-critical leadership responsibilities to be
> neglected; underdeveloped successors; static planning [which is
> based on thinking about the present and not the future needs];
> conformity risk [which is selecting people that are most like those
> making the selections]; finally culture-process alignment [execut-
> ing the succession management in ways that mirror the company
> values].

(1)

Bias in Succession Planning

The greatest risk for bias in the succession process is conformity and culture-process alignment. "Both ethnic minorities and the members of the White-majority group show a pro-White leadership bias in the categorization of universally valued leadership traits" (Gundemir et al. 2014, 8). People in organizations are more inclined to lean on a default view of leadership that reflects the dominant White culture. In a study on *homophily*, "which can be defined as the tendency for people to prefer to associate with others who are similar in status or beliefs, values and attitudes" (Golik and Blanco 2021, 2), a variety of homophily attributes play a role in talent management and identification (18). In fact, "[s]ince talent decision-making processes are boundedly rational, talent spotters/decision-makers tend to focus on candidates that are proximate and/or familiar with or fit their existing worldviews" (15). Auster and Prasad (2016) say that "[s]ocial categorization and stereotyping of visible and invisible markers also generate similarity/attraction and dissimilarity/repulsion, thereby increasing the likelihood of bias" (185).

To put this in perspective, one example of an area of dissimilarity and bias in the workplace is hair texture and styles typically worn by members of minority groups. In a study by Dawson et al. (2019), they observed "that how individuals think and feel about their hair is largely influenced by a labeling process, such that hair that is different from the Eurocentric norm of 'smooth and straight' is stigmatized as unprofessional and less beautiful" (398). Due to the increasing prevalence of discrimination related to ethnic hairstyles, the CROWN Act was introduced in California in January 2019 and signed into law on July 3, 2019, "the inaugural CROWN Act expanded the definition of race in the Fair Employment and Housing Act (FEHA) and state Education Code, to ensure protection in workplaces and K-12 public and charter schools" (About – The Official CROWN Act).

Putting into Practice

Step 1: Identify bias in the current talent review process

Although "[t]he Talent Review Meeting is also designed to increase the visibility of talent in the organization; increase the validity of the succession plans, high potential identification, and develop action plans" (Sims 2010, 25), the process is fraught with bias. In their summary of an incident that highlighted the importance of interrogating explicit and implicit systems and structures in organizations, Maitland and Steele (2020) indicate how an executive misjudged a diverse employee's "commitment" to the organization during a talent review. Initial discussions of the diverse candidate highlighted that this employee had continually exceeded performance expectations. However, one executive stated that this diverse employee was not promotion material since she left the office at 5 p.m. every day. "Because of hidden individual and systemic bias about what 'commitment' and 'leadership' looked like, the company could have been deprived of top leadership material" (Maitland and Steele 2020, 63), a stark example of Auster and Prasad's social categorization and stereotyping, and Golik and Blanco's homophily. This case also highlights implicit versus explicit expectations for success and promotion. Although the diverse employee did exceptional work, an explicit requirement for promotion, the implicit expectation to demonstrate organization commitment was to work past 5 p.m. A different and perhaps more interesting conversation might have been to explore how this employee exceeded expectations during normal business hours while her peers needed to stay late to accomplish the same results.

Step 2: Develop strategies to mitigate bias

Managing change through an OD approach begins with some basic assumptions grounded in Burke's (1994) criteria: "it must (1) respond to an actual and perceived need for change on the part of the client, (2) involve the client in the planning and implementation of the change, and (3) lead to change in the organization's culture" (9).

With this foundation, developing more equitable approaches in talent reviews requires:

- Recognition of a need for change in the talent management process in your organization.
- The involvement of the people affected by the proposed change.
- A transformation to the culture, not simply process improvement.

Without your organization's willingness to engage in all three of these elements, your company may not be ready to leverage an OD approach for change in talent strategy, because OD should be used only when there is an interest in a fundamental change to an organization's culture.

If you are seeking a step-by-step guide on how to go about this change process, you are not alone. However, "[p]hases is a more appropriate term than steps for describing the flow of events in OD work. Steps imply discrete actions, while phases better connote the reality of OD practice – a cycle of changes" (Burke 1994, 80). These phases ought to be grounded in a framework. "Without a framework for understanding, the data an OD practitioner collects about a client organization may remain nothing more than an array of personal comments of the who-said-what-about-whom variety" (96). Frameworks also guide the questions asked. Although details on the following diagnostic frameworks are beyond the scope of this chapter, they are presented here for your reference:

- Weisbord's Six-Box Model (1976)
- Nadler and Tushman's Congruence Model (1989)
- Burke and Litwin's Model (1989, 1992, 2002)
- Galbraith's Star Model (2002)
- Cheung-Judge and Holbeche OD Evaluation Model (2011)

It is important to highlight that the most important aspect of your work will be the level and approaches to inclusion built into your interventions, the stakeholder engagement.

Step 3: Publish updated talent review process

In 2020, the murder of George Floyd spawned an avalanche of interest in all things related to diversity, equity, and inclusion. Some common and immediate actions taken by companies were the creation of Diversity/Equity/Inclusion/Belonging staff positions, and public declarations of commitment to increasing the representation of people of color. However, without a thorough examination of the organizational structures and HR processes that can perpetuate and sometimes hide discriminatory or biased practices, those first steps will do nothing to ensure an inclusive and equitable talent management process. Since many organizations take a highly confidential approach when conducting talent reviews, a radical shift toward transparency with this process is the first real action that will facilitate the accountability needed to mitigate bias. Your employees should be informed there are yearly discussions with senior leaders to identify future leaders and they ought to know how it works. By allowing employees' and other key stakeholders' insight into the talent review process, your organization will build a solid foundation of trust and accountability needed for a successful organizational transformation. Using the five phases in design thinking – an inclusive process to develop or refine content grounded in the user experience outlined in Table 8.1 and found in Appendix E – your organization can leverage specific actions to develop your equitable approaches to talent reviews. See Chapter 7 for the preparation needed by the practitioner leading an equity-focused change initiative.

Some potential outcomes are:

■ Establishing a transparent talent review process by informing the organization that talent reviews occur and inviting feedback from across the organization on how to make it more equitable.
■ Creating a self-nomination process for employees to be considered during a talent review.
■ Applying the same antidiscrimination policies used in the talent acquisition to talent reviews.
■ Applying or developing the same diverse slate requirements used in talent acquisition.
■ Outlining measures of accountability for inclusive practices in talent reviews as part of managing by objectives and rewards and recognition for all parties involved a talent review.
■ Establishing a role specifically aimed at identifying and calling out bias during talent reviews.
■ Moving beyond data points on the percentage of people of color in a particular role, group, or department to the experiences of people of color connected to retention.
■ Establish periodic audits to evaluate advancement decisions to ensure adherence to antidiscriminatory approaches.
■ Ensuring staff development facilitates the inclusion of diverse talent through initiatives that require managers to rotate the team member involvement on projects.

Although training is one of the low-level, micro-approaches to managing inclusion (Mor Barak 2005), it can also be a helpful starting point. Golik and Blanco (2021) emphasized the need to train line managers on homophily biases to help reduce the negative consequences of homophily when identifying talent. Otherwise, important and qualified social groups will be excluded from leadership and those selected will continue to choose those who are like themselves.

Step 4: Evaluate results

As mentioned in previous chapters, you should evaluate the effects of changes you made to the talent review process.

There is a tool, appearing in Appendix E, that tracks with the step-by-step approach toward implementation described in this chapter.

Key Questions about the Chapter

1. Did you know what a talent review was before you read this chapter? Does your company have talent reviews? If so, how would a transparent approach to talent reviews shift the culture at your organization?
2. Where have you seen homophily demonstrated implicitly or explicitly in your organization?
3. What are implicit cultural expectations related to promotions held by your organization?
4. Who is the steward to the data related to the representation of diverse talent in your company? Is that data easily accessible or highly confidential? What would knowing this information do for stakeholders across your organization?
5. Which of the five phases in Table 8.1 would you find easiest to accomplish? Which would be the most challenging and why?

Works Consulted

"About: The Official CROWN Act." n.d. *The CROWN Act*, June 17, 2021, https://www.thecrownact.com/about.

Al Ariss, Akram, Wayne F. Cascio, and Jaap Paauwe. 2014. "Talent Management: Current Theories and Future Research Directions." *Journal of World Business* 49 (2): 173–179.

Auster, Ellen R., and Ajnesh Prasad. 2016. "Why Do Women Still Not Make It to the Top? Dominant Organizational Ideologies and Biases by Promotion Committees Limit Opportunities to Destination Positions." *Sex Roles* 75: 177–196.

Berger, Lance A., and Dorothy R. Berger. 2004. *The Talent Management Handbook: Creating Organizational Excellence by Identifying, Developing, & Promoting Your Best People*. Madison, WI: CWL Publishing Enterprises, Inc.

Brandemuehl, Jenny. 2009. "Talent Reviews and Succession Planning Matter More During Tough Economic Times." *T+D* 63 (6): 17.

Burke, Wyatt Warner. 1994. *Organization Development: A Process of Learning and Changing*. Boston, MA: Addison-Wesley Publishing Company.

Burt, Tequia. 2005. "Leadership Development as Corporate Strategy: Using Talent Reviews to Improve Senior Management." *Healthcare Executive* 20 (6): 14–18.

Dawson, Gail A., Katherine A. Karl, and Joy V. Peluchette. 2019. "Hair Matters: Toward Understanding Natural Black Hair Bias in the Workplace." *Journal of Leadership & Organizational Studies* 26 (3): 389–401.

Effron, Marc, and Miriam Ort. 2010. *One Page Talent Management: Eliminating Complexity, Adding Value*. Boston, MA: Harvard Business School Publishing Corporation.

Fernandez-Araoz, Claudio, Boris Groysberg, and Nitin Nohria. 2011. "How to Hang on to Your High Potentials." *Harvard Business Review* 89 (10): 76–84.

Golik, Mariela, and Maria Rita Blanco. 2021. "Homophily: Functional Bias to the Talent Identification Process?" *Personnel Review*. Vol. ahead-of-print No. ahead-of-print.

Gundemir, Seval, Astrid C. Homan, Carsten K. W. de Dreu, and Mark van Vugt. 2014. "Think Leader, Think White? Capturing and Weakening an Implicit Pro-White Leadership Bias." *PLOS One* 9 (1): 1–10.

Maurer, Roy. 2020. "Leadership Succession Risks and What HR Can Do About Them." *SHRM.*.

Maitland, Alison, and Rebekah Steele. 2020. *Indivisible: Radically Rethinking Inclusion for Sustainable Business Results*. Canada and UK: Young & Joseph Press.

Mor Barak, Michalle E. 2005. *Managing Diversity: Toward a Globally Inclusive Workplace*. Thousand Oaks, CA: Sage Publications, Inc.

Rothwell, William J. 2015. *Effective Succession Planning: Ensuring Leadership Continuity and Building Talent from Within*. 5th ed. New York: Amacom.

Rothwell, William J., Jacqueline M. Stavros, and Roland L. Sullivan. 2016. *Practicing Organization Development: Leading Transformation and Change*. 4th ed. Hoboken, NJ: Wiley.

Sims, Doris. 2010. *The Talent Review Meeting Facilitator's Guide: Tools, Templates, Examples, and Checklists for Talent and Succession Planning Meetings*. Bloomington, IN: AuthorHouse.

Stadler, Karien. 2011. "Talent Reviews: The Key to Effective Succession Management." *Business Strategy Series* 12 (5): 264–271.

Chapter 9

Step 8: Promoting Your Organization's Talent

Barbara R. Hopkins

Contents

Scenarios in Promotions

Imagine having the occasion to promote someone from within the organization to a leadership position. It is the opportunity of a lifetime for a rising star and has the potential to lead to even higher levels of administration. The manager takes a careful look at the pool of applicants and sees a familiar name. Although others on the list have equally impressive qualifications, the manager remembers hearing from a close colleague this candidate worked well in a different office, was always on time, and maintained

DOI: 10.4324/9781003184935-12

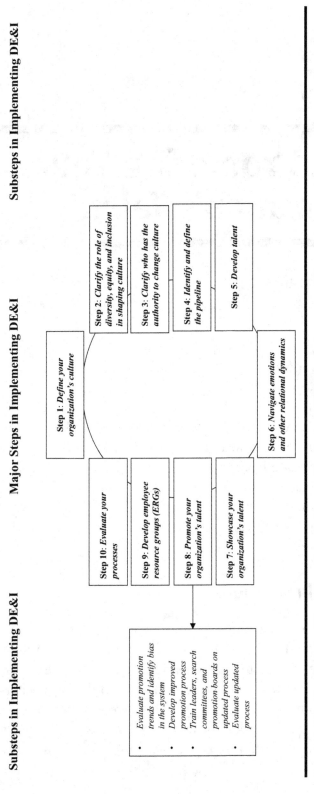

Frontmatter Figure 9.1   The diversity, equity, and inclusion (DE&I) roadmap model.

collaborative relationships with coworkers. The manager completes the interviews and selects the familiar candidate because there is confidence this candidate will fit in well with the department.

In another scenario, imagine the candidate pool includes a 60-year-old employee who has been with the organization for over 25 years. Although the employee has an impressive work history, the manager wonders if the employee knows the company and would be sufficiently innovative. The manager also wonders if the employee will retire soon, forcing yet another search to fill the same position. With this in mind, a younger candidate is selected for longevity and fresher ideas.

Finally, imagine a situation where the candidate pool includes a well-qualified employee of Asian descent. Although the skills and abilities are a great match for the department, the hiring supervisor realizes there are no other employees of Asian descent in the department and fears the candidate would feel isolated and uncomfortable. To spare the candidate from discomfort, the supervisor instead selects an employee who more closely matches the demographic makeup of the department.

In reviewing the above scenarios, is there anything wrong? Is one of them more understandable or more acceptable than the others? These circumstances show prejudice by the hiring supervisor, despite the seemingly reasonable justifications for the decisions made. This is because these situations show forms of bias. And while the terms "prejudice" and "bias" tend to quickly generate labels such as "racist," the fact is that many biases are not intentionally applied and people use them without even realizing it. This is called *implicit bias*.

What Does the Research Say?

When promoting employees from within the organization, the goal should be to find the best talent who can move the organization forward. To do that, there must be an opportunity for everyone who might be interested or eligible to be considered in the pool of candidates. However, research shows that unconscious bias remains an obstacle to adopting fair practices in hiring – even when hiring from within the organization.

Many forms of literature discuss bias regarding categories such as race, ethnicity, gender, disability, or identity. These preferences are buried deep within every person based on prior experiences and upbringing. They become evident when in a situation that involves someone different. It could be men preferring not to hire women or those who are able-bodied preferring not to hire those with disabilities.

Often society deems bias as a negative trait. And those practicing these biases are prejudiced or discriminatory. However, bias is a neutral concept found in everyone and is not something that can simply be turned off. The unconscious nature of this form of preference is rooted in science.

Clohisy et al. (2017) share that the human brain is flooded with millions of pieces of information. However, only a minuscule amount of that information can be processed simultaneously. To compensate, the mind takes shortcuts and relies on these subconscious biases to make connections and reduce the vast energy it takes to decide. Swart et al. (2015) share common psychological concepts which result from internal preferences. One such concept is the halo effect. Research has shown that individuals who are considered attractive are thought to have positive characteristics unrelated to looks such as intelligence and trustworthiness. This effect may also refer to those who are attractive in other ways besides physical appearance. For example, if a coworker's personality makes her likable, one may be more inclined to accept an idea or a proposal from that person.

So, even though bias is hardwired into the human brain to aid complex processing, it could also unintentionally create errors in judgment. This means that sometimes "following one's gut" could lead to a path that does more harm than good. For example, a candidate named John could remind a manager of a bully named John from high school. Intellectually, the manager knows this is not the same person. However, if that manager was a consistent victim of the high school bully, a natural dislike of the name (and any associated person) may have developed subconsciously. This would explain why John, the candidate, just "doesn't feel right" to the manager and could be overlooked for a job promotion.

Yet, if being biased is a natural inclination, then why does it matter? Why try to minimize something that human minds were designed to do? The answer lies in the organizational impact of bias. When left unchecked, this phenomenon affects employee morale, organizational productivity, and even organizational success.

Even the appearance of bias may influence employees to withhold innovative solutions for the organization or neglect to refer well-qualified colleagues to work for the organization (Hewlett et al. 2017). Employees in companies where there is diverse leadership are more likely to be engaged. Many minorities find it difficult to see themselves in a leadership position when no one in leadership has the same look or characteristics they do.

Putting into Practice

Step 1: Evaluate promotion trends and identify bias in the system

Now that there is an understanding of bias and its impact on the promotional process, what can be done to mitigate this systemic issue? There are numerous possibilities available to answer this question, but the solution for any organization will depend on the institutional culture and commitment from leadership. To aid with this solution, a few steps can be followed to help guide this work so it is customized to meet the needs of any company or association.

Many institutions begin this process by cultivating awareness. Remember that bias is unconscious – so many managers and supervisors are not even aware they are committing this act. However, everyone has some bias at some point and for some reason. Understanding this idea in a nonjudgmental way is the first step to ensuring progressive mindfulness surrounding this topic.

In order to help gauge awareness, an assessment could be completed to gather a sense of awareness from an organizational perspective. There are multiple resources to assist with this task. The Society of Human Resource Management (SHRM 2021) has assessments, research, and other tips available for review. (See also the Resource list at the back of this book.) There are also organizations founded specifically for diversity, equity, and inclusion collaborations and resources such as CEO Action for Racial Equity and Coequal. These groups were initiated to ensure accessibility to ideas and best practices regarding equity within organizational structures and processes.

Although these resources are valuable, remember that, even with the many assessment tools available, the best source of knowledge about bias in a particular organization is its employees. A survey of employees in all departments and at all levels will provide valuable information about the perception of bias in the organization. The critical idea of this assessment step is to learn about the diversity within one's organization and determine the needs of the populations of employees (Rothwell et al. 2017).

Step 2: Train leaders, search committees, and promotion boards on updated process

After taking the time to make the assessments in Step 1, the organization must do something with the information collected. If employees will take the time to share this personal information, leaders must review the results and commit to acting on them (Roepe 2021). Some companies have committed to making this information public, so they are held accountable for improving the data published. This data should be used to develop improved promotion processes.

Once an improved promotion process is developed, the next step recommended is to implement training. The purpose of the training is to help supervisors understand the subtlety and power of bias in their decision-making so that they can try to minimize the negative impacts of this phenomenon. However, those who develop the training must be careful about how this professional development is provided to employees. Some initial workshops to give information is great to increase awareness, but it should be part of an overall program that includes additional opportunities to engage with others in ways that change attitudes and behaviors. The reason bias is so impactful is because it is instinctive and part of routine human behavior. Participants should be guided to find ways to break those routines and broaden their perspectives so they understand why the new practices are important.

Step 3: Implement practices to improve promotion process

After developing a robust training program, practices should be implemented to encourage changes in corporate culture that will reinforce training concepts and assist with a more equitable promotion process.

This step will require some research into activities and procedures being used by other organizations. For example, some companies use published rubrics to make everyone aware of the criteria used in promotional decision-making (Roepe 2021). Others offer regular workshops on key skills needed to move ahead such as budgeting, conflict resolution, and leadership development. Further examples include a "blind" application process where names and identifying information are removed from applications and/or resumes, using a diverse team to guide hiring decisions instead of relying on only one perspective, and giving decision-makers a vocabulary list of phrases to describe an applicant based on behaviors rather than labels. The selection of these or any other practices will depend on the organizational culture, needs, and membership.

Once the appropriate practices are determined, there should be a systematic implementation of the practices developed. In other words, all employees should know and understand how the promotion process works along with the expectations from leadership.

Step 4: Evaluate updated process

Finally, a critical step to remember is to evaluate the process to ensure it is providing the desired (fair) results you are looking for. This means deciding on metrics that may be used to determine if the promotion plan is generating the desired results. It also means share the metrics and goals with the entire institution so all are aware of the progress. Incorporating this review in the normal procedures is essential to ensuring equity in the promotion process.

All of these steps can be visualized simply in Figure 9.1. Following these easy guidelines can help you develop a promotional process that meets the needs of the organization and also advocates for the needs of organizational members. Further, the tool in Table 9.1 will assist with making notes on how you want to accomplish the steps in this chapter. Using this and the key questions at the end of the chapter will allow you to customize a plan that will help in promoting your organization's talent in a way that minimizes the effects of natural biases.

Furthermore, there is also a tool, appearing in Appendix E, that tracks with the step-by-step approach toward implementation described in this chapter. If you complete that tool and the others in chapters following this one, you will have the foundation for a proposal to your organization's management for installing an effective DE&I effort.

Figure 9.1   Continuous improvement for DE&I.

Table 9.1 Checklist for Equity in Promotions
Use this checklist to guide development of an equitable promotion process

Be aware	
Do you know the diversity within your organization?	
Do hiring managers and supervisors know about unconscious bias?	
Train	
Are managers provided regular trainings or refresher sessions regarding implicit bias?	
Does your training program allow activities or discussions among all employees?	
Does your training program promote cultural change in promotional practices?	
Practice	
Is there commitment from top leadership to employ equity and inclusion practices?	
Do all employees have the same opportunity to learn about new internal postings?	
Has your organization recently explored best practices to improve equity in the promotional process?	
Check	
Is there a mechanism for all employees to share feedback regarding the promotion process without fear of retaliation or consequence?	
Is there a regular, systematic review of the promotion process to ensure effectiveness?	

Key Questions about the Chapter

1. If your organization were to mirror the diversity in your community, what would it look like?
2. How does your organization mitigate unconscious bias in the promotion process?
3. What efforts does your organization make to ensure all employees receive professional development opportunities that would allow them the skills and experience necessary for advancement?
4. What is the perception of your organization's managers regarding the fairness of the promotion process? How does that compare to the perception of other employees?
5. How often are promotional policies and processes reviewed for fairness and application of current best practices?

Works Consulted

Clohisy, Denis R., Michael J. Yaszemski, and Joanne Lipman. June 2017. "Leadership, Communication, and Negotiation Across a Diverse Workforce." *The Journal of Bone & Joint Surgery* 99-A, no. 12: 1–5.

Hewlett, Sylvia A., Ripa Rashid and Laura Sherbin. 2017. *Disrupt Bias, Drive Value: A New Path Toward Diverse, Engaged, and Fulfilled Talent.* Los Angeles: Rare Bird Books.

"Implicit Bias." n.d. *Merriam-Webster.com Dictionary*, Merriam-Webster, Accessed March 17 2021. https://www.merriam-webster.com/dictionary/implicit%20bias.

Roepe, Lisa Rabasca. "Barriers for Black Professionals." Posted February 6, 2021. https://www.shrm.org/hr-today/news/all-things-work/pages/racism-corporate-america.aspx.

Rothwell, William, Angela Stopper, and Jennifer Myers. Eds. 2017. *Assessment and Diagnosis for Organization Development: Powerful Tools and Perspectives for the OD Practitioner.* New York: Productivity Press.

SHRM. 2021. https://www.shrm.org/ResourcesAndTools/hr-topics/Pages/diversity-equity-and-inclusion.aspx

Swart, Tara, Kitty Chisholm, and Paul Brown. 2015. *Neuroscience for Leadership: Harnessing the Brain Gain Advantage.* New York: Palgrave Macmillan.

Chapter 10

Step 9: Developing Employee Resource Groups

Wayne Gersie

Contents

DOI: 10.4324/9781003184935-13

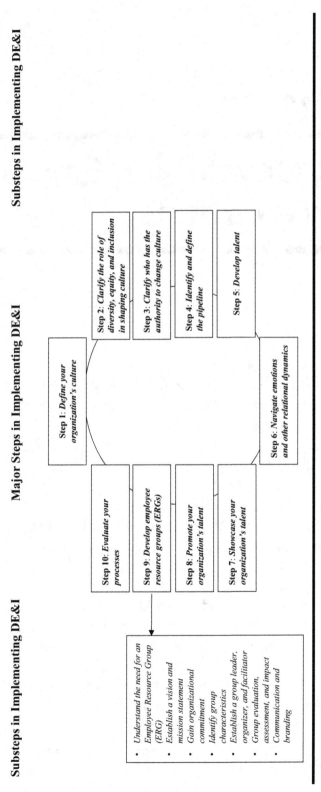

Frontmatter Figure 10.1   The diversity, equity, and inclusion (DE&I) roadmap model.

This chapter offers organization development (OD) practitioners background on Employee Resource Groups (ERG) along with information on best practices to speed their use. Here we will explore the importance of ERGs as part of an enduring OD strategy that is facilitative, rather than directive, ensuring stakeholder buy-in and ultimately a sense of belonging for the workforce. As with the origination of ERGs, which will be discussed later in this chapter, the value proposition of such groups is often realized because of national events. Some such events awaken the focus on the importance of diversity, equity, inclusion, and sense of belonging and lead to the consideration of ERGs as the solution toward DE&I goals. Done correctly, these groups can increase productivity and, ultimately, the bottom line.

Since their inception, ERGs have been referred to by various names based on their charge and evolution within the needs of the industry. For this chapter, ERGs are what researchers (Kaplan et al. 2009; McGrath Jr and Sparks) define as "employee groups within an organization created to provide resources for the workforce and other stakeholders within the organization." ERGs are primarily voluntary, employee-led groups that can vary from a few members to thousands (Friedman and Craig 2004; Kaplan et al. 2009). They serve members with common social identities (e.g., gender, generation, and race), interest in common causes, and hobbies. Their common theme is to foster a diverse and inclusive work environment within the context of the organization's mission, values, goals, business practices, and objectives.

A Case for Employee Resource Groups

Two years ago, Jeff Green became the first Chief Diversity Officer (CDO) of the McDowell Company, a midsize defense contractor in a small town in Central Ohio. The Chief Executive Officer (CEO), a retired senior commissioned officer, upon the recommendation by the company's board of directors (BOD), created this new leadership position. The CEO and the BOD recognized that to remain competitive and relevant, it was imperative to develop a diverse workforce that would bring different lived experiences to problem-solving and therefore out-innovate competitors, as others in the industry already. The hiring of a thought leader on DE&I who would lead a strategic vision on DE&I would be paramount. And so, to address this need, Jeff was hired as a member of the senior leadership team as the first CDO.

At this time, the McDowell Company's workforce was mainly composed of White males – 93%. According to company information on employee demographics, 1% were African Americans, 1% Latinx persons, and 1% Asian Americans. Representation by Native and Indigenous Americans was nonexistent. The administrative support staff was 100% female; of the 241 identified managerial roles, women held six positions, and people of color, two. Finally, the 13-person senior leadership team consisted of ten White males, one African American male new to the team, and one White female – the chief human resources officer. Against this backdrop, Jeff began his inaugural position, becoming the second Black male in senior leadership.

In his second month with McDowell, Jeff hired a third party to facilitate the development of an employee climate survey to gain better insight into employees' perceptions of their work environment. This climate survey would also serve as a pseudo-needs assessment for McDowell Company and its stakeholders. By the fourth month, the survey was launched and members at all levels of the organization's workforce were invited to participate. Incentives were included to increase the response rate. The survey presented both quantitative and qualitative employee inquiries about the work environment, with specific questions on their perception of bias in the workplace. The survey remained open for one month.

When the analysis of the survey began, the McDowell Company had acute, systemic, and structural inequities and pockets of sexist, homophobic, and racist climates. These behaviors permeated from entry level to the highest levels of the organization. Similar structural issues existed related to hiring, promotions, and succession planning. Besides concerns related to discrimination of marginalized and underrepresented groups, there was also a fear of retaliation related to expressing management concerns.

Along with those who chose to openly express these concerns in the survey, some chose not to express certain opinions by selecting the "do not wish to disclose" option in the survey responses. It became very clear to Jeff that the survey data gave further voice and context to the impact of the demographic makeup of the McDowell Company.

Armed with this new knowledge, four months into the job, Jeff navigated and facilitated a course of action and developed a vision that aligned with and supported the McDowell Company's stated and aspirational goals related to DE&I. Like any successful OD practitioner, Jeff would need to consider foundational to successful outcomes. The guiding questions would be: (1) What organizational interventions would help move the current organizational climate toward its aspirational goals? (2) How would he facilitate an organizational change that would be enduring in workspaces that require innovation? (3) How could Jeff best serve as a facilitator rather than dictator/ director to optimize stakeholder buy-in? (4) How would he get stakeholders in a position of privilege and agency to realize that DE&I was beneficial to them and also persuade use of their levers of power to ensure these organizational and cultural changes happened? In his mind, the ultimate measure of success would be to initiate and develop a sense of belonging among those harmed by the current cultural norms at McDowell.

Jeff soon realized that a key solution to the McDowell Company's challenges was to ensure those who were systematically affected by inequities within the company, which affected their recruitment, retention, and promotion, would have a voice in disrupting these dysfunctional patterns and influencing the organization in a positive direction. He would need to create a platform through which their stories could be heard and their contributions would be part of the systemic changes that needed to take place.

One evident challenge found in the climate survey feedback revolved around issues of gender inequity. With that knowledge, Jeff invited a group of women from all levels of the organization to discuss the survey results, which by then had been published and shared company-wide. Jeff understood that to influence organizational buy-in, this group would need a forum where they could be heard and given a clear avenue to contribute to the strategic vision that ultimately helped change the climate. Jeff supported the ERG to the Director, who then committed to providing support and resources to the ERG. This included allowing released time for group members to convene and a line item in the budget to which the work hours conducted on behalf of these initiatives could be charged. This group's value was recognized with a direct reporting line to the company's CEO and CDO. The ERG would be self-directed and advise the CEO, CDO, and other members of senior leadership on initiatives that included key performance indicators used to assess organizational development (OD) and progress toward its DE&I goals. Hence, the McDowell Company Gender Employee Resource Group (GERG) was formed.

Within a year of the formation of this group, it was formally charged by the CEO with helping to tackle the top challenges that emerged from the survey results. Issues such as equitable parental leave benefits, intentional recruiting to broaden prospects and ensure diverse applicant pools, blind screening processes to improve equity in hiring, equitable processes for promotions, and other endeavors were implemented. The GERG has proven invaluable in instigating valuable initiatives and making progress toward a more diverse, inclusive, and equitable organization.

Serving as a great example, the GERG, as one of the company's first initiatives, tackled inequities within the company, starting with the maternal leave policy. Under the existing policy, expecting mothers were granted no paid maternal leave and, instead, only used a very limited number of vacation and sick days post-pregnancy. This inflexible policy resulted in new mothers exhausting all sick and vacation during a time of mandatory leave. They were forced to rush back to work sooner than was typically ideal for them and often had no paid leave balance upon their return. And fathers had no right to any leave after the birth of a child. The GERG gathered and provided qualitative and quantitative data on the positive impact of a paid parental leave benefit and worked with company management to develop its policy. By utilizing an ERG, a benefit that disrupted inequity and improved morale, a strong recruiting and retention tool had been born.

The Evolution of Employee Resource Groups

A bridge is repaired only when someone falls into the water. – *Somali Proverb*

At the most basic level, ERGs provide a social network for marginalized employees. And there is a potential for building a network of advocates, allies, and influencers, beyond the affinity group, that may interrupt climate and environmental issues which may have helped to form the ERGs. It is widely recognized that underrepresented groups have little to no access to informal interaction networks (Ibarra 1993). The importance of these networks for minority groups cannot be overstated as the formation of ERGs alone can almost singlehandedly address the deficit of informal social networks.

Since their creation, ERGs have become a best practice for many companies. As they evolved, many versions of ERGs have become integral in plans for inclusiveness. ERGs have moved beyond cultural and other identity groups, and they now include groups based on other commonalities or interests, such as parenting, wellness, or environmental activism. ERGs have evolved to include an emphasis on community volunteer work, and some companies have created entire employee volunteer networks.

The success of ERG groups in the United States expanded beyond the borders to become a global phenomenon, with international ERGs taking on a similar function to that found among them today. Specifically, over the past 25 years, ERGs have become a corporate DE&I best practice, including their emergence in Fortune 500 firms and small businesses (Friedman and

Deinard 1996). As ERGs expanded globally, so did the audiences they served – including a focus on encouraging employees to identify and participate in hobbies and other interests (Mercer 2011).

What the Research Says about Employee Resource Groups

The origins of the first ERGs are rooted in national and local events related to racial events. Since their inception, the charge of ERGs has continued to evolve. These developing charges of ERGs resulted in name changes to match the charges to groups. The original term for ERGs, "caucus group," has been replaced by various names that include affinity groups, employee networks, employee councils, employee forums, and business resource groups to comply with the ever-changing functions of these groups. For a long time, the term "affinity group" was the predominantly accepted term. Eventually, this designation was replaced by the now more commonly used term, "employee resource group" (Briscoe and Safford 2015).

The early focus of ERG groups is still the standard today, though variants exist. As ERGs have evolved, so have their original purposes. These groups now tackle organization development concerns that go beyond DE&I. ERGs have become an industry staple and strategy to create a healthy and productive climate. The success of ERGs is tied to how companies leverage them to ensure enduring organizational inclusiveness. ERGs can transform companies from reactionary environments that utilize one-off interventions to companies that leverage an OD perspective and subsequent enduring systemic changes.

Since the inception of ERGs, DE&I has been a key focus of these groups. Recent events like the murders of Ahmad Aubrey, Brianna Taylor, George Floyd, as well the insurrection on the U.S. national capitol building on January 6, 2021, may too reflexively pivot companies' attention to contemplate how well they serve their diverse workforces. These events trigger company leadership to ponder whether their organizations facilitate actions, training, and strategies culturally responsive to those in their workforce and customer base and in the communities they serve. This contemplation may cause company leaders viewing ERGs to think of it as a DE&I strategy for their organization. Company executives continue to come to these questions after tragic or alarming events.

The definition of insanity is to do the same thing and expect a different result. How will this time be different? Are the results a symptom of a cause and are ERGs a part of a whole? Regardless, the key question is to determine how to leverage ERGs effectively toward a culturally responsive DE&I strategy. To determine the efficacy of ERGs in organizations, a review of the existing research is necessary.

Despite the prevalence of ERGs since the 1960s, little research has been done on their evolution, effectiveness, and impact. Researchers argue that little to no scholarly work has been dedicated to this topic. This failure is a missed opportunity to produce a significant body of work on the importance of ERGs to the individuals who join these groups, to organizations, and the workforce in those organizations. What makes this dearth of information even more surprising has been HR practitioners' and OD professionals' abundant interest in the effectiveness of ERGs (Friedman and Holtom 2002).

Researchers posit that while the ERG trend continues to grow, the scholarly work on ERGs has not kept up (Welbourne et al. 2017). In a review of the literature, researchers (Briscoe and Safford 2015; Friedman and Deinard 1996; Mercer 2011; Welbourne et al. 2015) found that in the little scholarly work focused on ERGs, the primary emphasis has been placed on specific types of ERGs, followed by observational research, followed by a very limited emphasis on theory. Within this body of work, themes and ideas have varied. The methodology used in the reviews includes case studies, structured and semistructured interviews, surveys, archival data sets, and mixed-method approaches that include both quantitative (Wang and Schwarz 2010) and qualitative (Colgan and McKearney 2012) data collection methods.

Categories of Employee Resource Groups

When exploring the characteristics of existing ERGs, researchers have pointed to three predominant types (Welbourne and McLaughlin 2013). These are social-cause-centered, professional-centered, and attribute-centered ERGs. *Social-cause-centered ERGs* are concerned with a specific social issue such as the environment, or economic- or health-related issues. *Professional-centered ERGs* focus on interests related to specific professional fields such as the engineering profession, management, or administration. The third category is *attribute-centered ERGs*, which focus on personal and prescribed social identities that might include protected classes such as gender, race, veteran status, and so forth. Attribute-centered ERGs are similar to the original ERGs of the 1960s.

Attribute-Centered ERGs and the Impact on DE&I

Beyond being the most researched groups, attribute-centered ERGs also receive the most criticism or present the most potential legal exposure because they are perceived as exclusive to underrepresented group members (Lambertz-Berndt 2016). Attribute-centered ERGs offer a safe space for members to discuss shared experiences and various opportunities within the company. And these groups can lead to community-building from personal relationships at work to a broader network of spontaneous connections. Group members can exchange strategies and best practices on how to navigate issues unique to their social identity and opportunities for mentoring and support. The relationships developed through participation in attribute-centered ERG groups can cause enhanced career development through community-building and, ultimately, increased retention of members from this group. These groups can provide feedback to management and communicate complaints about bias-based behavior (Friedman and Deinard 1996), although the main focus of these groups is not advocacy.

Theoretical Approaches to Studying ERGs

No guiding theory or conceptual framework is dedicated to the study of ERGs (Welbourne et al. 2015, 2017). In addition, there have been a few studies in which research models are used to describe the effectiveness of ERGs or use theory when examining ERGs. Those studies that have done so are varied. For example, researchers (Friedman and Craig 2004) who have tested whether those who join network groups feel dissatisfied have used cognitive-dissonance theory (Festinger 1957). In another study, researchers examined the growth of ERGs and their results using negotiation and social movement theory (Scully 2009). Researchers also applied social network theory and theory to explore how female participants in an ERG group affected its success or failure (Bierema 2005)

Individual Benefits and Organizational Benefits of ERGs

Scholarly work on ERGs has largely focused on how they benefit individual group members and impact organizations. Research highlighting impacts on individuals stresses personal benefits, which include leadership development and cultural competency, and the creation of strong networks within their community – an added advantage in corporate branding (Kaplan et al. 2009). Additional research has pointed to other benefits of ERGs, such as providing social and professional support to group members, along with mentoring and visibility, including opportunities to interact with senior leadership (Van Aken et al. 1994).

Turning to ERGs' benefits to organizations, research has shown that ERGs are an effective means of creating a more culturally responsive workforce that can disrupt inequitable behaviors and shift organizational culture toward antiracism (Van Aken et al. 1994). Other organizational benefits include positive cultural shifts that increase productivity and stimulate innovation (Welbourne et al. 2017). Researchers also suggest that ERGs potentially improve recruitment to develop a more diverse workforce (Connelly and Kelloway 2003). ERGs are essential to fostering a climate that promotes a sense of belonging and disrupts an unwelcoming climate for underrepresented employees (Kaplan et al. 2009).

ERGs as an Outcome of an Organizational Development Strategy

If leveraged appropriately, ERGs can be part of a measurable and enduring OD approach. To optimize their effectiveness, ERGs should be a component of an overall strategy to improve recruitment, retention, promotion, and sense of belonging. As with any successful OD strategy, ERGs can become part of a long-term change effort directed toward individuals, groups, and the organization – but only if they are utilized to improve decision-making, problem-solving, and organizational culture (Rothwell and Sredl 1992). Finally, to have the greatest impact, ERGs need to be well-planned, have an organization-wide impact, be managed from the top-down, need increase organizational effectiveness intended to exert an impact, and, ultimately, need to be part of an intentional intervention approach that uses behavioral science-based knowledge.

The historical context of developing ERGs and a review of the limited scholarly work on these groups are very relevant and insightful in determining the charge of ERG formations and how it relates to company values and goals. This context demonstrates that ERGs have the potential to disrupt behaviors counter to optimal OD goals and values, especially in DE&I. The DE&I competencies are an essential part of 21st-century workforce development, and ERGs should play a major role in fostering these competencies. In addition, ERGs cannot be viewed as "magic bullets." Company leadership should have a facilitative rather than directive function in ERG development.

How companies charge and leverage the availability and creation of ERGs are critical to creating an inclusive and welcoming business environment. Further, ERGs that support the recruitment and retention of a diverse workforce bring a greater competitive edge in innovation. Until this point is embraced, continued cyclical reactions to national and local events will drive the impact of ERGs on group members and influencing the success of DE&I initiatives and the endurance of company goals.

Putting into Practice

Step 1: Understand the need for an ERG

The creation of an ERG has to be driven by a specific purpose and goal. This can be accomplished only if the stakeholders of an organization are intentional and develop a thorough process that begins with understanding its needs before the formation of any ERG. The first thing OD professionals must realize is that information gained when exploring the need for an ERG sets the foundation for all future decisions. What are the group's charge, vision, and mission? They must consider how this ERG can best serve stakeholders but, more important, ensure an enduring organizational impact. Finally, throughout the planning and launching of an ERG, OD professionals must ensure that the purpose of the ERG aligns with the organization's values and goals to facilitate the desired organizational development and performance outcomes. To achieve the desired alignment, an assessment of stakeholder needs is required at the outset.

The origins of ERGs at Xerox were driven by factors outside the company. The race riots of that era triggered a reactionary leadership response. They sought to provide a safe space for their African American workforce in a time of need in response to an external event affecting many of its employees. Even as ERGs evolved, their formations were often born out of external factors, and as such the creation of such groups continued to be a reactionary behavior. The result was sometimes ineffective and short-lived ERGs. Those considering implementing an ERG should not fall into this trap if the ERG is intended to improve organizational performance over a continued time and support a long-lasting sense of belonging. One must begin with exploring organizational needs.

Needs assessment is an essential process in the performance improvement of organizations. If an ERG is to be folded into company-wide performance-based strategic goals, a need assessment must be conducted. Current company DE&I gaps and challenges must be identified before determining how an ERG could help mitigate issues and/or pivot these gaps into pillars of best practices and desired performance. To demonstrate and identify a need for an ERG, decision-makers should be guided by these three questions:

- *What are gaps and challenges in existing versus aspirational strategic business needs related to company DE&I that the ERG can support?*
- *What are gaps and challenges in existing versus aspirational individual workforce performance needs and/or competencies related to DE&I that the ERG can support?*
- *What are gaps and challenges in existing versus aspirational training related to DE&I that the ERG can support?*

Differentiating between DE&I required needs and desired outcomes is essential to developing enduring impact (Roberson et al. 2013). Another key is creating a workforce culturally responsive to the needs of stakeholders who continue to be more diverse as demographics are ever-changing. Equally critical is the recognition that, unlike the original versions of ERGs where external factors influenced their creation, this approach of including a comprehensive needs assessment before an ERG was launched will cause informed, strategic influences throughout developing the ERG. Armed with this data and knowledge, only then can the OD professional and organization move forward with providing a clear vision, mission, and charge for the ERG.

Step 2: Establish a vision and mission statement

Researchers agree that developing a vision and a mission is influenced by the necessity to detect gaps and challenges in existing versus aspirational strategic goals (Calder 2014). Once the organizational environment is assessed, a mission statement is then created as an overarching theme under which an ERG will execute its charge (Powers 2012). Key to developing any mission and vision in alignment with the goals of the stakeholder. When ERGs succeed, participating employees, nonparticipating employees, and company leadership all play a role in the ERG direction.

Even though ERGs are employee-run and address employee concerns, the outcomes of the ERG need to align with the company's strategic imperatives and performance goals. When ERGs function in a manner in which all stakeholders' directions are aligned with company performance goals, a winning proposition for all parties is realized.

Step 3: Gain organizational commitment

When charging an ERG, OD professionals need to make a compelling case to the company leadership regarding the need for organizational commitment, which is foundational to ERG success. Organizational commitment should not only be financial but must also incorporate other actions and behaviors that demonstrate dedication to the success of the group. Leaders should inspire and communicate across the organization a common vision and shared aspirations for the ERG. The ERG should be given a variety of resources to support its vision and make it a reality. Leaders must further show true commitment by empowering and enabling the group. The ERG must be given the agency to influence company strategic goals related to DE&I through challenging the status quo and developing innovating new strategies. An organization must utilize employee knowledge and expertise. It is imperative that the group's efforts to change, grow, and improve be leveraged. When the group trusts there is shared power and their efforts and contributions will lead to transformation, there can be remarkable success and rewards.

When organizational commitment is lacking and the agency is not granted to the ERG, the group is much more likely to be susceptible to failure. If ERGs are superficial performative maneuvers rather than a true attempt at a meaningful change that includes an organizational commitment to DE&I, they can become repositories of resentment. ERGs can unintentionally become nothing more than a safe space or a retreat from an unwelcoming work climate. In these instances, an ERG can quickly lose sight of its initial vision and mission and accelerate the attrition of those it was charged to support and retain. ERGs need to serve both as an advisory group to the organization and a support group to its participants, and a genuine and broad institutional commitment to ERGs is required if an organization seeks to meet its goals and reach its aspirations (see Figure 10.1).

Step 4: Identify group characteristics

When recruiting and selecting members for ERGs, OD professionals must identify the individual characteristics that will ensure overall group success.

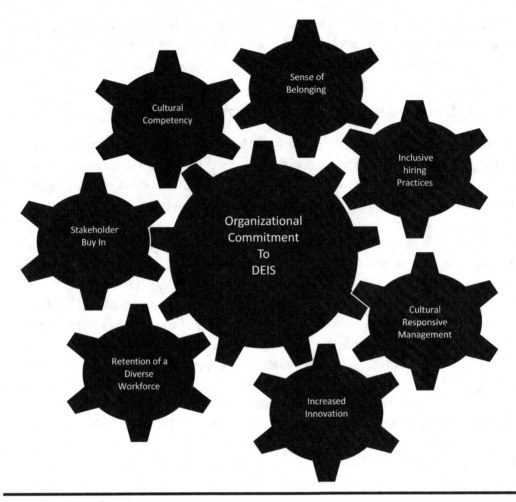

Figure 10.1   Organizational commitment to DE&I.

Applying the group effectiveness model to ensure optimum group context and process structure will enhance ERG members' ability to impact and influence OD (Sundstrom et al. 1990). OD professionals should try to ensure these groups are not monolithic and include not only underrepresented members of the workforce. Impactful ERGs should also include allies with privilege, who are well-positioned to help raise the level of DE&I consciousness of their peers and contribute to the cultivation of an environment where underrepresented members are empowered through this engagement with allies from privileged identities.

When considering membership, stakeholders from all levels and areas of the organization should be suggested for their potential to bring unique and varied contributions to the group. Finally, a critical characteristic is company leadership that plays a facilitative rather than a directive role. Creativity and innovation emerge when group members realize they are "steering the ship" and may develop diverse and culturally sensitive ideas. An OD professional must recognize these characteristics to maximize company return on investment to the ERG.

Step 5: Establish a group leader, organizer, and facilitator

Essential in a high-functioning group is the ability of a group leader or facilitator to maximize group performance to benefit the organization. To influence ERG outcomes favorably, the "group lead" must understand, recognize, and execute the responsibilities with which the group is tasked. In the planning stages and throughout development, the role the group leader will play in the group dynamics and process should be considered. The vision and mission will bear out not only the charge of the group but also the ideal characteristics for the leader of the group.

Upon determining the group charge, the ERG group leader will be guided by several factors. The first and most important question is whether the group leader is a functioning member of the group alongside the others, participating in all activities, or a neutral participant, who strictly organizes and facilitates the group process and logistics. In the most likely scenario, the DE&I ERG will be a self-directed group that would benefit from an organizer and a facilitator. This party would guide the group focus when appropriate, while not overly influencing group decisions or taking excessive control. A second consideration when identifying a leader in the group structure and membership. If the ERG is to include employees from all levels of the organization, including management, it may affect what is disclosed in group meetings. A skilled group leader is needed to build trust and navigate situations that may arise related to confidentiality and/or concerns of retaliation that could arise based on information or opinions shared by group members. Finally, it is especially critical in DE&I ERGs that the group leader be capable and willing to disrupt inequities and implicit biases within the group process to model the aspirational behavior for others. They must lead by example.

Step 6: Group evaluation, assessment, and impact

To have the most intentional positive impact, ERGs should be an outcome of an organizational-wide assessment and developed strategic initiative.

Success can be measured through key performance indicators and feedback. To assess the impact of ERGs, comprehensive formative and summative data should be collected consistently. Data should also be collected in both quantitative and qualitative methods (Rothwell et al. 2017). The qualitative data must be gathered to give voice to experiences that provide leadership a broader contextual understanding of the DE&I-wide view of their organizations. Assessment tools and data points may be pulse surveys, focus group interviews, data collected from exit surveys, and tracking of demographic-related hiring, promotion, and retention. To measure the true impact, data should be disaggregated to ensure that it represents key constituents whose experiences otherwise may be overlooked. As with any initiative, continued assessment of the ERGs impact is necessary. Over time one needs to measure whether the group is still meeting a need, operating successfully, and promoting and contributing to the aspirational workplace.

Step 7: Communication and branding

A final key consideration when launching and implementing ERGs is an effective communication and branding plan. When organizations fail to communicate and brand impactful practices related to DE&I, the assumption by stakeholders is that nothing is happening in this space and such practices do not exist. Branding and communicating successful initiatives spearheaded by ERGs helps build trust and respect and identifies DE&I as a core value of the organization. In addition, branding and communication of impactful ERG outcomes will promote a sense of belonging for employees and will improve morale, performance, and retention. ERG wins must be shared across the organization. Not only should the group's activities and role be transparent, but steps should be taken to inform the organization's community of successful measures taken and practices implemented so ERG contributions are realized and the value to the organization is highlighted.

Use the tool to make notes on how you want to accomplish the steps in this chapter. These steps will help in developing ERGs.

Chapter Tools

CHAPTER 10 TOOL 1: LAUNCHING EMPLOYEE RESOURCE GROUP TOOLKIT

Pre-formation stage

Demonstrate need to leadership and stakeholders
- Initiate needs assessment (Pulse survey, Focus Groups, Exit Survey, Demographic data, etc.)
- Gaps and challenges in existing versus aspirational goals

Offer value proposition of DEIS on OD and performance to leadership
- Stimulates innovation
- Increased productivity
- Business imperative
- Higher retention
- Increase in cultural competent and therefore cultural responsive workforce

Secure leadership support and resources
- Agency to impact institutional direction and performance
- Release time to participate
- Report structure to leadership

Secure stakeholder buy-in
- Demonstrate leadership commitment
- Share need assessment results
- Offer value proposition to stakeholders

Promote, launch, recruit
- Recruit members at all levels of the organization and across job function
- Recruit to ensure multi underrepresented groups have a critical mass
- Invite allies to join

Formation stage

Establish group mission and vision
- Serves as an advisory group to the organization or support group to its participants or both
- Align group outcomes with the company strategic imperatives and performance goals
- Company leadership plays a facilitative rather than a directive role in group charge

Group characteristics
- Not a monolithic underrepresented member group (diverse perspective with the underrepresented group)
- Includes allies with privilege
- Stakeholders from all levels and areas of the organization and across job functions

Group leader/facilitator role
- Maximize group performance for the benefit of the organization
- Establish clear understanding whether they are member of the group or a neutral participant, who strictly organizes and facilitates the group process and logistics
- Must understand, recognize, and focus the group on the execution of the responsibilities with which it is tasked
- Not overly influencing group decisions or taking excessive control
- Willing to disrupt inequities and implicit biases within the group process to model the aspirational behavior for others

---

Post-formation stage

Post-assessment
- Collect formative and summative data during entire process
- Collect quantities and qualitative data
- Data should be disaggregated to ensure that it is representative of key
- Publish data

Communication and branding
- Develop an effective pre-launch communication and branding plan that clearly articulates a value proposition of the ERG as well as organizational buy-in to it
- Branding and communicating strategies should highlight the successful outcomes of ERGs by demonstrating key performance indicators
- By highlighting successful ERG outcomes, leadership may build trust with employees and demonstrate commitment of DEIS as a core value of the organization

CHAPTER 10-TOOL 2: LAUNCHING EMPLOYEE RESOURCE GROUP TOOLKIT

Pre-formation stage Demonstrate need to leadership and stakeholders	Formation stage Establish group mission and vision	Post-formation stage Post-assessment
Offer value proposition of DEIS on OD and performance to leadership		
	Group characteristics	Communication and branding
Secure leadership support and resources		
Secure stakeholder buy-in	*Group leader/facilitator role*	
Promote, launch, recruit		

There is also a tool, appearing in Appendix E, that tracks with the step-by-step approach toward implementation described in this chapter. If you complete that tool and the others in chapters following this one, you will have the foundation for a proposal to your organization's management for installing an effective DE&I effort.

Key Questions about the Chapter

1. How does an ERG relate to DE&I?
2. When would ERGs be most helpful to workers from diverse groups?

3. An earlier chapter mentioned the shadow organization, the ghost job. How does the shadow organization and ghost job relate to the ERG as described in this chapter?

Works Consulted

Bierema, Laura L. 2005. "Women's Networks: A Career Development Intervention or Impediment?" *Human Resource Development International* 8, no. 2: 207–224.

Briscoe, Forrest and Sean Safford. 2015. "Employee Affinity Groups: Their Evolution from Social Movement Vehicle to Employer Strategies." *Members-only Library* 14, no. 1–2.

Calder, William B. 2014. "Achieving an Institution's Values, Vision, and Mission." *College Quarterly* 17, no. 2: n2.

Colgan, Fiona, and Aidan McKearney. 2012. "Visibility and Voice in Organisations: Lesbian, Gay, Bisexual and Transgendered Employee Networks." *Equality, Diversity, and Inclusion: An International Journal*.

Connelly, Catherine E. and E. Kevin Kelloway. 2003. "Predictors of Employees' Perceptions of Knowledge Sharing Cultures." *Leadership & Organization Development Journal*.

Festinger, Leon. 1957. *A Theory of Cognitive Dissonance*. vol. 2. Stanford, CA: Stanford University Press.

Friedman, Ray and Caitlin Deinard. 1996. "Black Caucus Groups at Xerox Corporation." *Managerial Excellence Through Diversity: Text and Cases*: 300–313.

Friedman, Raymond A. and Kellina M. Craig. 2004. "Predicting Joining and Participating in Minority Employee Network Groups." *Industrial Relations: A Journal of Economy and Society*, vol. 43, no. 4: 793–816.

Friedman, Raymond A. and Brooks Holtom. 2002. "The Effects of Network Groups on Minority Employee Turnover Intentions." *Human Resource Management*, vol. 41, no. 4: 405–421, doi:https://doi.org/10.1002/hrm.10051.

Ibarra, Herminia. 1993. "Personal Networks of Women and Minorities in Management: A Conceptual Framework." *The Academy of Management Review* 18, no. 1: 56–87, JSTOR, doi:10.2307/258823.

Kaplan, M. M. et al. 2009. *The Catalyst Guide to Employee Resource Groups*. New York: Catalyst.

Lambertz-Berndt, Megan Mary. 2016. "Communicating Identity in the Workplace and Affinity Groups Spaces."

McGrath Jr, Roger and William L. Sparks. 2005. "The Importance of Building Social Capital." *Quality Progress* 38, no. 2: 45.

Mercer. 2011. "Ergs Come of Age: The Evolution of Employee Resource Groups." *Author Geneva*.

Powers, Edward L. 2012. "Organizational Mission Statement Guidelines Revisited." *International Journal of Management & Information Systems (IJMIS)* 16, no. 4: 281–290.

Roberson, L., Kulik, C. T. and Tan, R. Y. (2013). Effective diversity training. In Q. M. Roberson (Ed.), *The Oxford Handbook of Diversity and Work* (pp. 341–365). Oxford: Oxford University Press.

Rothwell, William J. and Henry J. Sredl. 1992. *The ASTD Reference Guide to Professional Human Resource Development Roles and Competencies.* vol. 1. Amherst, MA: HRD Press.

Rothwell, William, Stopper, Angela and Myers, Jennifer. Eds. 2017. *Assessment and Diagnosis for Organization Development: Powerful Tools and Perspectives for the OD Practitioner.* New York: Productivity Press.

Scully, Maureen A. 2009. "A Rainbow Coalition or Separate Wavelengths? Negotiations among Employee Network Groups." *Negotiation and Conflict Management Research* 2, no. 1: 74–91.

Sundstrom, Eric et al. 1990. "Work Teams: Applications and Effectiveness." *American Psychologist* 45, no. 2: 120–133, doi:10.1037/0003-066X.45.2.120.

Van Aken, Eileen M et al. 1994. "Affinity Groups: The Missing Link in Employee Involvement." *Organizational Dynamics* 22, no. 4: 38–54.

Wang, Peng and Joshua L Schwarz. 2010. "Stock Price Reactions to GLBT Nondiscrimination Policies." *Human Resource Management: Published in Cooperation with the School of Business Administration, The University of Michigan and in alliance with the Society of Human Resources Management* 49, no. 2: 195–216.

Welbourne, Theresa M. et al. 2015. "Employee Resource Groups: An Introduction, Review and Research Agenda." *Academy of Management Proceedings* 1: 15661–11594.

Welbourne, Theresa M. et al. 2017. "The Case for Employee Resource Groups: A Review and Social Identity Theory-Based Research Agenda." *Personnel Review* 46, no. 8: 1816–1834, doi:10.1108/PR-01-2016-0004.

Welbourne, Theresa and Lacey McLaughlin. 2013. "Making the Business Case for Employee Resource Groups." *Employment Relations Today* 40, no. 2: 35–44, doi:10.1002/ert.21409.

Chapter 11

Step 10: Evaluating Your Processes

Christina Pettey

Contents

DOI: 10.4324/9781003184935-14

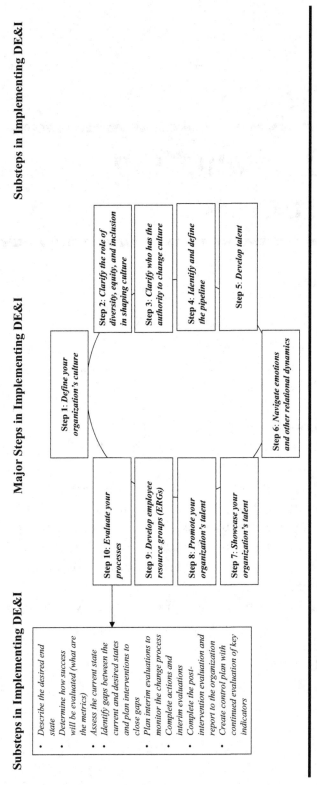

Substeps in Implementing DE&I

Major Steps in Implementing DE&I

Substeps in Implementing DE&I

Step 1: *Define your organization's culture*

Step 2: *Clarify the role of diversity, equity, and inclusion in shaping culture*

Step 3: *Clarify who has the authority to change culture*

Step 4: *Identify and define the pipeline*

Step 5: *Develop talent*

Step 6: *Navigate emotions and other relational dynamics*

Step 7: *Showcase your organization's talent*

Step 8: *Promote your organization's talent*

Step 9: *Develop employee resource groups (ERGs)*

Step 10: *Evaluate your processes*

Substeps in Implementing DE&I

- *Describe the desired end state*
- *Determine how success will be evaluated (what are the metrics)*
- *Assess the current state*
- *Identify gaps between the current and desired states and plan interventions to close gaps*
- *Plan interim evaluations to monitor the change process*
- *Complete actions and interim evaluations*
- *Complete the post-intervention evaluation and report to the organization*
- *Create control plan with continued evaluation of key indicators*

Frontmatter Figure 11.1   The diversity, equity, and inclusion (DE&I) roadmap model.

Case Study

Alexis was the HR Manager for a medium-sized food processing facility with 400 employees. As tensions grew between different people in her community, the management team recognized the need for culture change in their facility. The Plant Manager approached Alexis and asked her to lead the effort since she was the only one in management with any training or experience in organization culture change initiatives. Alexis happily agreed and went to work researching best practices for diversity and inclusion programs. She changed their recruiting processes, assigned diversity training to all plant employees, and set up affinity groups. After one year, the board asked for a report of how the culture had been improved.

Unfortunately, while Alexis had been doing a lot to improve her workplace, she didn't have a way to measure any progress made. She thought her recruiting improvements would attract more diverse applicants. But they were not collecting EEO data during the application process and so she could not confirm if it did. She thought the affinity groups would help minority employees feel more included, but she could find no measurements to support that assumption beyond a few quotes from participants.

Alexis suddenly realized that, although evaluation is often seen as the final step in an intervention (Jones and Rothwell 2017), without planning it is difficult to complete the evaluation due to missing information or an absence of pre-implementation data. Had Alexis planned her culture change with the end in mind and concrete goals, her evaluation report would have spoken directly to the areas of improvement her organization had agreed to target. This chapter will explain why it is so important to plan the evaluation process from the very beginning and why evaluation should be happening throughout the implementation process (Rothwell et al. 2021)!

Evaluation Research

Decades of research have shown the importance of evaluating results. Evaluation can help us review the impacts of our efforts to confirm the interventions have achieved the desired results (Kirkpatrick 1998). Continued assessments of process data can show performance over time to determine whether changes are self-sustaining within current processes or if improvement was fleeting and the organization will need additional interventions to create lasting change (Jeffrey 2005). They help us confirm that the changes didn't create new problems or compound existing ones (Nicholas 1979). And finally, a measurement of improvement can show a return on investment for time and effort put into change initiatives (Park 2017) and should include intangible attributes such as reduction of risk that comes from having a variety of perspectives (Hood 2019).

Specifically with organization culture change initiatives, evaluation is important because change happens so slowly that it's difficult to see improvement except in retrospect, which can be mistrusted unless there is a concrete measurement. This is especially true with DE&I improvements since many related initiatives are often implemented in sequence. The long-term change process with many stages can be affected at each stage by many organizational variables (Fouche et al. 2004). Evaluation of the effectiveness of one will affect how subsequent initiatives are handled. Lack of evaluation could lead to repeating mistakes or missing unanticipated negative consequences (Nicholas 1979). And if goals and outcomes are not clearly defined, those evaluating the effort "may draw improper conclusions" (Park, 2018, 75).

According to M.J. Park (2017), a "multiphase approach of evaluation" for organization development (OD) interventions is recommended: preintervention evaluation, intraimplementation evaluation, and postintervention evaluation. In a preintervention evaluation, "assessments of the *potential* tangible and intangible influences on the implementation process and the success of the change effort are recommended" (18). The results of the preintervention evaluation are then used to create objectives and goals for the change effort. The intraimplementation evaluations allow continual feedback throughout the change process. A final postintervention evaluation measures the improvement and ensures accountability and can highlight intangible results (21).

Plan the end evaluation from the beginning because we often need to capture new or different data to obtain the information we plan to measure. In 1978, Kerry Bunker spoke of the importance of defining measurable independent criteria while planning a change because "success and strategies for measuring them must be built into the change process if one hopes to generate results which are internally and externally valid." Agreeing on an evaluation plan before beginning an intervention promotes commitment from stakeholders and increases success. When responsibility for diversity improvements is assigned and tracked, there is a significant increase in managerial diversity – more than social programming or training created (Kalev et al. 2006).

Although we have discussed diversity, equity, and inclusion efforts as one overarching topic in this book, these are three distinct topics and therefore should be considered and evaluated separately. This begins with discussing the definition of each term as an organization since individual expectations associated with each term can vary (Roberson 2006). The glossary of this book will help people in your organization understand various interpretations of each term and determine which definition will be used in your organization.

Putting into Practice

Taking on a DE&I culture change initiative is a whole-scale organizational change effort. The prospect of measuring and evaluating progress for such a nebulous concept can feel daunting. The key to managing it is planning and organizing the evaluation activities. When I joined Kwik Lok Corporation as the Director of Human Resources, the company had embarked on a full change to its vision, mission, and values. The owners knew they wanted to focus on equitable practices and increased diversity in the workforce. My job was to create the overall strategy and recommend change initiatives. None of the owners or leadership team had experience leading DE&I change efforts, and I needed to describe how we would measure and evaluate as part of our strategy.

The model in this chapter is just one method to evaluate your organization. It follows the basic scientific method and takes specific steps from both the Action Research Method and Six Sigma Define, Measure, Analyze, Improve, and Control (DMAIC) processes. The generality of each step makes it possible to use for every level of activity, from the overarching DE&I strategy to culture goals to specific interventions.

1. Describe the desired end state.
2. Determine how success will be evaluated.
3. Assess the current state.
4. Identify gaps between the current and desired states and plan interventions to close gaps.
5. Plan interim evaluations to monitor the change process.
6. Complete actions and interim evaluations.
7. Complete the postintervention evaluation and report to the organization.
8. Create control plan with continued evaluation of key indicators.

Before describing what is involved in each step, I want to point out
there can be several evaluation activities going on at once, as shown in
Figure 11.1. These evaluation activities happen simultaneously, each at a different point in the planning and evaluation process. As each postintervention evaluation is completed, it rolls up as input into the postintervention
evaluation of the goal or strategy it supports.

The tool associated with this chapter is a great starting point to collect
information from each step in the model. This will assist you in tracking
your goals, how you will measure them, and what actions are required for
each.

Step 1: Describe the desired end state

The first step is to consider what the desired end state looks like. Because
corporate culture is nebulous and often difficult to define, I find it helpful to
use Appreciative Inquiry prompts for the dream phase. Appreciative Inquiry
is a method of organization development that focuses on using an organization's strengths to meet its goals. Defining the dream state helps stakeholders create a vivid description of how people in the organization behave
and how they interact, which can then pinpoint behaviors or organizational
states that can be measured. The facilitator encourages stakeholders to
describe a positive end state while the facilitator probes for details to identify themes (Cooperrider et al. 2008).

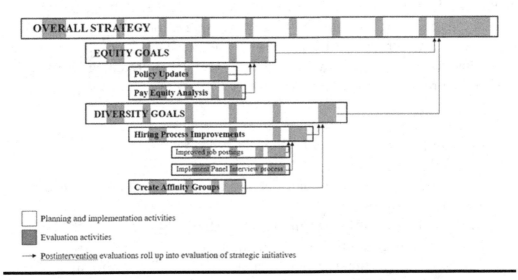

Figure 11.1   Concurrent evaluation strategies. Copyright Christina Pettey, 2021.

When considering the need to evaluate culture, the facilitator should probe for specific behaviors in the dream state. If stakeholders describe it as a feeling of "openness," ask what specific behaviors will lead to that feeling. It may be organization members reporting they can "be themselves" or that they may bring up ideas and concerns. Maybe they envision organization members discussing social issues. For each component of the dream state, dig down to a few specific behaviors that create or reinforce the environment envisioned. Consider which aspects of the dream state relate to the organizational mission or strategy. For a company that values innovation, a diverse workforce can fuel the creativity they want. Consider what types of diversity in employees will be important in each department or team.

Although this activity can feel less strategic to certain personality types in management positions, it is a great way to dig for specific behaviors while maintaining the positive creative atmosphere that is inherent when describing an ideal future. Co-owner of Kwik Lok Corporation Stephanie Paxton-Jackson said:

> It was extremely valuable to start with what our dream culture looked like. Then, we dug deeper to identify more specific behaviors we wanted to see in our culture. This gave us the concrete information we would need to reinforce what we envisioned for Kwik Lok's future culture.

Step 2: Determine how success will be evaluated

When all intervention activities are complete, how will you know the interventions succeeded? This question is why culture change efforts are best suited to an OD approach. Stakeholders often expect different results or different amounts of change to consider a change successful. Involving all stakeholders in the evaluation plan upfront ensures that the planned measurements used will show improvements where each stakeholder expects to see them. CEO of Kwik Lok Corporation Don Carrell stated, "Organizational culture is difficult to define and difficult to change. Creating an evaluation plan from the beginning helped us to come up with concrete actions and measurements to target the improvements we wanted to see." There are many types of measurements. As you read through the descriptions in this section, consider which will be important for your organization to measure.

Primary metrics are used as objectives for improvement. These are the specific areas that can be measured to show improvement. Often moderating variables increase the strength or effect of two other variables. They may be tracked to analyze and improve the impacts of a change effort targeted at improving a primary variable. Common moderating variables are personal characteristics or groupings. A secondary metric is a variable that could be hurt by the change effort. In process improvements, a secondary metric is often tracked to ensure the change effort has not had an unexpected negative impact. I would like to note here that with any culture change, there are both positive and negative impacts. Create realistic goals and consider during the planning process how to mitigate the negative impacts.

To put those definitions into context, the examples below are possible metrics or variables to watch during an effort to implement panel interviews:

- *Primary metric*: Diversity of interviewees compared to the diversity of hires
- *Moderating variables*: Department, Hiring Manager
- *Secondary metric*: Cycle time for interviews

Besides the outcome variables described above, process variables can show how the intervention itself is being received by the organization. These are often surveys asking organization members how well they understand the changes or measures of voluntary participation in change efforts.

Data collection can be quantitative or qualitative. Quantitative data collection includes survey data and records. Quantitative data refers to things you can count, such as the number of hires or days to fill a position. Qualitative data collection targets deeper, more personal, information. This can be collected through interviews and observations or from open survey responses.

Get stakeholder buy-in when defining measurements. For diversity, what personal characteristics should be monitored to ensure adequate opportunity and representation? Gender, ethnicity, and disability are commonly tracked categories, but diversity also includes hidden characteristics such as socioeconomic background, personality, first language, and health conditions.

While the opportunities for measurements of culture are endless, here are a few possible metrics by category to consider. Remember that some data may not be available now but could be collected going forward – don't leave out a measurement just because it doesn't currently exist.

Diversity:
- Percent of the workforce by diversity characteristics
- Percent of leadership by diversity characteristics
- Applicants by diversity characteristics
- Hire rates by diversity characteristics – both by percent of hires and versus applicant pool
- Attrition rates and reasons by diversity characteristics
- Differences in performance by diversity characteristics
- Percent of diversity groups in customer base
- Supplier diversity
- Types of community advocacy and philanthropy

Equity:
- Perception of barriers and opportunities to career progression
- Promotion rates by diversity characteristics
- Consider visible, semivisible, and invisible attributes
- The adverse impact of processes on certain groups
- Inclusive language in job postings, policies, and organization communications
- Reduction in discrimination and harassment complaints and litigation
- Types of rule violations and discipline given, reviewed by diversity characteristics

Inclusion:
- Perceptions of employees and stakeholders
- Descriptions of the "ideal employee"
- Representation of diversity in marketing materials
- Response to new ideas or feedback
- Respect for differences in ideas and opinions
- Attributes of leaders – supporting employees, modeling behaviors, etc.
- Access to information
- Employee understanding of different communication styles and perceptions

Change process:
- Understanding of the dream state and goals of the change initiative
- Buy-in by stakeholders and employees

- Group performance
- Impact on individual behaviors
- Alignment of implicit behavior norms with stated organizational goals and objectives
- Attrition
- Absenteeism
- Employee relations complaints

Once the metrics have been selected, it is helpful to create key performance indicators (KPIs). This takes data from measurement to an assessment of whether the data shows the organization is meeting its goals. KPIs always have a target goal, and often have levels of performance defined.

An example of a possible KPI for recruiting could be focused on increasing diversity in applicant pools. The goal would be to strategically post positions to attract underrepresented candidates. Before determining what the target percentage is, understand where the organization is to create a goal that is realistic. In this situation, underrepresented candidates account for 20% or less of each applicant pool. The organization wants to increase that to 50%.

KPI: Percentage of applicant pool – underrepresented candidates
    Target: 50%

- Green: >50%
- Yellow: >35%
- Red: <35%

KPIs should be monitored on an ongoing basis, and as historical measurements are collected, the organization can see progress toward the goal state. If measurements do not show progress, this will signal the need to review actions being taken to determine if something additional must impact the end state being sought.

Step 3: Assess the current state

Ideally, we would use the same measurements defined for the end state to evaluate the current state of the organization. Unfortunately, when beginning a culture improvement effort, we often find data lacking. Think creatively of all the places where culture data might be contained. Employee surveys and employee relations issues are great starting points. Performance reviews, while about individual performance, might indicate what is valued in the organizational culture.

I have found that deep-dive interviews can give a good insight into the current culture if members of the organization feel comfortable sharing. When planning interviews, consider how many employees will need to be interviewed to represent all members of the organization. Then code and analyze their responses to find themes. Here are questions I have compiled for trying to understand the current state of an organization's culture:

Diversity:

- What groups are considered underrepresented in the organization's community, country, or industry? Are these groups adequately represented in the organization?
- How are underrepresented groups represented in each *level* of the organization? If they are clustered in the lower levels and sparse in organizational leadership, are there expectations in those higher-level positions that influence employees to opt out?
- What aspects of the hiring process attract underrepresented applicants? What aspects might deter them? (These might be things like salary history, drug offenses, biased language, unnecessary requirements such as degree or GPA, or when interviews are scheduled.)
- Do job descriptions have measurable standards that can be evaluated without bias?
- What does the organization do if the applicant pool isn't as diverse as desired?
- Are hiring decisions made by one person or a group of people?
- Do hiring managers understand unconscious bias and address that awareness when making hiring decisions?
- What programs are in place to increase diversity in the organization?
- When looking at attrition, are underrepresented groups leaving at a rate higher than other groups? Does exit interview data indicate why?

Equity:

- Are disciplinary measures given consistently for the same violations, or is there a sense of favoritism?
- What rules are ignored? What behaviors are rewarded?

- What is the process for awarding raises and bonuses?
- If there is a process for in-line promotions, what are the requirements and how are promotions approved?
- What do employees see as barriers in their career progression?
- Do benefits include nontraditional family members?

Inclusion:

- Do people feel they can "be themselves" at work?
- How does the organization deal with change?
- Is feedback given and received regularly?
- How would managers describe an employee who would be a "good fit" in the organization?
- Do managers and employees understand and respect different communication styles and perceptions?
- Do policies and communications contain language that would exclude certain groups?
- How is friction between employees handled? What is the process for investigating complaints of bias or racism?
- Are stereotypes used in everyday conversation?
- Where are members of your diversity groups working? If they are clustered in certain departments, is there an aspect of that department's culture that attracts them or aspects of other departments that deter them?
- Is there a certain leadership or personality style of top-level leaders, and does that influence what is required for success in the organization?

Step 4: Identify gaps between the current and desired states and plan interventions to close gaps

Once you know what you value in the organization and how you can measure it, you can determine where current practices match the desired end state and which do not. After you have identified the gaps, work with organizational leadership to evaluate the importance of each gap to the organization's success and the expected difficulty the organization will have with each piece of culture change. Consider which gaps are related that might be affected by the same intervention. You can consider how much time/effort might be involved for each, but realize that without having implementations already planned (which should not have happened yet), the strategic plan is a roadmap that will be a living document, updated at each subsequent evaluation point. After prioritizing what improvements are needed, the focus shifts to how those aspects can be improved.

Remember during this step that individuals and groups in the organization may have varied interpretations of the different words or goals in your dream state and measurements. This may be identified as a gap in knowledge, but it also might simply be a natural starting point in an organization that hasn't openly discussed the terms previously. Kimberly Paxton-Hagner is both co-owner and Chair of the Board of Directors for Kwik Lok Corporation. When asked about her experience with DEI changes over the past year, she said:

> Shared language can give us insight into the current state of a culture. During one-on-one listening sessions as the new board chair, I noticed certain words and ideas repeatedly used. Employees liked that it felt "more open" which made them feel safe to "share ideas". A common theme emerged around contributing and feel part of a team. Frequently used words help us see what our employees value. This shared language can serve as our cultural building blocks.

Planning an intervention should begin with identifying and including all stakeholders. This is a key aspect of organization development. Consider who will champion the change and include these people in the improvement team, but also consider who will give the most resistance and include them too! Getting buy-in from these individuals early in the process improves the likelihood that the change will be widely accepted in the organization.

There are many options for analyzing a particular gap and planning an intervention to improve that aspect of the organization's culture. Which tool will work best depends largely on the facilitator's comfort level with the tool and the team's interaction style. Consider:

- *SWOT Analysis (Strengths Weaknesses Opportunities Threats)*: This assesses what aspects of the organization to leverage and what negative impacts are likely to occur and will need to be considered.
- *5 Why's/Fishbone*: This tool helps the group dig deeper into a problem to find the root causes.

- *House of Quality*: This is a planning matrix that compares customer needs and requirements, prioritization of needs and requirements, technical difficulty, and competitive benchmarking to pinpoint possible areas of focus.
- *XY Matrix or Failure Modes and Effects Analysis (FMEA)*: This tool walks through each step in a process (or each aspect of a culture, in this case) and identifies possible types of failure, causes of failure, what current controls are, and recommended actions. Measurements for severity, occurrence, and detection multiply into an overall score to pinpoint the highest areas of concern.
- *Training Needs Analysis*: This tool assesses the need for training based on knowledge, skills, and abilities and then creates clear objectives that can be used for designing or assigning training.

Step 5: Plan interim evaluations to monitor the change process

Before taking any actions, a plan needs to be made regarding when and how progress will be measured. This differs from the overall evaluation at the end of an intervention. Intraimplementation evaluations allow course correction if changes are not being embraced by the organization and can give early warnings if the changes are causing unanticipated problems.

Interim evaluations are twofold – they look at whether the organization is improving in the defined behavior or organization state, and they also look at how the change process is being managed and accepted within the organization. First, define leading indicators that will show progress toward the end goals. These may be metrics related to your key metric, the key metric itself, or metrics to evaluate the rollout process and how employees are reacting to it. Second, consider whether your organization would prefer to use specific goals or if they feel more comfortable with ranges of desired improvement. Third, look for iterative changes in the defined metrics. If the result is not what was expected, the group may consider tweaking the intervention to consider the new information received in the intraimplementation evaluation.

Plan regular coordination with stakeholders to maintain engagement and commitment through a lengthy effort. This will help confirm the success of actions taken and assuring leadership and the team that their efforts are having a positive impact. It is often helpful to schedule a full culture evaluation once a year to show yearly progress compared to the initial baseline data from Step 3.

Step 6: Complete actions and interim evaluations

Now the fun part – you can get to work implementing the interventions you have planned! For each intervention, consider who needs to be updated on results. How often and in-depth the updates need to be will depend on the stakeholder. Since you will likely have several interventions happening simultaneously or in sequence, it is very helpful to have a master tracking sheet to keep all the moving parts organized. An example is included for your use on page 187.

During each intervention, remember to complete interim evaluations to ensure that the activities are having the anticipated impact. If the results are not what you expected, pull the planning team back together to review the metrics and determine whether the plan needs to be changed. Remember that your tracking sheet should be a living document, and dates may move as new information is reviewed and changes to the interventions are made.

Step 7: Complete the postintervention evaluation and report to the organization

Once an intervention is complete, it is tempting to leave it behind and move on to the next project. However, the benefits of a postintervention evaluation exceed the time and effort it takes to complete it. Without a final report, it may be difficult to respond to questions received later about the success of the intervention. If the impact of time and money spent is unclear, it may make leadership support more difficult to gain for the next project. And finally, any issues with the rollout of the intervention won't be properly captured and applied to future efforts.

When completing the postintervention evaluation, involve all stakeholders. Having the team complete the evaluation and present findings to organization leadership builds ownership throughout the organization and improves long-term success.

Step 8: Create a control plan with continued evaluation of key indicators

While new habits take many weeks or months to take hold, reverting to previous behaviors can happen quickly. Once the organization has embraced the change and its continued success is being managed by members of the organization, make sure there is continued monitoring. A control plan takes the KPIs and identifies the range expected for each, and then describes corrective actions to be taken if the measurement falls outside of the expected range.

As in the other steps, consider both the original KPIs and secondary metrics. Plan who will monitor the metrics and who they will report periodic results to. The organization should have a plan ahead of time that determines how much fluctuation will require additional intervention and how that will be initiated and managed.

With a long-term control plan in place, the intervention and assessments are executed! But even though the change effort is complete, culture is constantly in flux. Continue to measure and monitor those areas important to your organization, and you'll be able to guide the culture.

Key Lessons

The key to a successful evaluation is to plan the end from the beginning. When thinking of individual behavior in organizations, I often think of the Eli Goldratt quote, "Tell me how you measure me, and I will tell you how I will behave" (1990, 26). Effective evaluation is a continuous process, planned from the beginning of the project and implemented at each step in different ways. By involving stakeholders in planning how behavior will be measured and reporting on progress continually throughout the change effort, we will increase our chances of success.

Key Questions about the Chapter

1. What will be considered a success for your organization?
2. How can that change be measured?
3. What variables can be measured throughout the effort to show progress?
4. Can KPIs be created and tracked for those variables?
5. How often will you need to demonstrate progress?

Chapter Tool

CHAPTER 11 TOOL 1: EVALUATION PLANNING AND TRACKING TOOL

	Target characteristic of end state	How will success be evaluated?	Current state of that characteristic	Gaps between current state and end state	Planned intervention(s) to close the gap	Interim evaluation metrics	Status of actions	Next evaluation	Control plan
Example	Open communication at all levels of the organization	Count of employee questions during meetings – goal is interactive discussions, with target of three questions during meeting	Currently employees do not ask questions during meetings, and questions at the end of meetings are rare. Current count is 0–1 questions per meeting	Employees do not feel that questions are welcome. Managers do not ask for questions during presentations	Managers will plan two points per meeting to invite attendees to give feedback.(Lead: Alexis P.)	Number of times managers invite feedback; number of questions per meeting	Start date January 2022 – End date est. June 2022	1/30/22 (interim evaluation)	TBD
1									
2									
3									
4									
5									
6									
7									
8									
9									
10									

There is also a tool, appearing in Appendix E, that tracks with the step-by-step approach toward implementation described in this chapter. If you complete that tool you will have the foundation for a proposal to your organization's management for installing an effective DE&I effort.

Works Consulted

Adamson, Maria, Elisabeth K. Kelan, Patricia Lewis, Nick Rumens, and Martyna Slíwa. 2016. "The Quality of Equality: Thinking Differently about Gender Inclusion in Organizations." *Human Resource Management International Digest* 24, 7: 8–11.

Althof, Holly. 2020. "Viewpoint: Belonging is the Missing Piece in the Fight for Inclusion." *SHRM*. August 21, 2020. https://www.shrm.org/ResourcesAndTools/hr-topics/behavioral-competencies/global-and-cultural-effectiveness/Pages/Viewpoint-Belonging-Is-the-Missing-Piece-in-the-Fight-for-Inclusion.aspx.

Bernstein, Ruth Sessler, Morgan Bulger, Paul Salipante, and Judith Y. Weisinger. 2020. "From Diversity to Inclusion to Equity: A Theory of Generative Interactions." *Journal of Business Ethics* 167: 395–410.

Bunker, Kerry A. 1978. "Evaluation as a Systemic Component of Organizational Change Efforts." *Proceedings of the Human Factors Society Annual Meeting* 22, 1: 404–408.

Caven, Valerie and Stefanos Nachmias, eds. 2018. *Hidden Inequalities in the Workplace: A Guide to the Current Challenges, Issues and Business Solutions.* Cham, Switzerland: Palgrave Macmillan.

Cooperrider, David L., Diana Whiney, and Jacqueline M. Stavros. 2008. *Appreciative Inquiry Handbook for Leaders of Change, 2nd Edition.* Brunswick, OH: Crown Custom Publishing.

Dobbin, Frank, Soohan Kim, and Alexandra Kalev. 2011. "You Can't Always Get What You Need: Organizational Determinants of Diversity Programs." *American Sociological Review* 76, 3: 386–411.

Fouche, Christa, Cherylene de Jager, and Anne Crafford. 2004. "The Evaluation of a Diversity Program." *SA Journal of Human Resource Management* 2, 2: 37–44.

Fujimoto, Yuka and Charmine E.J. Härtel. 2017. "Organizational Diversity Learning Framework: Going Beyond Diversity Training Programs." *Personnel Review* 46, 6: 1120–1141.

Goldratt, Eliyahu M. 1990. *The Haystack Syndrome: Sifting Information Out of the Data Ocean.* Croton-on-Hudson, NY: North River Press.

Hamdani, Maria Riaz and M. Ronald Buckley. 2011. "Diversity Goals: Reframing the Debate and Enabling a Fair Evaluation." *Business Horizons* 54: 33–40.

Hood, Angela. July 16 2019. "Slow to Embrace Diversity in the Workplace? It's Probably Affecting Business." *Fast Company.* https://www.fastcompany.com/90376242/diversity-in-the-workplace-is-a-smart-business-practice

Jeffrey, Arthur. 2005. "Integrating Organization Development and Six Sigma: Six Sigma as a Process Improvement Intervention in Action Research." *Organization Development Journal* 23, 4: 20–31.

Jones, Maureen and Rothwell, William. Eds. 2017. *Evaluating Organization Development: How to Ensure and Sustain the Successful Transformation.* New York: Productivity Press.

Jones, Maureen Connelly. 2017. "Reporting Results to Stakeholders" In *Evaluating Organization Development*, Jones, Maureen C. and William J. Rothwell, Eds. New York: Productivity Press.

Kalev, Alexandra, Erin Kelly, and Frank Dobbin. 2006. "Best Practices or Best Guesses? Assessing the Efficacy of Corporate Affirmative Action and Diversity Policies." *American Sociological Review* 71, 4: 589–617.

Kalinoski, Zachary T., Debra Steele-Johnson, Elizabeth J. Peyton, Keith A. Leas, Julie Steinke, and Nathan A. Bowling. 2013. "A Meta-analytic Evaluation of Diversity Training Outcomes." *Journal of Organizational Behavior* 34, 8: 1076–1104.

Kirkpatrick, D. 1998. *Evaluating Training Programs: The Four Levels.* San Francisco, CA: Berrett-Koehler.

Knouse, Stephen B. and James B. Stewart. 2003. "'Hard' Measures that Support the Business Case for Diversity: A Balanced Scorecard Approach." *The Diversity Factor* 11, 4: 5–10.

Kulik, Carl T. and Loriann Roberson. 2008. "Common Goals and Golden Opportunities: Evaluations of Diversity Education in Academic and Organizational Settings." *Academy of Management Learning & Education* 7, 3: 309–331.

Leigh, Jennifer M., Ester R. Shapiro, and Sherry H. Penney. 2010. "Developing Diverse, Collaborative Leaders: An Empirical Program Evaluation." *Journal of Leadership & Organizational Studies* 17, 4: 370–379.

Nicholas, J.M. 1979. "Evaluation Research in Organizational Change Interventions: Considerations and Some Suggestions." *Journal of Applied Behavioral Sciences* 15, 1: 23–40.

Park, M.J. 2017. "Why Evaluate Organizational Change Efforts?" In *Evaluating Organization Development*, Jones, Maureen C. and William J. Rothwell, Eds. Boca Raton, FL: CRC Press.

Roberson, Quinetta M. 2006. "Disentangling the Meanings of Diversity and Inclusion in Organizations." *Group & Organization Management* 31, 2: 212–236.

Rothwell, William, Imroz, Sohel, and Bakhshandeh, Behnam. Eds. 2021. *Organization Development Interventions: Executing Effective Organizational Change.* Boca Raton, FL: Productivity Press.

Smith, Jessi L. and Meghan Huntoon. 2014. "Women's Bragging Rights: Overcoming Modesty Norms to Facilitate Women's Self-Promotion." *Psychology of Women Quarterly* 38, 4: 447–459.

Tayar, Mark. 2017. "Ranking LGBT Inclusion: Diversity Ranking Systems as Institutional Archetypes." *Canadian Journal of Administrative Sciences* 34: 190–210.

FUTURE TRENDS IN DE&I

This part offers eight predictions for the future of DE&I. The final chapter lists trends affecting the future of DE&I and encourages DE&I facilitators to position their organizations to address these trends:

- *Trend 1*: Generational differences should be considered in DE&I efforts.
- *Trend 2*: Artificial intelligence and robots will create new DE&I challenges in the workplace.
- *Trend 3*: Diversity fatigue will grow as a factor affecting DE&I efforts.
- *Trend 4*: Building diversity on the board of directors will become an issue.
- *Trend 5*: Labels will change.
- *Trend 6*: Notions of diversity will evolve over time.
- *Trend 7*: The shrinking globe will affect DE&I.
- *Trend 8*: Gender identity and orientation will be a continuing focus for the future.

DOI: 10.4324/9781003184935-15

Chapter 12

Trends in Diversity, Equity, and Inclusion

Jamie Campbell

Contents

DOI: 10.4324/9781003184935-16

The preceding chapters of this text have given you the tools, tactics, and tips sufficient to create a DE&I effort or establish a corporate culture that fosters positive attitudes in celebration of diversity and diverse groups. This chapter examines trends that may shape the future of diversity in the United States. It should prompt useful reflections on how best to position your DE&I effort for the future.

Trends

A *trend* refers to the general shape of unfolding events. While many organizational leaders often think of a trend as a future continuation of the past, that is growing less common (Chron Contributor 2021). Today's world is typified by *black swan events*, minor situations that spiral out of control into often unexpected and nightmarish proportions, and a VUCA environment, where VUCA stands for *V*olatile, *U*ncertain, *C*omplex, and *A*mbiguous. Minor events may lead to surprising consequences. The recent pandemic is often cited as a black swan event. Evidence of the VUCA workplace can be seen when a business is sold without warning (an example of volatility), a sudden downsizing occurs (an example of uncertainty), the impacts of work-from-home are felt by workers or organizations (an example of complexity), and the consequences of ambiguity are felt (an example would be the length of the COVID-19 pandemic, which is not clear).

Organizations like the World Future Society (see www.worldfuture .org), the Association of Professional Futurists (see https://www.apf.org/?), LaFutura (see https://www.lafutura.org/), and others publish trends and sponsor conferences, journals, and online discussions about the future. These organizations offer many predictions of the future. Some predictions are optimistic and exciting; others are pessimistic and depressing. Regardless of the emotions the trends may evoke, they do provide a starting point for environmental scanning and efforts to plan.

Trends in DE&I efforts will not rely solely on statistical descriptions of present events. For instance, black swan events may prompt new issues in DE&I. (Who would have thought that diversity issues could be prompted by issues like differences between those who wear masks and those choosing not to do so, or those who receive vaccinations and those who do not?)

Before this chapter turns to examining trends in DE&I, consider the impact of social events on various groups by completing the Activity in Table 12.1. Using news sources, populate the left column of the table with

Table 12.1   Empirical Trends Mapping: Using Social Events to Predict the Next Trends in Workplace Diversity

Directions: Use this activity to help you predict the impact of social events on diversity, equity, and inclusion efforts in your organization. For each social event you can think of in the left column below, brainstorm what groups will be affected, why the impacts will be important, how the social event will impact members of your team, how conditions can be improved for your team, and what external support can be provided to help workers and the community. The first two lines below are filled out with some relevant examples so that you may see how this table might be used to prompt reflection and planning.

	What is the social event?	What groups will be impacted by the social event?	Why will the impacts be important?	How will the social event impact members of your team?	How can conditions be improved for your team?	What external support can be provided to help workers and the community?
1	The George Floyd murder	African Americans, LatinX	Communities see their lack of value in society, bias in workplace intensified	Trauma, fear of certain types of authority, distrust of majority persons	Engage employees around topic and preform internal climate check	
2	Stonewall riots	LGBTQI+	Identity and expression in all aspects	Stress of not being able to express themselves	ERG	
3						
4						
5						
6						

recent events. Then follow the directions in Table 12.1 to brainstorm on how current events may affect people in your organization.

Two examples have been done for you in Table 12.1, but what other events will affect the DE&I effort in your organization?

In understanding trends, you will need to consider the future and try to figure out what to do next to position your organization's DE&I effort for the future. Think about the trends shaping the future. Then, for each trend, consider how traditional human resource issues such as recruitment, selection, onboarding, training, appraising/managing performance, rewarding performance, and offboarding should be changed to position the organization to address DE&I. Use the activity in Table 12.2 for that purpose. While there are no right or wrong answers, some answers to the Activity may do better in positioning your DE&I effort to deal with future trends.

Eight Trends Shaping the Future of Diversity, Equity, and Inclusion

Consider eight possible trends that may well shape the future of diversity, equity, and inclusion efforts in many organizations. They are listed below. Each trend is described and then the trend's possible impacts on DE&I efforts are discussed.

Trend 1: Generational differences should be considered in DE&I efforts

Five generations are in today's workplaces (Figure 12.1):

- *Traditionalists*, whose members were born between 1927 and 1946
- *Baby Boomers*, whose members were born between 1947 and 1964
- *Generation X*, whose members were born between 1965 and 1980
- *Millennials*, whose members were born between 1981 and 2000
- *Generation Z*, whose members were born between 2001 and 2020

While much has been written on the differences (and, more rarely, the similarities) of these generations, the risk exists that members of each generation will be stereotyped as like all other members of the same group. Making that same mistake leads to sweeping generalizations about members of various races, genders, sexual orientations, veteran's status, and so forth. Great

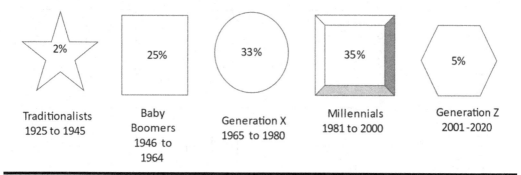

Figure 12.1 Generational groups in the workplace. Copyright 2021 by Jamie Campbell.

care should be taken to avoid stereotyping when considering the shared characteristics of members of the same generation.

The best way to avoid stereotyping is to *talk to people*. Communication can build bridges, create common bonds, and lead to shared interests. Facilitate communication among and between generational groups by:

- Engaging group members in activities – not traditional team-building – outside the workplace that can generate community. That can include hosting lunches, dinners, and family/partner center programs for all employees
- Talking to people by posing such important questions as:
  - Why are you here?
  - What makes you tick?
  - What topics are important to you, and why are they important?
- Integrating teaching and learning sessions for all about different eras

Trend 2: Artificial intelligence and robots will create new DE&I challenges in the workplace

Artificial intelligence (AI) refers to nonhuman entities, creations of technology, that can replicate human problem-solving and decision-making. How should artificial technological entities – whether resident and embedded within computer systems or else self-propelled such as robots or androids – be treated? Should they have the same rights as humans? Should the feelings of artificial entities be considered in the workplace, and (if so) how? If artificial entities are treated differently from humans, is that acceptable – or not?

Table 12.2 Repositioning Traditional HR Activities to Support the Future Diversity, Equity, and Inclusion Effort

Directions: Brainstorm a list of social trends in the left column below. For each trend, describe how you believe that the organization should change traditional HR activities – such as recruitment, selection, onboarding, training, appraising/ managing performance, rewarding performance, and offboarding – to position the organization to support the future diversity, equity, and inclusion effort.

Trends	What changes should be made to transitional HR activities to position the organization to support the future diversity, equity, and inclusion?						
List some trends below:	Recruitment	Selection	Onboarding	Training	Appraising/ managing performance	Rewarding performance	Offboarding
1							
2							
3							
4							
5							
6							
7							
8							
9							
10							

If human rights conflict with nonhuman rights, how are the conflicts resolved? What rights should nonhuman entities enjoy, and does the level of intelligence of a nonhuman entity matter in making that determination? For instance, if an AI can "think like a human," should it be "treated like a human"? If an AI cannot think like a human, should it be treated differently? Is it acceptable to take away the rights of nonhuman intelligences?

The age of AI and androids is upon us. Self-driving vehicles will soon become commonplace. Robots are already vacuuming carpets, mopping floors, and mowing grass. The future will only lead to a growing prevalence of robots and other artificial intelligence in workplaces. That fact may well revolutionize the needs of DE&I efforts in organizations.

Trend 3: Diversity fatigue will grow as a factor affecting DE&I efforts

Haven't we done enough already? That question, and those like it, are becoming popular when marginalized, underrepresented persons state they are still not experiencing equitable treatment in organizational settings. Those who are DE&I practitioners know that corporate culture change does not happen overnight, and it does not happen by itself. Changes in culture are said to be marathons, not sprints.

However, everyone can grow tired of a continued emphasis on DE&I. *Diversity fatigue* in the workplace is worthy of consideration. The term diversity fatigue refers to feelings of anxiety and weariness that accompany efforts to celebrate diversity, achieve equity, and encourage inclusion.

Diversity fatigue is sometimes regarded as an issue primarily affecting white males (Madison and Kofman 2018; Miranda-Wolff 2019). In her book *Black Fatigue* (2020), Mary-Frances Winters details how the issue that engages, informs, and inspires diversity efforts can become traumatic, tiring, and even life-threatening. Every person you encounter in your organization will be affected differently by the culture shift and diversity work associated with DE&I efforts.

Combat diversity fatigue much as a runner would combat physical fatigue:

- *Stretch*: Try new topics. They may be uncomfortable, but these new topics can help to reach higher levels of community.
- *Pace*: Do not send everything out to see what "sticks". Instead, engage programs in a manner that will inform the members but will not overwhelm them.

- *Refresh*: Do different things to keep the energy levels of the community up. Continuing the same one program will "dry-out" the diversity efforts.
- *Stay on course*: Do not treat a misstep as a total failure. Instead, make the mistake, correct it, and then move forward.
- *Finish strong*: Review the programs. Assess but do not critique. Then prepare for the next event.

Trend 4: Building diversity on the board of directors will become an issue

The boardroom remains a place often not regulated for diversity. National Public Radio reports that 29.6% of companies on the Standards and Poor 500 do not have at least one diverse board member (Gura 2021). Just as there is a business case to be made for diversity with the organization, there is also a case to be made for diversity on the board of directors of organizations. As organizational leaders set out to make their organizations more diverse, they should pay attention to the top echelons. Carter, Simkins and Simson (2003) point out that there is a direct correlation between board diversity and company performance. While many employees do not know who is on their organization's board of directors, top performers usually do know. If diverse group members cannot see representation at the top of their organizations, why should they remain in such an organization? Organizational leaders slowly realize that their organizations are not immune from being regarded as reflections of the communities which they serve. This recognition is now being operationalized at the top and at the bottom. It is a viewpoint that will only grow more intense as future census results reveal that the United States is becoming more diverse. So too should U.S. companies.

Building diversity at the top can be facilitated by:

1. Creating internal programs that teach organizational members how to serve as board members.
2. Encouraging HR units to develop long and short lists of potential board members.
3. Encouraging board members to serve as mentors for "rising stars."
4. Mentoring need not occur between members of the same race or gender.

5. Establishing lines of communication between the current board members, stockholders, and employees.

Trend 5: Labels will change

This book opened with Overview chapter entitled "What's in a Name?" This chapter made the point that the name of a DE&I effort is a strategic decision that affects the future of the culture change effort in much the same way as the name of a product may affect the willingness of customers to buy that product.

Words matter. Words can hurt people – or help them. And the same principle applies to DE&I efforts. What they are called can affect the willingness of others to participate in them and to support them.

What your DE&I effort should be called is a topic discussed early in this text. But what happens when the meaning of the words evolves? The "I" in DE&I has stood for inclusion, but what happens when it becomes "Belonging"? Remember we define "inclusion" as *including* people at or in places of power or prestige. However, the concept of inclusion is evolving and growing into more than its original meaning. Think about this point, the "A" in LGBTQIA means _____ but it also could mean _____ . If you need some help with that fill-in, review https://outrightinternational.org/content/acronyms-explained. As you build programs, remember words, like actions, matter. Make sure the words you are using are impactful and not harming to the communities you are trying to support.

This can be facilitated by:

1. Developing a DE&I committee tasked with researching and defining what the organization should call the initiative. Members should represent all parts of the organization (that is, from C-Suite to general employees).
2. Reviewing your strategic plan on diversity. If none exists, create one.
3. Seeking other organizational DE&I units. Review them and use their best practices for your organization's efforts.

Trend 6: Notions of diversity will evolve over time

To continue to grow to be inclusive, you should be looking to make sure that your programs are including everyone.

Diversity is moving beyond the basic recognition of difference. Through an early chapter in this text, you learned there are many ways to grasp building or strengthening an existing DE&I effort. Diversity is not just the "Big Three" – gender, race, orientation. Many issues are often overlooked in diversity matters. We have discussed age, but there is also:

■ *Neurodiversity*: A term coined by Judy Singer to mean the virtually infinite neurocognitive variability within Earth's human population. It points to the fact that every human has a unique nervous system with a unique combination of abilities and needs (Singer 2020). Figure 12.2 summarizes key aspects of neurodiversity. Neurodiversity should not be confused for or with mental illness. They are two separate topics. Additional information can be found at the Neurodiversity Hub (https://www.neurodiversityhub.org/). See "Neurodiversity and other conditions" 2021; Robinson 2013; Russell 2020; Singer 2020; "What is neurodiversity" n.d.)(adhdaware.org.uk 2021)

■ *Socioeconomic Status*: Income disparities and wage gaps are front and center in the workplace – and now more than ever before. Each income-level experiences varied challenges.

■ *Religion*: Religion is one of the three topics best left undiscussed in workplaces. Salary level and politics are the other two topics best left

Aspects of Neurodiversity

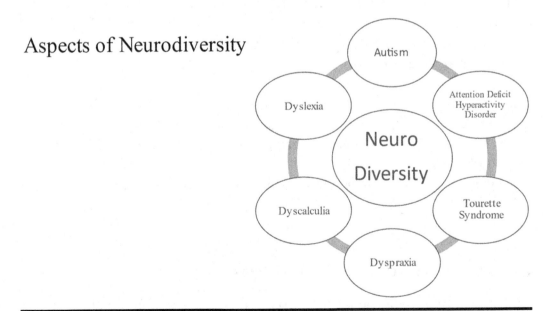

Figure 12.2   Aspects of neurodiversity. Copyright 2021 by Jamie Campbell. Adapted from Genius Within.

undiscussed. As the workplace becomes more global, spiritual issues are bound to come up. The workplace environment has varied impacts on different faiths.

This trend can be facilitated by:

1. Keeping up to date on DE&I vocabulary.
2. Observing the wages paid to entry-level employees.
3. Observing all holidays of faith with explanations from Employee Resource Groups.

Trend 7: The shrinking globe will affect DE&I

The pandemic, which prompted many organizations to draw on technological work methods to achieve work results, has changed how people interact. Interacting differently through various platforms – such as videoconferencing, audioconferencing, texting, and emailing – changes how people experience workplace diversity, equity, and inclusion.

When people work across national cultures, that also affects DE&I efforts. Diversity does not mean the same thing in the United States as it does in some other places. In China, 95% of the nation is from the same ethnic group. People from different genders are also treated differently in various national cultures. Globalization has prompted many organizations to realize that DE&I efforts need to be grounded in the local realities of where business operations occur.

Workers are used to working across functions and teams, but they must also learn to work across time zones, borders, and geographical locations. What happens when diversity is just about ethnic backgrounds or gender? Diversity in the United States has been covered in this text. Ideas of culture and what it takes to change diversity culture have been examined in this book. Yet in many places in the world, ethnicity is more important than racial or gender characteristics.

How can DE&I be facilitated in globalized settings? It can be facilitated by:

1. Developing cultural exchanges among teams.
2. Having in-person site visits from teams at various global locations.
3. Setting up social programing events, even those online, with team members in different places.

Trend 8: Gender identity and orientation will be a continuing focus for the future

When to disclose one's sexual orientation can be one of the toughest decisions that gay men, lesbians, queer persons, and persons who are transitioning may face. It can involve emotional turmoil and prompt fear of retaliation and rejection (Griffith and Hebl 2002). However, it is increasingly acceptable to reveal sexual orientation because of the Civil Rights Act, Title VII, and evolving public attitudes. Organizations, if they are to attract and retain top talent, must be welcoming places where workers can be themselves.

A welcoming culture can be facilitated by:

1. Encouraging all persons to use pronouns appropriate to themselves in virtual meetings.
2. Asking workers to state what pronouns they prefer to be used when referring to them during meetings.
3. Creating events for life partners in workplace settings.
4. Educating employees about live names and dead names.
5. Making sure health care benefits cover partners.

A Tool for Reflecting on the Future of DE&I

Use the tool to contemplate possible trends affecting the future of DE&I. Then plan how your organization may be positioned to address these trends as they unfold.

CHAPTER 12 TOOL: A TOOL FOR REFLECTING ON THE FUTURE OF DE&I

Directions: Use this tool to guide your thinking and reflection on diversity, equity, and inclusion trends affecting your organization. For each trend listed under column 1 below, describe under column 2 the likely impacts of that trend on your organization, and describe under column 3 what actions should be taken to position your organization's diversity, equity, and inclusion effort to deal with the trend and its likely impacts. In the blank spaces under column 1 below, add other trends that occur to you.

Diversity, equity, and inclusion trends	How will the trend likely impact your organization?	What actions should be taken to position your organization's diversity, equity, and inclusion effort to deal with the trend and its likely impacts?

1	Generational differences should be considered in DE&I efforts		
2	Artificial intelligence and robots will create new DE&I challenges in the workplace		
3	Diversity fatigue will grow as a factor affecting DE&I efforts		
4	Building diversity on the board of directors will become an issue		
5	Labels will change		
6	Notions of diversity will evolve over time		
7	The shrinking globe will affect DE&I		
8	Gender identity and orientation will be a continuing focus for the future		
9			
10			

Key Questions about the Chapter

1. Can DE&I trends in the marketplace be predicted?
2. What factors may affect DE&I in the workplace?
3. Can you determine what is DE&I?
4. What trend may be more important than others? Why do you think so?
5. How will artificial intelligence and robotics affect DE&I efforts in workplaces?
6. What is the best way to onboard new employees? Why do you think so?
7. How can managing across continents be done effectively across cultures?

Work Consulted

Carter, David A., Betty J. Simkins, and W. Gary Simpson. "Corporate governance, board diversity, and firm value." *Financial Review* 38, no. 1 (2003): 33–53.

Chron Contributor. n.d. "Definition of business trends." CHRON. *Small Business Chron*, May 2021. https://smallbusiness.chron.com/definition-business-trends -3399.html

Griffith, Kristin H., and Michelle R. Hebl. "The disclosure dilemma for gay men and lesbians: 'coming out' at work." *Journal of Applied Psychology* 87, no. 6 (2002): 1191.

Gura, Daniel. 2021. "You Can Still Count The Number Of Black CEOs On One Hand." National Public Radio. NPR, May 27, 2021. https://www.npr.org/2021 /05/27/1000814249/a-year-after-floyds-death-you-can-still-count-the-number-of -black-ceos-on-one-ha.

Madison, Amber, and Liz Kofman. n.d. "5 ways to fight 'diversity fatigue.'" *Culture Amp*, January 2018. https://www.cultureamp.com/blog/fight-diversity-fatigue

Miranda-Wolff, Alida. n.d. "What is diversity fatigue, anyway?" *Chief Learning Officer*, January 2019. https://www.chieflearningofficer.com/2019/01/28/what-is -diversity-fatigue-anyway/

"Neurodiversity and other conditions." n.d. *ADHD Aware*, January 2021. https://adh-daware.org.uk/what-is-adhd/neurodiversity-and-other-conditions/

Noble, Nicole, Ashley Penner, and Logan Winkleman. n.d. "Current trends in diversity recruiting practices." *Naceweb.org*, February 2020. https://www.naceweb .org/diversity-equity-and-inclusion/trends-and-predictions/current-trends-in -diversity-recruiting-practices/

Nordmeyer, Billie. n.d. "Business trend analysis." CHRON. *Small Business Chron*, February 2021. https://smallbusiness.chron.com/business-trend-analysis-72438 .html

Public Affairs Council. n.d. "2021 DEI trends in public affairs report." January 2021. https://pac.org/wp-content/uploads/dei-trends-in-public-affairs.pdf

Robinson, John Elder. n.d. "What is neurodiversity? Neurodiversity means many things to people. Here's my first-person definition." *Psychology Today*, October 2013. https://www.psychologytoday.com/us/blog/my-life-aspergers/201310/ what-is-neurodiversity.

Russell, Ginny. "Critiques of the neurodiversity movement." *Autistic Community and the Neurodiversity Movement* 2020 (2020): 287.

Singer, Judy. n.d. "What is neurodiversity." *Judy Singer on Neurodiversity*, March 2020. https://neurodiversity2.blogspot.com/p/what.html

Stahl, Ashley. n.d. "What's to come in 2021 for diversity, equity and inclusion in the workplace." *Forbes*. April 2021. https://www.forbes.com/sites/ashleystahl/2021 /04/14/whats-to-come-in-2021-for-diversity-equity-and-inclusion-in-the-work-place/?sh=2585d93c7f26

Wentling, Rose Mary, and Nilda Palma-Rivas. "Current status and future trends of diversity initiatives in the workplace: Diversity experts' perspective." *Human Resource Development Quarterly* 9, no. 3 (1998): 235–253.

"What is neurodiversity." n.d. *Genius Within*. https://www.geniuswithin.co.uk/what -is-neurodiversity/

Winters, Mary Francis. 2020. *Black Fatigue: How Racism Erodes the Mind, Body, and Spirit*. San Francisco, CA: Berrett-Koehler.

RESOURCES TO SUPPORT IMPLEMENTATION OF A DE&I EFFORT

This part provides resources to help facilitators who are implementing a DE&I effort. The appendices in this section are:

- *Appendix A*: Glossary of terms
- *Appendix B*: Diversity, equity, and inclusion (DE&I) culture audit
- *Appendix C*: Diversity resources
- *Appendix D*: Frequently asked questions about diversity, equity, and inclusion (DE&I)
- *Appendix E*: Tools to guide implementation

DOI: 10.4324/9781003184935-17

Appendix A: Glossary

Chief Diversity Officer (CDO): refers to a manager charged with facilitating and/or managing an organizational DE&I effort.

Corporate culture: refers to the unspoken but often shared views that stem from the shared experiences of people in the same organization. To change corporate culture, change the experiences of the organizational members. Successful experiences register as "what to do" in corporate culture; failed experiences register as "what not to do" in corporate culture.

Cross-cultural: refers to differences among, and across, cultures.

Cross-cultural competence: is understood to mean the ability to work effectively with different cultures.

Cultural communication: is about how culture affects the way people communicate. Generally it is what people say, who talks, how people use pacing and pauses in communicating, how people listen, what tones that people use in their talk, what is considered conventional language, and how directly and forthrightly people speak.

DE&I: stands for diversity, equity, and inclusion.

Diversity: refers to the demographic composition of a community, a constituency within a larger community, a state, a nation, etc. Diversity as a goal for communities may refer to the heterogeneity of members from different groups or identities and active efforts to ensure people from historically underrepresented groups. It does not and cannot apply to an individual. An individual cannot be diverse, despite the increasingly popular use of the term to refer to individuals of color. The backgrounds and identities of an organizational community, taken together, constitute diversity. Because of the positive benefits of compositional diversity for learning, discovery, and problem-solving,

DOI: 10.4324/9781003184935-18

organizations often identify goals of increasing the diversity of their members in backgrounds, identities, and perspectives.

Equity: refers to fairness in policies, procedures, and practices. The organizational goal is typically to ensure equal access to the programs, services, support, and opportunities appropriate to a constituency, role, or work.

Employee Resource Group (ERG): refers to a worker group composed of people who share common characteristics or interests.

Homophily: refers to the tendency of decision-makers to select someone like themselves. It is sometimes called the "like me bias" to indicate that people choose people like themselves.

Implicit bias: refers to biases not intentionally applied but that people use without even realizing it.

Inclusion: refers to the culture of an organizational community and how much people from all groups are welcomed and valued for who they are. Often, the organizational goal is to ensure that neither background nor identity stands in the way of belonging and success and that everyone can play a role in shaping the environment, not as individuals stripped of their identities, but as people whose cultures and perspectives make the organization better.

Microaggression: is a term that usually refers to slights that occur daily that are often unconscious by those who demonstrate them. They concern verbal slights or other slights that show negative feelings about people from otherwise historically marginalized groups.

Multicultural: has many meanings. In one sense it refers to a process whereby people who represent different heritages work together harmoniously without giving up their individual ethnic identities.

Social justice: speaks to the balance between individuals and society. It has to do generally with comparing how wealth is distributed among people, how personal liberty is handled, and how well people are given fair opportunities to various privileges.

Unconscious bias: concerns the tendency to make biased decisions without even realizing it.

Appendix B: Diversity, Equity, and Inclusion (DE&I) Audit

William J. Rothwell

Contents

DOI: 10.4324/9781003184935-19

Directions: For each item appearing in the left column below, rate it in the right column using the following scale: **0 = I don't feel this item applies to my organization; 1 = Very poorly; 2 = Poorly; 3 = Somewhat well; 4 = Adequately; 5 = Very well.** When you finish, add up your scores from items 1–10 and place them in the box at the bottom of the page. Then score the culture audit for DE&I on the next page. There are no "right" or "wrong" answers in any absolute sense, but realize how perceptions about the DE&I climate may vary across your organization – and use that to provide the basis for action to improve the culture and climate.

How well do you feel your organization …	Rating scales						
	0	1	2	3	4	5	
1	Has defined the culture?	0	1	2	3	4	5
2	Has clarified the role of diversity, equity, and inclusion in shaping culture?	0	1	2	3	4	5
3	Clarified who has the authority to change culture?	0	1	2	3	4	5
4	Identified and defined the pipeline?	0	1	2	3	4	5
5	Develops talent?	0	1	2	3	4	5
6	Navigates emotions and other relational dynamics?	0	1	2	3	4	5
7	Showcases your organization's talent?	0	1	2	3	4	5
8	Promotes your organization's talent?	0	1	2	3	4	5
9	Develops affinity groups?	0	1	2	3	4	5
10	Evaluates your processes	0	1	2	3	4	5
Total		**Total from the rating scales above**				**Multiply score to the left by 2 =**	

Scores

If your organization scores ...	Then ...
100–92	Congratulations! Your organization has an excellent climate to support DE&I
91–82	Good! Your organization has a good climate to support DE&I
81–72	OK. Your organization climate to support DE&I is about average. You need to work on it
71–62	Not good. Your organization's climate is below par on DE&I. Take action based on the pattern of items rated poorly on the audit above
61 and below	Your organization fails the audit. Take immediate corrective action

Appendix C: Resources for Diversity, Equity and Inclusion (DE&I)[*]

Contents

---

[*] All websites accessed on August 16, 2021.

DOI: 10.4324/9781003184935-20

Selected Competency Models for DE&I Practitioners

- *Creating a Competency Model for Diversity and Inclusion Practitioners*
  https://www.conference-board.org/pdf_free/councils/TCBCP005.pdf
- *Competencies for Diversity and Inclusion*
  https://www.naca.org/resources/Documents/Competencies_for_Diversity
  _and_Inclusion.pdf
- *Institute for Diversity Certification*
  https://www.diversitycertification.org/competencies
- *The Conference Board: Creating a Competency Model for Diversity and
  Inclusion Practitioners*
  https://wff.yale.edu/sites/default/files/files/conference%20board%20-
  %20creating%20a%20competency%20model.pdf
- Ratts, Manivong, Singh, Anneliese, Butler, S., Nassar-McMillan,
  Sylvia, and McCullough, Julian. 2016. *Multicultural and Social Justice
  Counseling Competencies: Practical Applications in Counseling.*
  American Counseling Association. https://ct.counseling.org/2016/01/
  multicultural-and-social-justice-counseling-competencies-practical-appli-
  cations-in-counseling/
- TRIEC. *Inclusive Workplace Competencies.* https://triec.ca/wp-content/
  plugins/competency/TRIEC-Inclusive-Workplace-Competencies.pdf
- White, Whitney. 2020. *Five Essential Leadership Competencies of an
  Effective D & I Practitioner.* http://www.talent2025.org/uploads/files/DI
  -Guidbook.v1.5C.optimized.pdf

Selected Organizational Diversity Standards

- *The Standards for Assessing Diversity Policies and Practices*
  https://www.fdic.gov/about/diversity/the-standards.pdf
- *ISO Standard for Diversity*
  https://www.ansi.org/news/standards-news/all-news/2021/05/5-4-21-new
  -iso-standard-supports-diversity-and-inclusion-in-the-workplace

Selected Diversity Audits

- *Diversity for Social Impact*
  https://diversity.social/diversity-audit/

- *21 Questions to Ask in a Corporate Culture Audit*
  https://www.thoughtfarmer.com/blog/14-questions-corporate-culture
  -audit/
- *The Diversity Audit Tool*
  https://www.ryerson.ca/content/dam/diversity/academic/Diversity
  %20Assessment%20Tools%20A%20Comparison_2011.pdf

Job Descriptions for DE&I Officers

- Kansas State University. *Chief Diversity Officer* (CDO).
  https://www.k-state.edu/president/initiatives/diversity-inclusion/Chief
  -Diversity-and-Inclusion-Officer.pdf
- Duke University School of Medicine, *Chief Diversity Officer* (CDO).
  https://wff.yale.edu/sites/default/files/files/CDO%20Job%20Description
  %20FINAL%2011_15_10.pdf

Diversity and Inclusion Self-Assessment

- *Diversity and Inclusion Self-Assessment*
  https://www.naceweb.org/career-development/organizational-structure/
  diversity-and-inclusion-self-assessment/
- Washington College. *Diversity Self-Assessment.*
  https://www.washcoll.edu/_resources/documents/Diversity%20Self
  -Assessment.pdf

Selected References about Diversity Metrics

- Palios, Stephen. 2021. *What D & I Metrics You Should Use*
  https://crescendowork.com/guide-start-diversity-inclusion-strategy/diver-
  sity-inclusion-metrics-use

Selected Journals about DE&I

- *Cultural Diversity and Ethnic Minority Psychology*
  https://www.apa.org/pubs/journals/cdp?utm_campaign=apa_pub-
  lishing&utm_medium=cpc&utm_source=google&utm_content=cdp

_googlesearch_grant_02192020&gclid=CjwKCAjwjdOIBhA_EiwAHz8
xm4ZObrzOLdGFW4MZzzWn9Lze9rMw5THycatwOjw7ZGSezlj3BQX
01xoCeVsQAvD_BwE

- *Education, Citizenship and Social Justice*
  https://us.sagepub.com/en-us/nam/journal/education-citizenship-and
  -social-justice
- *Education and Urban Society*
  https://journals.sagepub.com/home/eus
- *Equality, Diversity and Inclusion*
  https://www.emeraldgrouppublishing.com/journal/edi
- *Journal of Cross-Cultural Psychology*
  https://journals.sagepub.com/home/jcc
- *Journal of Diversity in Higher Education*
  https://www.apa.org/pubs/journals/dhe
- *Journal of Hispanic Higher Education*
  https://journals.sagepub.com/home/jhh
- *Journal of Multicultural Counseling and Development*
  https://onlinelibrary.wiley.com/journal/21611912
- *Race, Ethnicity and Higher Education*
  https://www.birmingham.ac.uk/research/crre/race-ethnicity/index.aspx

List of Selected Conferences about DE&I

- *8 Diversity Conferences Not to Miss in 2021* https://blog.powertofly.com/
  diversity-conferences-2021

Free Training about DE&I

- *8 Free Online Training Courses about DEI*
  https://www.businessinsider.com/free-online-courses-diversity-equity
  -inclusion-2020-10

Master's Degree Programs in DE&I

- 6 Masters Degrees in Diversity, Equity and Inclusion or Related Fields
  https://www.masterstudies.com/Masters-Degree/Diversity-Studies/

List of Professional Associations about DE&I

■ **List of associations**: https://diversity.ucdavis.edu/organizations

Selected Lists of Key Books on DE&I

■ Jadczak, Felicia. 2019. *Diversity, Equity, and Inclusion Books We're Reading.* https://shegeeksout.com/diversity-equity-inclusion-books -reading/

Selected Key Articles on DE&I

■ *Diversity, Equity and Inclusion Reading List.* 2021 https://libguides .library.umkc.edu/DEI_Reading_List
■ Wright, James. 2019. *Top 50 Diversity, Inclusion & Belonging Articles of 2019*
https://www.linkedin.com/pulse/top-50-diversity-inclusion-belonging -articles-2019-james-wright/

Selected Key Websites on DE&I

■ American Nuclear Society. Diversity, Equity and Inclusion Educational Resources. https://www.ans.org/communities/diversity/resources/
■ Educause https://www.educause.edu/about/diversity-equity-and-inclu-sion/resources

Selected Videos about Diversity, Equity, and Inclusion

■ Basics of Organization Development
https://www.youtube.com/watch?v=VDduIzjAjWE
■ Change Management Is Not Organization Development
https://www.youtube.com/watch?v=a-R-J79dPb8
■ Defining Diversity, Equity and Inclusion
The Difference between Diversity, Inclusion and Equity
https://www.youtube.com/watch?v=spBB68Wv7KM

- How to Begin the Conversation on Diversity & Inclusion in the Workplace
  https://www.youtube.com/watch?v=hs4q3aYMnP0
- The Case for Diversity Programs
  Don't Put People in Boxes
  https://www.youtube.com/watch?v=zRwt25M5nGw
- The Business Case for Inclusion and Diversity
  https://www.youtube.com/watch?v=3U5cXxoTn7k
- Measuring Diversity Programs
  Measuring the Success of Diversity & Inclusion Initiatives
  https://www.youtube.com/watch?v=O2mvCwPJz-Q
- Facilitating Transformative Learning
  The Science of Diversity and Inclusion Initiatives: Sparking Transformative Solutions
  https://www.youtube.com/watch?v=mDRwVLxbpR8
- Step 1: Defining Your Organization's Culture
  Include: Building a Diverse Corporate Culture
  https://www.youtube.com/watch?v=MYauOQ204VA
- Step 2: Clarifying the Role of Diversity, Equity, and Inclusion in Shaping Culture
  How to Start a Cultural Transformation?
  https://www.youtube.com/watch?v=zClAdLw4yRI
- Step 3: Clarifying Who Has the Authority to Change Culture
  How to Get Serious about Diversity and Inclusion in the Workplace
  https://www.youtube.com/watch?v=kvdHqS3ryw0
- Step 4: Identifying and Defining the Pipeline
  How Do You Build a Recruiting Pipeline That Is Diverse Enough?
  https://www.youtube.com/watch?v=V4r6bS0stIM
- Step 5: Developing Talent
  Robert Harris on Developing People
  https://www.youtube.com/watch?v=K-HZqbAfsDI
- Step 6: Navigating Emotions and Other Relational Dynamics
  Why Leadership on Diversity and Inclusion Requires Emotional Intelligence
  https://www.youtube.com/watch?v=9YeOc-6z-3s
- Step 9: Developing Affinity Groups
  The Importance of Affinity Groups
  https://www.youtube.com/watch?v=Kwf9vr4H7_I

- Step 10: Evaluating Your Processes
  Evaluating Internal Diversity Programs
  https://www.youtube.com/watch?v=c3-jFUnsn2g
- Trends in Diversity, Equity, and Inclusion
  Where Does Diversity and Inclusion Fit into the Future of Work?
  https://www.youtube.com/watch?v=CCHwSprkwj8

Appendix D: Frequently Asked Questions (FAQs) about Diversity, Equity, and Inclusion

Jamie Campbell, Phillip L. Ealy, and William J. Rothwell

Question 1: What is meant by such terms as *diversity, equity,* and *inclusion* (DE&I)?

Answer 1: The Glossary in this book provides suggested definitions. But it is helpful to engage your decision-makers in defining key terms as they apply to your organization. See the Overview in this book for a rationale for doing that and a tool to help facilitate the process.

Question 2: Is a DE&I program simply a fad?

Answer 2: No. But it can be if decision-makers regard DE&I as a quick fix or a public relations effort. Genuine commitment is tough to measure, but it can often be demonstrated by how many resources – time, money, and people – are devoted to the change effort. The same principle applies to DE&I efforts.

Question 3: What are the business reasons to launch and sustain a DE&I effort?

Answer 3: Diverse groups are more innovative than homogeneous groups. A major argument for diversity efforts is that they can lead to competitive advantage when the world's economy is focused on innovation rather than information, goods or services, or agriculture. Another argument for diversity efforts in organizations is that they can

DOI: 10.4324/9781003184935-21

open up access to groups traditionally overlooked to address talent shortages. Such groups may include people representing various races, genders, ages, religious affiliations, national heritages, veteran status, and much more.

Question 4: What is the difference between a DE&I *program* and a *corporate culture that supports DE&I*?

Answer 4: A *program* suggests a change effort with a beginning, middle, and end. But corporate culture is enduring. *Culture* consists of the unspoken rules that govern interpersonal relationships in an organizational context. A major goal of DE&I should be to move beyond a DE&I program to a corporate culture that supports DE&I as a taken-for-granted fact of the corporate culture.

Question 5: What are facts and figures on DE&I efforts in organizations?

Answer 5: Consider these facts and figures adapted from https://whatto-become.com/blog/diversity-in-the-workplace-statistics/

- About 43% of companies with diverse management teams had profits higher than those that did not.
- Companies demonstrating diversity are 35% more productive.
- Diverse teams are 87% better at decision-making.
- Organizations employing an equal mix of women and men yield 41% better results.
- Workers believe that diverse organizations are more competitive than those that do not.
- Organizations enjoying a high level of racial diversity garner 15 times the revenue as others.
- "Being too busy" is the most often cited reason by managers for not launching and/or sustaining a DE&I effort.
- Google has stated a goal of filling 35% of senior leaders from traditionally underrepresented groups by 2025.
- By 2044, the so-called "minorities" will be the majority in U.S. companies.
- 57% of workers in organizations today would prefer to see their organizations more diverse.
- Only 6.6% of Fortune 500 CEOs are women.
- 69% of executives today state that DE&I is the most important business issue.

Question 6: DE&I efforts in organizations sometimes provoke backlashes and resistance. Why is that, and what should be done about that?

Answer 6: Resistance stems from many sources. One is that organizational members may conflate a DE&I effort with undeservedly preferring representatives of various traditionally underrepresented groups to meet real or perceived "quotas." According to that view, merit is less important when making selection or promotion decisions than other factors such as race, gender, national origin, disability status, veteran status, and so on.

Question 7: Who should lead a DE&I effort?

Answer 7: Many DE&I efforts are led by a Chief Diversity Officer (CDO). Often, the person chosen as CDO is himself or herself a representative of an otherwise protected job class – but *does not have to be* a person from an underrepresented group.

Question 8: What should be examined in a DE&I effort?

Answer 8: All elements of the human resource system should be examined against DE&I issues. Consider recruitment, selection, onboarding, training, performance reviews, pay raises, promotion rates, corrective action, retention rates – and much more.

Question 9: When should a DE&I effort be launched?

Answer 9: There is no "right" or "wrong" time to launch a DE&I effort. But many DE&I efforts are launched in organizations immediately following a well-publicized crisis outside the organization (such as the police shooting an unarmed member of a traditionally underrepresented group), a crisis inside the organization (such as religious graffiti spray-painted on the side of the corporate headquarters), or evidence of systematic problems in the organization (such as engagement survey results that reveal worker perceptions of rampant discrimination in the organization).

Question 10: Where should a DE&I effort be launched?

Answer 10: DE&I should be launched wherever it may be needed.

Question 11: How should a DE&I effort be launched and sustained?

Answer 11: Many change models have been published. Any of them can provide guidance in formulating, implementing, and evaluating a DE&I effort because implementing and sustaining a DE&I effort is a change effort. This book is based on a change model for implementing a DE&I

effort. The steps described in this book, which will need to be customized and tailored to fit your organization, are:

- *Step 1*: Define your organization's culture.
- *Step 2*: Clarify the role of diversity, equity, and inclusion in shaping culture.
- *Step 3*: Clarify who has the authority to change the culture.
- *Step 4*: Identify and define the pipeline.
- *Step 5*: Develop talent.
- *Step 6*: Navigate emotions and other relational dynamics.
- *Step 7*: Showcase your organization's talent.
- *Step 8*: Promote your organization's talent.
- *Step 9*: Develop Employee Resource Groups.
- *Step 10*: Evaluate your processes.

Question 12: How does an OD approach to DE&I differ from other approaches?

Answer 12: Traditional change management approaches are often organized like projects. The managers/consultants behave like medical doctors who arrive at an organization with a perceived problem, conduct their diagnosis, offer recommendations, and then depart the organizational setting. But OD mostly does *not* rely on that approach. Instead, OD practitioners – and that can include those who practice DE&I – behave like facilitators who question people about what they believe their problems are, question people about what they believe their solutions should be, question people about what action plans should be used to implement solutions, and question people about what measures or metrics should be used to evaluate results. OD does not impose change on people; rather, OD facilitates change with and through people. The OD approach can be applied to DE&I efforts – but only if managers will accept the approach.

Question 13: How should a DE&I effort be evaluated?

Answer 13: At the outset of any change effort, change objectives should be established. It is very desirable if they are linked to the organization's strategic planning goals – perhaps as they are expressed in the organization's balance scorecard and cascaded down through the organization as key performance indicators (KPIs).

Question 14: Why do DE&I programs fail?

Answer 14: DE&I efforts fail when:

- Managers are not committed because they feel no need and see no need for the DE&I effort.
- Managers are not in agreement among themselves on the goals of the DE&I effort.
- No effort is made to clarify the roles expected of various stakeholder groups – such as CEO, senior team, HR, managers, and workers.
- No effort is made to hold people accountable for enacting their roles.
- No effort is made to align and link the DE&I effort to the organization's strategic goals.
- Workers are not clear what they should do differently.
- Consultants or facilitators confuse meeting their own needs with meeting client needs.

Appendix E: Tools to Guide Implementation

Philip L. Ealy and William J. Rothwell

Contents

This appendix provides many tools to aid Chief Diversity Officers and others to facilitate the implementation of a DE&I effort.

DOI: 10.4324/9781003184935-22

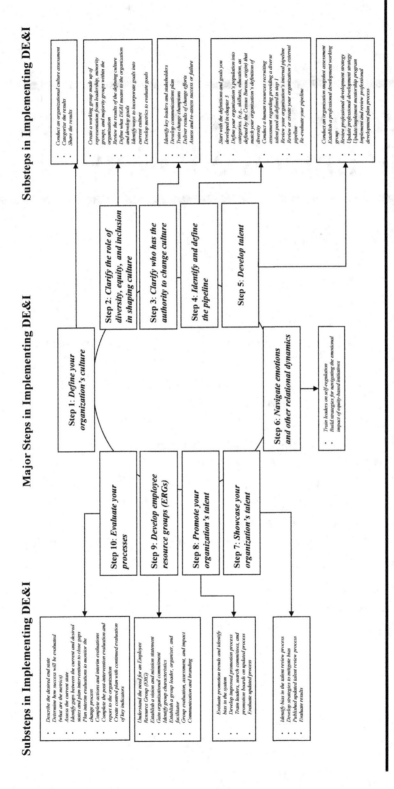

Final Figure   The diversity, equity, and inclusion (DE&I) roadmap model.

- *Step 1*: Tool to define your organization's culture
- *Step 2*: Tool to clarify the role of diversity, equity, and inclusion in shaping culture
- *Step 3*: Tool to clarify who has the authority to change culture
- *Step 4*: Tool to identify and define the pipeline
- *Step 5*: Tool to develop talent
- *Step 6*: Tool to navigate emotions and other relational dynamics
- *Step 7*: Tool to showcase your organization's talent
- *Step 8*: Tool to promote your organization's talent
- *Step 9*: Tool to develop employee resource groups
- *Step 10*: Tool to evaluate your processes
- Proposal format for building a culture that supports diversity, equity, and inclusion

Use the tools for Steps 1–10 to lay the groundwork for the information you prepare in the Proposal Format.

Tool 1: Tool to Define Your Organization's Culture

Directions: Use this tool to help you and your organization "define your organization's culture." That is Step 1 in the ten-step process to establish your diversity, equity, and inclusion effort. Carrying out Step 1 requires specific tasks in its own right. It does not happen on its own; rather, you and other leaders in your organization must guide it. For each step appearing in the left column below, take notes in the right column on your own plans to carry out each step. There are no right or wrong answers in any absolute sense. But to the extent you can customize these steps to fit your organization's culture, the more successful it is likely to be. Add, subtract, or combine steps – or resequence steps – as may be appropriate to you and your leaders. But at least this gives you a flexible action plan as a place to start.

What are the specific steps to take to define your organization's culture?		What, specifically, will you and your organization do to carry out the steps?
1	Conduct an organizational culture assessment	
2	Categorize the results	
3	Share the results	

Tool 2: Tool to Clarify the Role of Diversity, Equity, and Inclusion in Shaping Culture

Directions: Use this tool to help you and your organization "clarify the role of diversity, equity, and inclusion in shaping culture." That is Step 2 in the ten-step process to establish your diversity, equity, and inclusion effort. Carrying out Step 2 requires specific tasks in its own right. It does not happen on its own; rather, you and other leaders in your organization must guide it. For each step appearing in the left column below, take notes in the right column on your own plans to carry out each step. There are no right or wrong answers in any absolute sense. But to the extent you can customize these steps to fit your organization's culture, the more successful it is likely to be. Add, subtract, or combine steps – or resequence steps – as may be appropriate to you and your leaders. But at least this gives you a flexible action plan as a place to start.

What are the specific steps to take to clarify the role of diversity, equity, and inclusion in shaping culture?		What, specifically, will you and your organization do to carry out the steps?
1	Create a working group made up of representation from leadership, minority groups, and majority groups within the organization (as you defined in Chapter 2)	
2	Review the results of the defining culture from Chapter 2	
3	Define what DE&I means to the organization and develop goals	
4	Identify ways to incorporate goals into current culture (e.g., mission, vision, values)	
5	Develop metrics to evaluate goals	

Tool 3: Tool to Clarify Who Has the Authority to Change Culture

Directions: Use this tool to help you and your organization "clarify who has the authority to change culture." That is Step 3 in the ten-step process to establish your diversity, equity, and inclusion effort. Carrying out Step 3 requires specific tasks in its own right. It does not happen on its own; rather, you and other leaders in your organization must guide it. For each step appearing in the left column below, take notes in the right column on your own plans to carry out each step. There are no right or wrong answers in any absolute sense. But to the extent you can customize these steps to fit your organization's culture, the more successful it is likely to be. Add, subtract, or combine steps – or resequence steps – as may be appropriate to you and your leaders. But at least this gives you a flexible action plan as a place to start.

What are the specific steps to take to clarify who has the authority to change culture?		What, specifically, will you and your organization do to carry out the steps?
1	Identify key leaders and stakeholders	
2	Develop communications plan	
3	Train change champions	
4	Deliver results of change efforts (e.g., change forums and summits)	
5	Assess and reassess success or failure	

Tool 4: Tool to Identify and Define the Pipeline

Directions: Use this tool to help you and your organization "identify and define the pipeline." That is Step 4 in the ten-step process to establish your diversity, equity, and inclusion effort. Carrying out Step 4 requires specific tasks in its own right. It does not happen on its own; rather, you and other leaders in your organization must guide it. For each step appearing in the left column below, take notes in the right column on your own plans to carry out each step. There are no right or wrong answers in any absolute sense. But to the extent you can customize these steps to fit your organization's culture, the more successful it is likely to be. Add, subtract, or combine steps – or resequence steps – as may be appropriate to you and your leaders. But at least this gives you a flexible action plan as a place to start.

What are the specific steps to take to identify and define the pipeline?		What, specifically, will you and your organization do to carry out the steps?
1	Start with the definitions and goals you developed in Chapter 3	
2	Define your organization's population into categories (e.g., skill sets, education, as defined by the Census Bureau, origin) that match your organization's definition of diversity	
3	Conduct a human resources recruiting assessment regarding providing a diverse talent pool as defined in Step 1	
4	Review your organization's internal pipeline	
5	Review or create your organization's external pipeline	
6	Reevaluate your pipeline	

Tool 5: Tool to Develop Talent

Directions: Use this tool to help you and your organization "develop talent." That is Step 5 in the ten-step process to establish your diversity, equity, and inclusion effort. Carrying out Step 5 requires specific tasks in its own right. It does not happen on its own; rather, you and other leaders in your organization must guide it. For each step appearing in the left column below, take notes in the right column on your own plans to carry out each step. There are no right or wrong answers in any absolute sense. But to the extent you can customize these steps to fit your organization's culture, the more successful it is likely to be. Add, subtract, or combine steps – or resequence steps – as may be appropriate to you and your leaders. But at least this gives you a flexible action plan as a place to start.

What are the specific steps to develop talent?		What, specifically, will you and your organization do to carry out the steps?
1	Conduct an organization snapshot assessment	
2	Establish a professional development working group	
3	Review professional development strategy	
4	Update professional development strategy	
5	Update/implement a mentorship program	
6	Implement and review professional development plan process	

Tool 6: Tool to Navigate Emotions and Other Relational Dynamics

Directions: Use this tool to help you and your organization "navigate emotions and other relational dynamics." That is Step 6 in the ten-step process to establish your diversity, equity, and inclusion effort. Carrying out Step 6 requires specific tasks in its own right. It does not happen on its own; rather, you and other leaders in your organization must guide it. For each step appearing in the left column below, take notes in the right column on your own plans to carry out each step. There are no right or wrong answers in any absolute sense. But to the extent you can customize these steps to fit your organization's culture, the more successful it is likely to be. Add, subtract, or combine steps – or resequence steps – as may be appropriate to you and your leaders. But at least this gives you a flexible action plan as a place to start.

What are the specific steps to take to navigate emotions and other relational dynamics?		What, specifically, will you and your organization do to carry out the steps?
1	Train leaders on self-regulation	
2	Build strategies for navigating the emotional impact of equity-based initiatives	

Tool 7: Tool to Showcase Your Organization's Talent

Directions: Use this tool to help you and your organization "showcase your organization's talent" through talent reviews. Talent reviews is one of many ways an organization can showcase talent. That is Step 7 in the ten-step process to establish your diversity, equity, and inclusion effort. Carrying out Step 7 requires specific tasks in its own right. It does not happen on its own; rather, you and other leaders in your organization must guide it. For each step appearing in the left column below, take notes in the right column on your own plans to carry out each step. There are no right or wrong answers in any absolute sense. But to the extent you can customize these steps to fit your organization's culture, the more successful it is likely to be. Add, subtract, or combine steps – or resequence steps – as may be appropriate to you and your leaders. But at least this gives you a flexible action plan as a place to start.

What are the specific steps to showcase your organization's talent?		What, specifically, will you and your organization do to carry out the steps?
1	Identify bias in the talent review process	
2	Develop strategies to mitigate bias	
3	Publish updated talent review process	
4	Evaluate results	

Tool 8: Tool to Promote Your Organization's Talent

Directions: Use this tool to help you and your organization "promote your organization's talent." That is Step 8 in the ten-step process to establish your diversity, equity, and inclusion effort. Carrying out Step 8 requires specific tasks in its own right. It does not happen on its own; rather, you and other leaders in your organization must guide it. For each step appearing in the left column below, take notes in the right column on your own plans to carry out each step. There are no right or wrong answers in any absolute sense. But to the extent you can customize these steps to fit your organization's culture, the more successful it is likely to be. Add, subtract, or combine steps – or resequence steps – as may be appropriate to you and your leaders. But at least this gives you a flexible action plan as a place to start.

What are the specific steps to promote your organization's talent?		What, specifically, will you and your organization do to carry out the steps?
1	Evaluate promotion trends and identify bias in the system	
2	Train leaders, search committees, and promotion boards on updated process	
3	Implement practices to improve promotion process	
4	Evaluate updated process	

Tool 9: Tool to Develop Employee Resource Groups

Directions: Use this tool to help you and your organization "support and provide networking opportunities for your organization's talent." That is Step 9 in the ten-step process to establish your diversity, equity, and inclusion effort. Carrying out Step 9 requires specific tasks in its own right. It does not happen on its own; rather, you and other leaders in your organization must guide it. For each step appearing in the left column below, take notes in the right column on your own plans to carry out each step. There are no right or wrong answers in any absolute sense. But to the extent you can customize these steps to fit your organization's culture, the more successful it is likely to be. Add, subtract, or combine steps – or resequence steps – as may be appropriate to you and your leaders. But at least this gives you a flexible action plan as a place to start.

What are the specific steps to develop employee resource groups?		What, specifically, will you and your organization do to carry out the steps?
1	Understand the need for an ERG	
2	Establish a vision and mission statement	
3	Gain organizational commitment	
4	Identify group characteristics	
5	Establish a group leader, organizer, and facilitator	
6	Group evaluation, assessment, and impact	
7	Communication and branding	

Tool 10: Tool to Evaluate Your Processes

Directions: Use this tool to help you and your organization "evaluate your organization's processes." That is Step 10 in the ten-step process to establish your diversity, equity, and inclusion effort. Note that while this is Step 10, actions in this step happen at the beginning, and during the ten-step process. Carrying out Step 10 requires specific tasks in its own right. It does not happen on its own; rather, you and other leaders in your organization must guide it. For each step appearing in the left column below, take notes in the right column on your own plans to carry out each step. There are no right or wrong answers in any absolute sense. But to the extent you can customize these steps to fit your organization's culture, the more successful it is likely to be. Add, subtract, or combine steps – or resequence steps – as may be appropriate to you and your leaders. But at least this gives you a flexible action plan as a place to start.

What are the specific steps to evaluate your processes?		What, specifically, will you and your organization do to carry out the steps?
1	Describe the desired end state	
2	Determine how success will be evaluated (what are the metrics)	
3	Assess the current state	
4	Identify gaps between the current and desired states and plan interventions to close gaps	
5	Plan interim evaluations to monitor the change process	
6	Complete actions and interim evaluations	
7	Complete the post-intervention evaluation and report to the organization	
8	Create control plan with continued evaluation of key indicators	

Proposal Format for Building a Culture That Supports Diversity, Equity, and Inclusion

Directions: Use this tool to help you craft a proposal for building a culture that supports diversity, equity, and inclusion. For each question posed in the left column below, provide answers in the right column. As you answer the questions, you are developing a proposal for a DE&I program. There are no "right" or "wrong" answers. However, you would be well-advised to work with other key stakeholders to develop a proposal that meets the needs of your organization and fits the corporate culture. Add space if you wish. Add, subtract, or combine action steps as necessary to get stakeholder buy-in.

What key questions should be answered to build an effective proposal?		How do you answer the questions?
1	What goals are you seeking to achieve and why? How will the goals be measured?	
2	What steps will be taken to implement the DE&I corporate culture, and how will they be carried out?	
	When you answer these ten questions, consult the tools for each chapter as you do so	
3	1	*Define your organization's culture*	
	2	*Clarify the role of diversity, equity, and inclusion in shaping culture*	
	3	*Clarify with authority to change the organizational culture*	
	4	*Identify and define the pipeline*	
	5	*Develop talent*	
	6	*Navigate emotions and other relational dynamics*	
	7	*Showcase the organization's talent*	
	8	*Promote the organization's talent*	
	9	*Develop employee resource groups*	
	10	*Evaluate the processes*	

4	What is the time frame to implement the action steps? (*How long will it take to implement each step above?*)	
5	What is the budget to implement the action steps? (*Consider providing cost/benefit information.*)	
6	What staff will have to implement the action steps? (*For each step, indicate who will do it. Consider preparing a "responsibility chart" to show who does what.*)	

Index